Ultimate FinOps Earned Value Management

Optimise for Technology Business Value by Mastering Cloud Cost Management, FinOps, Earned Value Management, Unit Economics, and Forecasting

Anderson Candido Oliveira

www.orangeava.com

First Published: August 2026

Published By: Orange Education Pvt Ltd, AVA®

Address: 9, Daryaganj, Delhi, 110002, India

275 New North Road Islington Suite 1314 London,
N1 7AA, United Kingdom

ISBN (PBK): 978-81-69646-49-9
ISBN (E-BOOK): 978-81-69646-50-5

Scan the QR code to explore our entire catalogue

www.orangeava.com

Get a Free eBook

We hope you're enjoying your recent book purchase! Your feedback is incredibly valuable to us and helps other readers discover books that truly make a difference.

If you found this book useful or enjoyable, we'd greatly appreciate it if you could leave a short review with a 5-star rating on Amazon. Your review supports our work and allows us to reach more learners worldwide.

As a thank-you, we're happy to offer you a **free digital copy of this book** plus a **30% discount code** for your next purchase on our official websites:

www.orangeava.com

www.orangeava.in (For the Indian Subcontinent).

☑ **How it works:**

Leave your review on Amazon, take a screenshot of the confirmation or use the following link to submit the claim and email it to **info@orangeava.com.** Once received the required detail, we will send your rewards within 24 hours, **along with one month free subcription to the book on AVA SkillShelf!**

Claim Form
https://rebrand.ly/4d2477

Thank you for your support—it truly means a lot to us.

Colored images

Please follow the links or scan the QR codes to download the *Images* of the book:

https://github.com/orgs/ava-orange-education/repositories

The code bundles and images of the book are also hosted on ***https://rebrand.ly/35d574***

In case there's an update to the code, it will be updated on the existing GitHub repository.

Errata

We take immense pride in our work at **Orange Education Pvt Ltd,** and follow the best practices to ensure the accuracy of our content to provide an indulging reading experience to our subscribers. Our readers are our mirrors, and we use their inputs to reflect and improve upon human errors, if any, that may have occurred during the publishing processes involved. To let us maintain the quality and help us reach out to any readers who might be having difficulties due to any unforeseen errors, please write to us at:

errata@orangeava.com

Your support, suggestions, and feedback are highly appreciated.

Dedicated to

My Wife, Patricia and
My Sons, Caio and Breno.

My Beloved Parents:
Solange Oliveira and Nelson Oliveira (in Memoriam).

About the Author

Anderson Candido Oliveira is a renowned FinOps expert with over 25 years of experience in IT, financial operations, data analytics, and cloud cost management. As the founder of Zephyr Globe, he helps organizations maximize the value of their cloud investments by combining financial discipline, automation, governance, and operational excellence.

Throughout his career, Anderson has led FinOps initiatives for major global enterprises, delivering significant cost optimizations, and saving organizations millions of euros annually through strategic cloud financial management. His expertise spans cloud cost optimization, data-driven decision-making, cost allocation, and FinOps governance. He is a FinOps Certified Practitioner, FinOps Certified Engineer, and FinOps Certified FOCUS Analyst, reflecting his deep commitment to advancing best practices in cloud financial operations.

A respected speaker and thought leader, Anderson has presented at leading industry events, including FinOps XE Barcelona, the FinOps Community Day in Amsterdam, and the FinOps Portugal Meetup, where he shares practical strategies for aligning cloud spending with business value.

Through Zephyr Globe, Anderson also publishes articles, case studies, guides, and educational resources that help professionals and organizations navigate the evolving world of FinOps.

About the Technical Reviewer

Krishna Kandi has more than 22 years of experience in software design, software development, and system architecture across finance, communications, public safety, and enterprise technology domains. His work focuses on building reliable, high availability software systems with strong data integrity, secure processing, and long-term maintainability. He has extensive experience with secure financial data systems, including regulatory reporting, multi domain data synchronization, identity management, and high volume event driven processing. Mr. Kandi's responsibilities include designing application frameworks, implementing replication aware logic, improving data access patterns, and defining consistency rules for distributed data flows.

Krishna Kandi's career includes major modernization efforts involving FIN financial messaging systems, FIN Renewal, ISO 15022 message validation flows, distributed transaction systems, state-wide energy grid fault detection software, and unified cloud communications platforms. These systems require continuous responsiveness, precise processing, performance tuning, and strict reliability standards. His background includes deep expertise in distributed systems, high availability engineering, multithreaded processing, performance optimization, and end-to-end system design. He has also led engineering teams of more than 20 members, and contributed to real-time communication software used by a wide range of business clients.

Throughout his career, Mr. Kandi has been entrusted with responsibilities combining hands-on development, application architecture, technical leadership, and long range engineering planning. He continues to focus on reliable system design, software quality, engineer mentorship, and contributions to the broader engineering community through technical writing, papers, and participation in professional computing and engineering associations.

Acknowledgments

There are a few people whose steady support made it possible for me to complete this book. I am deeply grateful to my wife, whose encouragement and confidence in my work gave me the energy to carry this project forward. I am equally thankful to my sons for their patience and understanding, especially in the moments when writing demanded time that would otherwise have been theirs. Their love and support have meant more than I can express, and I carry that gratitude with me always.

I extend my sincere gratitude to the editors and technical reviewers whose expertise and guidance were essential in shaping this book. Their careful feedback, thoughtful suggestions, and commitment to quality encouraged me to refine each section and reach a higher level of clarity and precision. Their dedication not only strengthened the final work but also made the entire writing process genuinely rewarding. I am deeply thankful for everything they contributed.

Foreword

-Larry Advey,

Technology Advisor Council w/ FinOps Foundation | LinkedIn Learning Instructor | FOCUS Maintainer | AI Economics

https://www.linkedin.com/in/ladvey/

When I think about FinOps and, more importantly, how organizations can achieve true business value through it, very few people come to mind—and Anderson is at the top of that list. What sets him apart is his understanding that technology, engineering, finance, and FinOps only matter when viewed through the lens of value. Too often, organizations focus solely on cost visibility without addressing the more important question: how to create and measure value.

I had the opportunity to attend Anderson's breakout session at FinOpsX 2024, The Ultimate Business Value Indicator for Senior Leaders, where he explored topics such as Earned Value Management and introduced the Cost Performance Indicator. The depth of his knowledge and practical perspective were immediately evident. After the session,

Since then, I have had the pleasure of working with Anderson directly, and my respect for him has only grown. His contributions to unit economics, FinOps working groups, Zephyr Globe, Learning FinOps training, conference presentations, and his book Ultimate FinOps for Azure demonstrate a level of credibility and thought leadership that few professionals can match.

In this book, Anderson takes readers beyond traditional cost management, providing a comprehensive exploration of Finance, CapEx and OpEx, Earned Value Management, FinOps, Unit Economics, and, above all, business value. Whether you are new to FinOps or an experienced professional in finance, engineering, leadership, or technology, this book offers the essential insights such as without a clear understanding of value, even the best optimization efforts fall short.

Preface

For more than a decade, the cloud has been measured by what it costs. Teams track spend, monitor utilization, and celebrate savings. These signals are familiar and reassuring, but they answer only half of the question that matters. They tell us what we spent. They rarely tell us what that spend earned. This book is written to close that gap. It introduces FinOps EVM, a proven framework that connects cloud investment to business value, so that financial accountability and engineering delivery finally speak the same language. Whether you are a FinOps practitioner, a cloud architect, a finance leader, or a CFO, you will find a structured, practical path to measuring not just cost, but the value that cost creates.

The idea behind this book has a long history. Earned Value Management first intrigued me in 2002, during my first MBA in Project Management, where the Earned Value calculation itself was the hardest concept to grasp and, ultimately, the most rewarding to master. Over the next two decades I specialized in cost management, became a PMP instructor on the subject, and as a PMO Manager guided dozens of project managers in implementing EVM for value-based cost control. In December 2022, I first combined EVM with FinOps to associate business value measurement with cloud cost management. Since then I have applied these concepts across every FinOps implementation I have led, from startups to large corporations consistently with success. In 2024, I presented FinOps EVM at FinOps X in Barcelona, the largest FinOps event in Europe, and have shared it ever since through podcasts, webinars, and articles. This book is the structured, complete expression of that journey.

FinOps EVM adapts a discipline that has guided projects for over 60 years to the fast-moving, consumption-based reality of the cloud. Where traditional EVM tracks cost and schedule, FinOps EVM redefines how we measure value where flexibility and pay-as-you-go pricing change the rules. The book explains how to calculate the key indicators, how to apply them across organizations of any size, and how to use them to drive smarter decisions. It bridges finance, engineering, and product, connecting spend to the outcomes the business actually expects, so that being "on budget" becomes a relationship between cost and value rather than a blunt comparison of plan against actuals.

The journey is built to be hands-on. Each chapter builds on the one before, supported by exercises, templates, and automation-ready tooling that make the framework practical and scalable. You will move from foundations to calculation, from data and unit economics to budgeting and forecasting, and finally to the organizational change required to make value a shared operating model. A comprehensive set of appendices keeps you grounded in the language and logic of FinOps throughout.

The book is organized into seven parts, and contains ten chapters, followed by a set of appendices. The opening part introduces why cloud value needs a new lens. The parts that follow cover the foundations of EVM and FinOps, data and automation, governance through unit economics, financial planning, and organizational change. Hence, whether you are new to cloud financial management or refining years of expertise, this book will help you turn cloud spend into strategic impact. Here are the details of each chapter.

Chapter 1 establishes why value measurement in the cloud must be redefined. It traces the shift from capital expenditure to operational consumption, exposes the limits of traditional cost-focused FinOps, and shows the business impact of value that goes unseen, from missed optimizations to budget overruns and strategic misalignment.

Chapter 2 dives into the six-decade legacy of Earned Value Management in project management. It unpacks the core concepts of Planned Value, Earned Value, and Actual Cost, along with cost and schedule variances, drawing on historical context and practical examples to surface lessons proven over about 60 years of practice.

Chapter 3 introduces FinOps as both an operational framework and a cultural shift that embeds financial accountability into cloud computing. It covers the definition and guiding principles of FinOps, the FinOps lifecycle as a roadmap for maturing the practice, the key stakeholders and their roles, the FinOps maturity model for assessing where an organization stands, and the core capabilities of real-time monitoring, cost optimization, and forecasting.

Chapter 4 marks the pivotal moment where Earned Value and FinOps converge into a single construct: the FinOps EVM Framework. It translates Earned Value Data points such as Percent Complete, Actual Cost, and Planned Cost into the language of cloud operations, addresses the fundamental difference between the finite duration of a project and the ongoing nature of an operation, and works through the key assumptions and calculations, supported by practical exercises.

Chapter 5 expands the analytical toolkit beyond the foundational indicators, teaching the step-by-step calculation of the full EVM suite as it applies to FinOps such as: Schedule Variance, the Schedule Performance Index, Estimate at Completion, Estimate to Complete, Variance at Completion, and the To-Complete

Performance Index. It explains how each indicator behaves in traditional project management, and how to adapt it to cloud environments where the spend is continuous and variable, with practical exercises that turn the formulas into day-to-day decision-making.

Chapter 6 explores the data plumbing required for accurate EVM. It covers billing exports, tagging conventions, and telemetry sources, explains how to normalize disparate datasets, and provides an overview of native cloud services, third-party FinOps platforms, and BI dashboards, along with automating metric calculation and alerting.

Chapter 7 guides readers through defining, measuring, and operationalizing Unit Economics within the FinOps EVM framework. It explains the attributes of a strong model, distinguishes technical from business metrics, and shows how aligning the two becomes a reliable mechanism for demonstrating and tracking value in real environments.

Chapter 8 reframes traditional enterprise budgeting through the lens of FinOps EVM, showing that every EVM calculation depends on a baseline created during budgeting. It introduces the structure of enterprise, IT, and cloud budgets, the planning and execution lifecycle, and the personas who shape financial decisions. Above all, it shows how embedding Unit Economics into the plan turns the budget from a cost container into the value baseline that EVM later measures against.

Chapter 9 explains how FinOps EVM strengthens forecasting by combining consumption patterns, business assumptions, and EVM performance indicators into a single predictive model. Readers learn to build rolling forecasts, apply scenario modeling for growth and contraction, and improve accuracy through variance analysis and continuous refinement.

Chapter 10 offers change-management tactics to secure buy-in across finance, engineering, and leadership. It details training programs, certification pathways, and the creation of a FinOps EVM Center of Excellence, showing how to measure maturity through scorecards and continuous improvement loops, so that teams embrace the framework as a core operating model.

Finally, the **Appendices** Section furnishes practical reference materials to extend the book beyond its chapters. It includes the article, "*The Pursuit of Value in the AI Era*," a curated set of Unit Economics examples, a RACI chart for assigning FinOps EVM accountability, a consolidated reference of FinOps EVM formulas, and a comprehensive glossary of terms, giving readers quick access to the language, calculations, and roles that bring the framework to life!

DID YOU KNOW

Did you know that Orange Education Pvt Ltd offers eBook versions of every book published, with PDF and ePub files available? You can upgrade to the eBook version at **www.orangeava.com** and as a print book customer, you are entitled to a discount on the eBook copy. Get in touch with us at: **info@orangeava.com** for more details.

At **www.orangeava.com**, you can also read a collection of free technical articles, sign up for a range of free newsletters, and receive exclusive discounts and offers on Print Books and eBooks.

PIRACY

If you come across any illegal copies of our works in any form on the internet, we would be grateful if you would provide us with the location address or website name. Please contact us at **info@orangeava.com** with a link to the material.

ARE YOU INTERESTED IN AUTHORING WITH US?

If there is a topic that you have expertise in, and you are interested in either writing or contributing to a book, please write to us at **business@orangeava.com**. We are on a journey to help developers and tech professionals to gain insights on the present technological advancements and innovations happening across the globe and build a community that believes Knowledge is best acquired by sharing and learning with others. Please reach out to us to learn what our audience demands and how you can be part of this educational reform. We also welcome ideas from tech experts and help them build learning and development content for their domains.

REVIEWS

Please leave a review. Once you have read and used this book, why not leave a review on the site that you purchased it from? Potential readers can then see and use your unbiased opinion to make purchase decisions. We at Orange Education would love to know what you think about our products, and our authors can learn from your feedback. Thank you!

For more information about Orange Education, please visit **www.orangeava.com**.

Table of Contents

CHAPTER 1
A New Lens for Cloud Value

Introduction

Cloud adoption has transformed how organizations build, scale, and deliver. But the way cloud is measured, has not kept the pace. Many teams still rely on legacy metrics rooted in cost control. They track spend, monitor utilization, and report savings. These signals are familiar, but they do not tell the full story. Cloud is not just a cheaper data center. It is a strategic platform for agility, speed, innovation, and resilience.

This chapter challenges the assumption that cloud success is defined by cost reduction. That narrative is limiting. It leads to reactive decisions, misaligned incentives, and missed opportunities. Instead, we introduce a broader lens — one that focuses on the earned value. This means asking not just what was spent, but what was delivered. Did the cloud investment accelerate product launches? Improve customer experience? Enable new capabilities?

We begin by unpacking common misconceptions and misaligned KPIs. We explore how traditional metrics such as utilization and budget variance can distort decision-making. We share anonymized case studies that reveal how waste is often mistaken for success. And we introduce Earned Value Management as a framework to connect financial oversight with engineering delivery.

This chapter sets the foundation for a new approach to cloud governance. One that aligns teams, clarifies outcomes, and supports strategic growth. The chapters ahead will build on these ideas, offering practical tools and models to measure cloud value with precision. The goal is not just to manage spend, but to understand what that spend enables — and how to optimize it for impact.

Structure

In this chapter, we will cover the following topics:

- The Illusion of Cloud ROI

- The Shift from Cost to Value
- Symptoms of a Broken Lens
- Introducing Earned Value Management for FinOps

The Illusion of Cloud ROI

For years, cloud adoption has been sold as a cost-saving panacea. "Move to the cloud and save millions," they said. And many did. Migrating workloads, decommissioning data centers, and celebrating reduced capital expenditure. But, beneath the surface of those early wins, lies a troubling truth: traditional ROI models do not work in the cloud.

Cloud is not a one-time investment with predictable depreciation. It is a dynamic, consumption-based ecosystem, where the value is earned incrementally. The challenge is that it is often invisible. Yet, organizations continue to measure success using legacy metrics: budget variance, utilization rates, or cost per VM. These figures may look tidy in a spreadsheet, but they rarely reflect the business impact.

Consider this: a team spins up $50,000 worth of cloud resources to accelerate a product launch by three months. Was that spend "over budget"? Perhaps. But did it deliver competitive advantage, revenue acceleration, or market share? Almost certainly. The problem is not the spend. It is the lens.

Cloud ROI, as traditionally defined, is an illusion. It assumes linearity in a non-linear environment. It treats agility as a side effect, not a core value. And it ignores the earned outcomes that cloud enables: faster innovation, reduced time-to-market, and operational resilience.

To truly understand cloud value, we need a new lens — one that quantifies not just what we spent, but what we gained. That lens is Earned Value Management, which is adapted for the cloud era, and it starts with reframing the conversation from cost control to value realization.

Common Misconceptions: "Cloud Saves Money" versus "Cloud Delivers Value"

One of the most persistent myths in cloud adoption is the belief that cloud automatically reduces costs. This idea gained traction early, driven by comparisons to traditional infrastructure and the appeal of elastic pricing. But, when cost reduction becomes the primary success metric, organizations often miss the broader picture.

Cloud can reduce costs, but only under specific conditions. These include disciplined architecture, workload alignment, and continuous optimization. Without these, cloud spend tends to grow faster than expected. Decentralized provisioning, idle resources, and architectural drift contribute to this growth. The result is often sticker shock, followed by reactive cost-cutting that slows innovation.

This leads to a second misconception: that cloud value is defined by savings. In reality, value is measured by what the business gains. Faster deployment cycles, reduced time-to-market, improved scalability, and resilience, all contribute to value. These benefits are harder to quantify, but they are the reasons why cloud adoption continues to accelerate.

Imagine two teams. One reduces cloud spend by 20 percent through aggressive rightsizing. The other increases spend by 15 percent to support a product launch that accelerates revenue by six months. If the only metric is cost, the first team appears more successful. But, if the goal is business impact, the second team clearly delivers more.

This tension between cost and value reflects the maturity of an organization's FinOps practice. Early-stage teams focus on visibility and control. Mature teams prioritize unit economics, business alignment, and measurable outcomes. They treat cloud as a strategic enabler, not a utility.

Most reporting frameworks do not capture this shift. Finance teams track budget adherence. Engineering teams monitor performance. Executives look for business impact. Without a shared language, cloud success becomes fragmented. Moving from "cloud saves money" to "cloud delivers value" requires a change in mindset and measurement.

Organizations must redefine their metrics. Instead of asking whether spend decreased, they should ask whether delivery accelerated or customer experience improved. These questions demand new tools, better collaboration, and a willingness to challenge legacy thinking.

Cloud delivers value when it is aligned with business goals, governed with intent, and measured with precision. The savings narrative is outdated. The real opportunity lies in understanding what cloud enables.

Misreading Elasticity as Efficiency

Elasticity is one of cloud's most celebrated features. It promises flexibility, responsiveness, and control. Resources scale up to meet demand and scale down when no longer needed. On paper, this looks like efficiency. But in practice, elasticity is often misunderstood. It becomes a proxy for optimization, a shortcut for governance, and a mask for architectural drift.

Just because a system scales, it does not mean that it is efficient. Elasticity allows teams to provision quickly, but it does not guarantee that what is provisioned is necessary, right-sized, or aligned with business goals. A service that scales automatically may still be overbuilt. A workload that shrinks at night may still be idle during the day. Without intentional design, elasticity becomes reactive. It responds to usage patterns without questioning them.

This misreading creates blind spots. Teams assume that scaling equals control. Dashboards show dynamic resource allocation, and reports highlight automated adjustments. But no one asks whether the architecture supports long-term sustainability. No one checks whether the scaling events reflect real demand or poor design. Elasticity becomes a performance, not a strategy.

Consider a retail application that scales aggressively during peak traffic. The system performs well, and outages are avoided. But the underlying code is inefficient. The database queries are slow. The caching strategy is weak. The infrastructure absorbs the load, but the root causes still remain. Elasticity hides the problem. It delivers availability, but not optimization.

Another example: A data pipeline scales based on ingestion volume. The system adjusts automatically, and costs fluctuate accordingly. But the pipeline includes redundant steps, unnecessary transformations, and legacy dependencies. The scaling works. The spend looks controlled. But the value is diluted. Elasticity masks inefficiency.

To use elasticity well, teams must pair it with intent. This means designing for scale, not just reacting to it. It means auditing workloads, refining architecture, and aligning provisioning with outcomes. Elasticity should be a tool, not a crutch. When used with discipline, it supports resilience, agility, and cost control. When misread, it creates noise, waste, and false confidence.

Efficiency is not about movement. It is about purpose. Elasticity enables movement. But it is only the strategy which gives it a direction.

ROI Blind Spots in Lift-and-Shift Migrations

Lift-and-shift migrations are often positioned as quick wins. They promise speed, simplicity, and minimal disruption. Legacy applications are moved to the cloud with little to no refactoring. Timelines are met. Budgets are respected. The migration is declared a success. But beneath the surface, the return on investment is shallow.

The lift-and-shift model prioritizes movement over modernization. It transfers technical debt from one environment to another. Applications built for static infrastructure are dropped into dynamic ecosystems without adaptation. Auto-scaling is ignored. Licensing costs increase. Performance gains are limited. The cloud bill grows, but the value remains flat.

This creates blind spots. Teams celebrate delivery speed, while overlooking long-term inefficiencies. Finance sees budget adherence, but misses rising operational costs. Leadership sees progress, but it does not question sustainability. The migration is measured by completion, not by transformation.

Consider a financial services firm that moves 300 legacy applications to the cloud. The project finishes ahead of schedule. The team is recognized. But post-migration analysis reveals oversized instances, poor tagging hygiene, and no lifecycle policies. The cloud spend doubles within a year. Performance improvements are negligible. The migration delivered movement, not momentum.

Another example: A healthcare provider lifts its patient records system into the cloud. The infrastructure is replicated. The application runs. But latency increases. User complaints rise. The system was not optimized for cloud-native performance. The migration met its deadline, but failed its users.

Lift-and-shift migrations are not inherently flawed. They serve a purpose. They create momentum. But when they are treated as endpoints rather than starting points, they distort ROI narratives. They suggest success, while deferring value. They create the illusion of modernization without the substance.

To avoid these blind spots, organizations must pair migration with optimization. That means revisiting the architecture, rightsizing resources, and aligning workloads with cloud-native patterns. It means measuring success not by how fast applications moved, but by how well they perform, scale, and contribute to business goals.

ROI in cloud is earned through impact. Lift-and-shift is a step, not a finish line. The real value begins when migration leads to transformation.

The Shift from Cost to Value

For many organizations, the journey into cloud begins with a familiar compass: cost. Teams scrutinize invoices, flag anomalies, and celebrate savings as signs of success. Dashboards glow with budget adherence, and reports highlight the reduced spend as a proof of operational maturity. But beneath this surface lies a deeper truth: cost is only one dimension of cloud value — and often the least revealing.

Cloud is not just a cheaper data center. Nothing is so far from this (ask those companies that are repatriating to on-premise infrastructure just because of spiraling cost). It is a strategic enabler of speed, agility, innovation, and resilience. Yet, when success is measured solely by spend, these transformative qualities remain invisible. A cloud program might reduce costs while slowing delivery. It might optimize resources while stifling experimentation. In such cases, the metrics look good, but the business impact is muted.

True value emerges when cloud investments are tied to measurable outcomes. Did the infrastructure accelerate product launches? Did it improve customer experience, support scalability, or enable new capabilities? These are the questions that matter. And they require a shift, not just in metrics, but in mindset.

This shift demands new conversations across disciplines. Finance must move beyond budget variance and embrace performance indicators. Engineering must connect provisioning decisions to business goals. Leadership must ask not "How much did we spend?" but "What did that spend enable?" When these conversations evolve, so does the organization's ability to extract real value from cloud.

It also requires a broader understanding of what cloud is meant to achieve. Cloud is not a static asset; it is a dynamic platform for continuous delivery. Its value is earned incrementally – through faster deployments, resilient architectures, and empowered teams. Measuring this value means tracking velocity, feature adoption, uptime, and customer satisfaction. It means seeing spend not as a cost to control, but as an investment to optimize.

This section explores how organizations move beyond cost control and begin to quantify the value delivered through cloud strategy. It is a journey from reactive governance to proactive enablement. From savings to impact. From spend to significance.

The organizations that make this shift harness from it. They stop asking "How much did we save?" and start asking "How far did we go?" That is the real measure of cloud success.

Defining "Value" in Cloud Terms: Agility, Speed, Innovation, Resilience, and Business Outcomes

When it comes to cloud strategy, value is not a line item on a budget report. Cloud has reached the status of a multidimensional force that drives transformation. It cannot be captured by a single metric, or distilled into a simple equation. Instead, cloud value is a dynamic composite of agility, speed, innovation, resilience, and business outcomes. Each of them connected, makes each essential.

Agility is the ability to pivot without friction. It empowers teams to respond to market shifts, customer demands, and emerging opportunities without waiting for infrastructure to catch up. Speed is the heartbeat of modern delivery: the time it takes to move from concept to deployment, from idea to impact.

Innovation flourishes when experimentation is low-cost and low-risk, allowing bold ideas to be tested, refined, and scaled without fear.

Resilience ensures that the systems bend, but do not break. In other words, that they recover quickly, adapt under pressure, and maintain continuity in the face of disruption.

Business outcomes are the ultimate measure. They represent the tangible results that reflect whether cloud investments are fueling growth, enhancing customer experience, and advancing strategic goals.

Yet these dimensions are often overshadowed by cost reports. Organizations pore over invoices, scrutinize spend, and celebrate savings, while overlooking what those costs actually enabled. A spike in cloud usage might signal a surge in experimentation, a burst of innovation, or a critical product launch. A steady increase in spend could reflect rising customer demand, or an expanding market reach. But without context, these signals are misread. Spend becomes a warning sign, not a story of progress.

To truly define value in cloud terms, organizations must shift their lens from technical metrics to business impact. Here are some of the aspects that are worth tracking:

- Delivery velocity: This demonstrates how fast teams ship features.
- Uptime monitoring: It is responsible for monitoring the reliability of services under stress.
- Feature adoption tracking: This is the resonance of new capabilities with users.
- Customer Satisfaction: It is about listening to what the customer is saying, and feeling about the product and features. It may indicate the voice of the market.

But it does not stop there. Cloud decisions must be connected to product performance and market results. Did a new architecture reduce churn? Did a scalable platform enable global expansion? Did faster deployment cycles lead to competitive advantage? When cloud activity is aligned with these outcomes, value becomes visible. And once visible, it can be measured, optimized, and communicated across the business.

This is the foundation of earned value in the cloud. It is not about what was spent – it is about what was achieved, and equally about moving beyond efficiency to impact. Beyond control to contribution, and beyond savings to significance.

The organizations that embrace this definition do not just use cloud – they leverage it. They build cultures of experimentation, resilience, and speed. They align technology with strategy. And they measure their success not by what they saved, but by what they delivered.

Contrast: Capex-Era Metrics versus Cloud-Native Metrics

In traditional IT finance, CapEx-era metrics focused on fixed assets, depreciation schedules, and upfront investment. Success was measured by how well infrastructure costs were amortized over time. Procurement cycles were long, and capacity planning relied on forecasts that often missed the mark. The goal was predictability. Once the hardware was purchased, its cost was locked in, and any deviation from the plan was treated as an inefficiency.

Cloud-native metrics operate differently. Spend is variable, tied to usage, and influenced by architectural choices. Instead of tracking depreciation, teams monitor consumption. Instead of measuring asset utilization, they evaluate delivery velocity, feature adoption, and business impact. The emphasis shifts from ownership to enablement.

CapEx metrics reward stability. Cloud metrics reward adaptability. In the CapEx model, a server running at 80 percent utilization is considered efficient. In the cloud model, a service that scales to meet demand, and then shuts down is considered optimized. The underlying logic has changed.

This shift creates tension in reporting. Finance teams accustomed to fixed costs struggle to interpret variable spend. Engineering teams accustomed to speed and scale, struggle to explain the value in financial terms. Without alignment, cloud metrics are misread, and decisions are delayed.

To bridge this gap, organizations must adopt metrics that reflect the cloud realities. These include cost per deployment, cost per customer, and cost per feature. They also include earned value indicators that tie spend to outcomes. When metrics evolve, conversations improve. And when conversations improve, cloud strategy becomes measurable, defensible, and aligned with the business goals.

CapEx-era metrics served a different time. Cloud-native metrics reflect the pace and complexity of modern delivery. The organizations that make this shift are the ones that unlock real value.

Symptoms of a Broken Lens

Many organizations operate under the assumption that their cloud economics are under control. They monitor spend, track usage, and produce monthly reports that suggest stability. Dashboards show consistent costs. Reports highlight savings. Leadership sees predictability. But beneath these polished surfaces, the story is often incomplete.

Stable spend does not guarantee efficiency. It might conceal idle resources, abandoned environments, or any architectural drift. A savings report might celebrate cost reduction, while ignoring delayed delivery, degraded performance, or missed opportunities. When metrics are disconnected from outcomes, they create a false sense of control. The signals look clean, but the reality is quite messy.

This disconnect is not accidental. It is a symptom of a broken lens. Teams focus on what is easy to measure. Cost per service. Budget variance. Utilization rates. These metrics are familiar, accessible, and easy to report. But they rarely reflect what matters the most: business impact. The result is a fragmented view of cloud performance.

Without a framework that ties spend to value, decisions become reactive. Engineering defends provisioning choices without any business context. Finance questions invoices without delivery insight. Leadership asks for cuts without understanding trade-offs. The conversation stalls. The metrics dominate. And the outcomes disappear.

This misalignment shows up in patterns. These include dashboards that exclude development environments to simplify reporting, savings campaigns that degrade performance, and migration projects that celebrate speed, but ignore optimization. These are not isolated incidents. They are signals that the lens is focused on cost, not contribution.

When cloud reporting is misaligned with strategic goals, organizations lose clarity. They chase efficiency without impact. They celebrate savings without any progress. And they make decisions based on optics, not outcomes.

This section explores those patterns. It surfaces the blind spots. It challenges the metrics, and lays the groundwork for a new lens – one that connects spend to strategy, and reporting to reality.

The Danger of Efficiency Theater in Cloud Reporting

Cloud reporting often rewards optics over outcomes. Teams showcase dashboards with stable spend, high utilization, and reduced waste. These metrics look impressive, but they do not always reflect business impact. When reporting focuses on appearance rather than substance, it becomes an efficiency theatre: a performance that signals control without delivering value.

Efficiency theater thrives in those environments where cost is the dominant narrative. Teams optimize for visibility, not outcomes. They chase savings, suppress variance, and avoid experimentation. The result is a culture that celebrates predictable spend, while ignoring the missed opportunities. Innovation slows. Delivery stalls. And the metrics still look good.

Consider a team that rightsizes workloads aggressively to meet a quarterly savings target. The dashboard shows success. Spend drops. But performance degrades, customer experience suffers, and support tickets rise. None of these impacts appear in the report. The savings are real, but the cost to the business is hidden.

Another example: A dashboard excludes development and staging environments to simplify reporting. Spend appears stable, but 30 percent of cloud usage is missing. Leadership sees control. In reality, waste is growing off-screen.

Efficiency theater is not just misleading. It is dangerous. It creates false confidence, masks risk, and distorts decision-making. To move beyond it, organizations must connect metrics to outcomes. That means tracking delivery velocity, feature adoption, and customer impact – not just spend and savings.

Cloud reporting should reflect the reality, not a performance. When metrics align with a strategy, teams make better decisions. When they do not, the theater continues, and the value remains out of reach.

Examples of Misaligned KPIs

Many organizations believe that they are managing cloud spend effectively, because they track the common metrics, such as utilization, total spend, budget variance, and cost savings. These indicators are familiar, easy to report, and often used in traditional IT finance. But in cloud environments, they can mislead. When metrics are disconnected from business outcomes, they create noise instead of insight. This section breaks down four frequently used KPIs, and shows how they can distort decision-making, if not paired with a context.

Utilization

Definition: Measures how much of a provisioned resource is actively used.

Why it misleads: In cloud, unused capacity is not always waste. It may be intentional, designed to absorb the traffic spikes, or support a failover. High utilization can also signal a risk, if the systems lack the headroom to scale.

Example: A team provisions extra compute capacity for a retail application during the holiday season. Utilization averages 45 percent, but the buffer prevents outages during peak traffic. Finance flags the low utilization as an inefficiency, ignoring the business-critical role of availability. High utilization can also indicate that a workload is operating without enough buffer to absorb demand spikes, which increases the operational risk.

Total Spend

Definition: Measures the absolute amount paid for cloud services.

Why it misleads: Spend alone does not reveal whether the investment has delivered the value. A rising bill might reflect growth, innovation, or an increased customer demand. A flat bill might signal stagnation.

Example: A product team increases the monthly spend to support a new feature rollout. The feature drives higher customer engagement and retention. The spend is questioned, even though it directly supports business outcomes.

Budget Variance

Definition: Compares actual spend to forecasted budget.

Why it misleads: Cloud usage is dynamic. Forecasts are often based on static assumptions. Penalizing variance discourages agility and experimentation.

Example: A data team exceeds its budget after launching a new model into production. The model improves fraud detection, and reduces financial losses. The budget overrun is flagged, despite the clear business impact.

Cost Savings

Definition: Measures reduction in spend compared to a baseline.

Why it misleads: Savings are often celebrated without examining trade-offs. Cutting spend may delay delivery, reduce performance, or limit innovation.

Example: An infrastructure team rightsizes workloads and saves $100,000. However, the change introduces latency that affects the user experience. Support tickets increase, and customer satisfaction drops. The savings are real, but the cost to the business is hidden.

These KPIs are not inherently flawed. They become problematic, when used in isolation. Cloud value requires multidimensional analysis. Metrics must reflect business impact, not just technical efficiency. When KPIs are aligned with outcomes, they guide better decisions. When misaligned, they create friction, and missed opportunities.

Case Studies of Cloud Waste Masked as Success

Organizations often celebrate cloud initiatives, based on surface-level indicators, for example, reduced spend, stable dashboards, or rapid delivery. But beneath these polished metrics, inefficiencies can go undetected. The following anonymized case studies reveal how the cloud waste is frequently disguised as success, especially when teams rely on incomplete reporting or narrow KPIs. These examples are crafted to resonate with FinOps practitioners, engineering leaders, and executives, who grapple daily with the complex balance between cloud expenditure and business value.

Each case highlights a different scenario, where the traditional metrics painted a picture of control and achievement, while a deeper analysis exposed the missed opportunities, hidden costs, or strategic misalignment. From over-provisioned innovation labs to dashboards that omit critical environments, these stories underscore the need for a more nuanced lens. One that connects spend to outcomes, and performance to impact.

Case Study 1: The Over-Provisioned Innovation Lab

A global retail company launched an internal cloud sandbox for innovation. Teams were encouraged to experiment freely, with a minimal governance. Within six months, the initiative was hailed as a success. Hundreds of workloads were deployed, and the cloud spend increased by 40 percent. Leadership celebrated the surge as proof of a thriving innovation culture.

Behind the scenes, most workloads were abandoned after an initial testing. Persistent storage, idle VMs, and unused databases continued to accrue charges. No tagging policy was enforced, and no cleanup process was in place. The spend was real, but the value was speculative. The initiative lacked a mechanism to measure which experiments led to production features or business outcomes.

Case Study 2: The "Successful" Migration

A financial services firm completed a lift-and-shift migration of 300 legacy applications to the cloud. The project came in under budget, and ahead of the schedule. The migration was declared a success, and the team received executive recognition.

Post-migration analysis revealed that many applications were running on oversized instances, with no auto-scaling or optimization. Licensing costs increased due to poor architectural choices. The cloud bill doubled within a year, and performance gains were negligible. The success was based on the delivery speed, and not on operational efficiency, or long-term value.

Case Study 3: The Cost-Saving Campaign That Backfired

An infrastructure team launched a cost-saving initiative by aggressively rightsizing compute resources. The campaign reduced spend by 25 percent over two quarters. Finance praised the effort, and the team published a case study internally.

Soon after, customer-facing applications began experiencing latency spikes. Support tickets increased, and user satisfaction dropped. The savings were real, but the impact on customer experience was ignored. No one had measured the trade-off between the performance and the cost. The campaign was celebrated for its financial impact, but it eroded the business value.

Case Study 4: The Dashboard That Hid the Problem

A SaaS company built a cloud cost dashboard for executive reporting. It showed the stable monthly spend, consistent with forecasts. Leadership used it to validate cloud governance maturity.

However, the dashboard only included production environments. Development and staging environments were excluded, even though they accounted for 30 percent of the total spend. These environments had no lifecycle policies, and the resources were rarely decommissioned. The dashboard created a false sense of control. Spend looked predictable, but waste was growing in the shadows.

These examples show how cloud waste can hide behind metrics that appear successful. Without a framework to connect spend to outcomes, organizations risk celebrating inefficiency. That is why the earned value must become a part of the conversation — not just cost, but contribution.

Introducing Earned Value Management for FinOps

Cloud spend is often treated as a technical detail. Engineers provision resources, finance teams review invoices, and leadership asks whether the budget was respected. But this separation between the cost and delivery creates blind spots. Without a shared framework, it is difficult to answer the most important question: what did the cloud spend actually achieve?

Earned Value Management offers a way to close that gap. Originally developed for large-scale project management, EVM provides a structured method to compare the planned work, actual progress, and the associated cost. It introduces three core metrics: Planned Value (PV), Earned Value (EV), and Actual Cost (AC). These form the basis for performance indicators like Cost Performance Index (CPI) and Schedule Performance Index (SPI). In traditional settings, EVM helps project managers understand whether they are on track, over budget, or ahead of the schedule.

Key Definitions and Formulas

These core EVM elements provide the foundation for measuring cloud performance. The following definitions and formulas establish the basic structure, and the later chapters will explore each one in depth, showing how they adapt to cloud delivery, variable spend, and FinOps workflows.

- **Planned Value (PV):** The value of the work planned to be completed at a given point. Formula: PV = Planned Percent Complete × Budget at Completion
- **Earned Value (EV):** The value of the work actually completed. Formula: EV = Actual Percent Complete × Budget at Completion
- **Actual Cost (AC):** The cost incurred to deliver the work completed so far
- **Cost Performance Index (CPI):** Measures cost efficiency. Formula: CPI = EV : AC
- **Schedule Performance Index (SPI):** Measures schedule alignment. Formula: SPI = EV : PV

Tiny Worked Example

A team is running a cloud workload with a clear Unit Economics target for the month. The plan is to generate 1,000 units of value for a total cloud cost of 10,000. At the midpoint of the period, the workload was expected to have delivered 500 units of value for about 5,000 in cloud spend.

When they review the numbers, they see a different picture. The workload has delivered only 400 units of value so far, and the actual cloud cost has reached 6,000. The team has spent more than planned, and earned a comparatively less value than expected for that point in time. From a FinOps EVM perspective, the workload is underearning. The issue is not only the higher spend, but the gap between value delivered and value planned.

Now, imagine a variation, where the team spent only 4,000, and still delivered the same 400 units of value. The cost profile would look better, yet the workload would remain behind the value target for the period. The business would still be receiving a lesser value than planned. This illustrates a key point in FinOps EVM. Lower spend does not automatically means a better performance. What matters is whether the workload earned the value that was expected for that period, based on its Unit Economics objectives.

The succeeding figure illustrates how Planned Value, Earned Value, and Actual Cost interact over time to reveal cost and schedule performance.

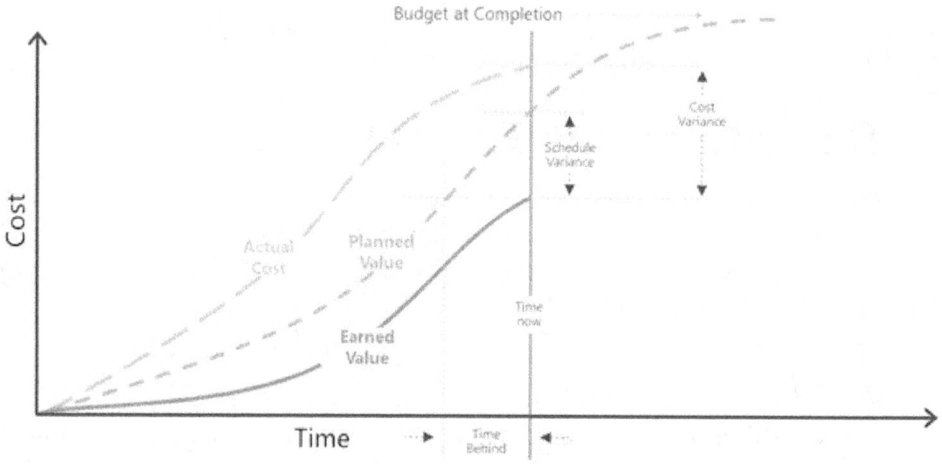

Figure 1.1: *Earned Value Management Template with Main KPI*

Applied to FinOps, EVM becomes a bridge between financial oversight and engineering delivery. It allows the teams to quantify cloud value in terms of outcomes, and not just spend. For example, if a product team planned to deliver five features in a sprint and completed three, the earned value reflects those three features. If the cloud cost, to support that sprint, was higher than expected, the CPI reveals whether the spend was justified. This approach shifts the conversation from "Did we overspend?" to "Did we earn what we planned?"

EVM also introduces accountability across the roles. Finance gains visibility into delivery progress. Engineering gains a context for the cost decisions. Leadership gains a way to measure cloud investments against the set business goals. Instead of debating line items, teams discuss earned outcomes. This is the foundation for strategic cloud governance.

This framework is especially useful in environments with variable spend and iterative delivery. Cloud resources scale up and down. Features are released continuously. Traditional budget tracking struggles to keep up the pace. EVM adapts by focusing on the value delivered, not just the resources consumed.

It is important to note that EVM in FinOps is not a direct lift from project management. The terminology and mechanics must be tailored to cloud realities. Planned Value might reflect forecasted deployment velocity. Earned Value could be tied to feature adoption, or customer impact. Actual Cost comes from usage-based billing. The key is to define these elements in ways that reflect how the cloud work is planned and measured.

This chapter introduces the concept. The later chapters will break down each component, showing how to apply them in cloud environments, and offering examples across maturity levels. The goal is not to replace existing FinOps practices, but to enhance them. EVM provides a lens to connect spend with strategy, delivery with accountability, and metrics with meaning.

When cloud value is earned, not assumed, organizations gain clarity. They stop reacting to invoices, and start managing the outcomes. That is the shift EVM enables. It is the foundation for cloud value management.

Conclusion

Cloud cost management is evolving. What began as a technical concern has become a strategic capability. Organizations can no longer rely on spend reports alone. They need a lens that connects cloud activity to business outcomes. That lens must be clear, multidimensional, and grounded in value.

This chapter introduced the foundational shift: moving from cost control to value realization. We examined common misconceptions, explored misaligned KPIs, and surfaced examples where waste was mistaken for success. We introduced Earned Value Management as a framework to bridge finance and delivery. And we outlined the symptoms that reveal when cloud reporting is out of sync with strategy.

These ideas are not abstract. They shape how teams collaborate, how leaders make decisions, and how organizations define success. But they require depth. The later chapters will unpack each concept with precision. We will define earned value in cloud terms, build practical models for measurement, and show how to apply them across maturity levels. We will explore how to align engineering velocity with financial accountability, and how to communicate cloud value in executive language.

This is not just a FinOps evolution. It is a leadership shift. The organizations that succeed in cloud are the ones that treat it as a business enabler. They build a shared understanding, challenge the legacy metrics, and measure what matters the most.

The chapters ahead will provide the tools, language, and frameworks to make that shift real. Whether you are leading a FinOps practice, advising executives, or building cloud-native products, the goal is the same: to earn value, not just spend money.

We will start with *Chapter* 2, that begins this progression by returning to the foundations of Earned Value Management, and clarifying the core metrics that will support the rest of the framework.

The lens is changing. It is time to focus on what cloud enables.

References

- Oliveira, A. C. (2024, November 7). A *Comprehensive Guide to FinOps Earned Value Management* - ZEPHYR GLOBE. ZEPHYR GLOBE. Retrieved April 11, 2026, from https://zephyrglobe.com/2024/11/07/a-comprehensive-guide-to-finops-earned-value-management/
- Jones, C. (2024, June 18). FinOps: Applying Earned Value Management to maximize ROI. Platform9. https://platform9.com/blog/finops-applying-earned-value-management-to-maximize-roi/
- McKinsey & Company. (n.d.). How to use FinOps to get the most value from cloud. McKinsey & Company. https://www.mckinsey.com/capabilities/tech-and-ai/our-insights/the-finops-way-how-to-avoid-the-pitfalls-to-realizing-clouds-value
- FinOps Foundation. (2023). Cloud FinOps: Collaborative, real-time cloud financial management. O'Reilly Media.
- Project Management Institute. (2017). A guide to the project management body of knowledge (PMBOK® Guide) (6th ed.). Project Management Institute.
- AWS Cloud Financial Management. (2022). Cloud value framework: Measuring business value of cloud. Amazon Web Services. https://aws.amazon.com/cloud-financial-management/cloud-value-framework/

CHAPTER 2
Foundations of Earned Value Management

Introduction

In the introductory chapter, we outlined the limitations of traditional financial governance in cloud environments. It introduced the need for a more adaptive framework: one capable of aligning financial accountability with the pace and complexity of modern operations. This need sets the stage for revisiting the foundational principles of Earned Value Management (EVM).

This chapter returns to the origins of EVM, tracing its evolution across six decades of project delivery. It begins by unpacking the core metrics: Planned Value, Earned Value, and Actual Cost. These elements form the basis for measuring performance against scope, schedule, and budget. Their interplay reveals cost and schedule variances, offering visibility into execution trends, before they escalate into risk.

Historical context is used not to romanticize legacy methods, but to clarify their original intent. EVM was designed to surface early warning signals, and enable corrective action. That function remains relevant. Through practical examples, we examine how these metrics have supported decision-making across industries, and delivery models.

Earned Value Management, as a framework, is ready for transformation. While its structure was built for static environments, its principles, especially the emphasis on measurable value, can be adapted to dynamic systems like the cloud. This foundation will be essential, as we explore how cloud-native operations challenge the conventional baselines, and redefine what it means to earn value.

By the end of this chapter, you will have a clear understanding of EVM's mechanics, and its enduring relevance, even as the context around it continues to evolve.

Structure

In this chapter, the following topics will be covered:

- The History of Project Management
- Earned Value Management Fundamentals
- Understanding Earned Value Management
- Earned Value Management in Action

The History of Project Management

You may be wondering that why we are stepping into the world of Project Management in a book focused on FinOps. It is a fair question. But this detour is intentional. There is a deeper thread running through both the disciplines: the pursuit of value. And that pursuit did not begin with cloud computing or cost allocation. It started long before, in environments where teams had to deliver outcomes with precision, accountability, and limited resources.

Understanding the evolution of Project Management helps us see how the idea of measuring value has matured. From ancient engineering feats to post-war industrial programs, the need to track progress, manage risk, and align execution with intent has always been there. What changed over time were the tools, the language, and the expectations.

This section invites you to look at that journey —not as a history lesson, but as a way to ground FinOps in something larger than itself.

This history matters, because the challenges that early project managers faced—uncertainty, shifting scope, limited visibility, and the need for objective performance signals—are the same challenges that we face in the cloud today, and the principles that they developed give us a proven foundation for measuring value in the environments defined by scale, speed, and constant change.

The principles that shaped Earned Value Management did not emerge in isolation. They were responses to real constraints and real complexity. And those same pressures exist today, just in different forms.

Before Project Management

Before Project Management became a formal discipline, it existed as a set of instincts, improvisations, and leadership practices embedded in the execution of complex human endeavors. Long before Gantt charts or critical paths, people were managing projects—they just did not call it that.

Thousands of years ago, civilizations undertook massive undertakings like the Pyramids of Giza, the Great Wall of China, and Roman aqueducts. These were projects in every sense: they had objectives, timelines, labor forces, and resource constraints. But, they were managed through command hierarchies, oral tradition, and sheer authority. There were no standardized tools, no performance metrics, and certainly no dashboards. Success depended on experience, intuition, and control.

Figure 2.1: *Great Wall of China near Jinshan Ling.*

(Source: Wikimedia Commons contributors, "File:20090529 Great Wall 8185.jpg," Wikimedia Commons, https://commons.wikimedia.org/w/index.php?title=File:20090529_Great_Wall_8185.jpg&oldid=989297254 (accessed October 31, 2025))

As societies industrialized, the scale and complexity of projects grew. The 18th and 19th centuries saw the rise of railroads, factories, and large-scale engineering feats. These efforts demanded more coordination, but management remained informal. Engineers and foremen relied on notebooks, sketches, and personal oversight. Planning was linear, and progress was tracked by walking on the site or checking the ledger.

Figure 2.2: *1965 Cadillac Production Assembly Line.*

(Source: Wikimedia Commons contributors, "File:1965 Cadillac production assembly line.jpg," Wikimedia Commons, https://commons.wikimedia.org/w/index.php?title=File:1965_Cadillac_production_assembly_line.jpg&oldid=892516217 (accessed October 31, 2025))

The early 20th century brought the first signs of structure. Henry Gantt introduced his now-famous chart in the 1910s, offering a visual way to track the tasks over time. It was a breakthrough, but still not a part of a broader discipline. Around the same time, Frederick Taylor's principles of scientific management began influencing how a work was organized, thus emphasizing efficiency and repeatability.

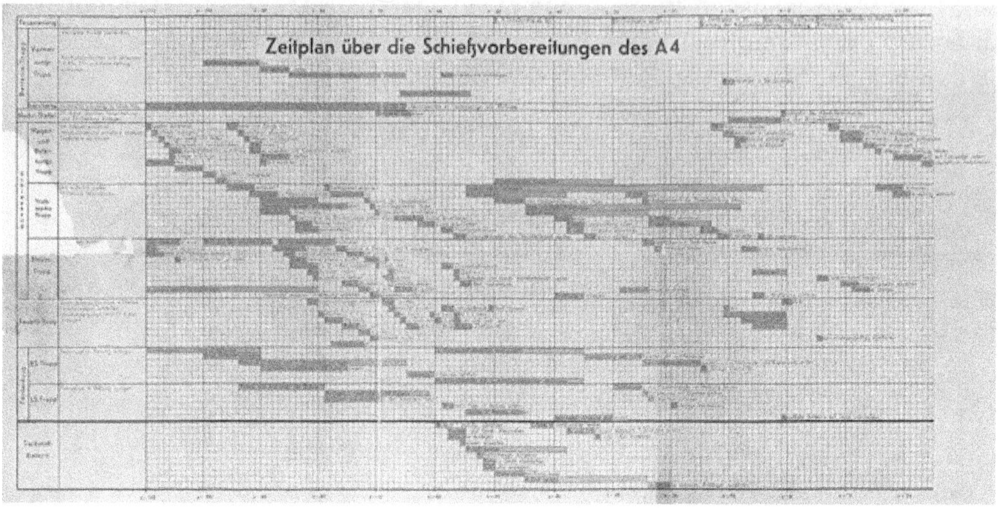

Figure 2.3: *Schedule of Shooting Preparations for the A4 - 1944.*

(Source: Wikimedia Commons contributors, "File:A4-Fibel 1944 2170.png," Wikimedia Commons, https://commons.wikimedia.org/w/index.php?title=File:A4-Fibel_1944_2170.png&oldid=994000490 (accessed October 31, 20))

The Rise of Project Management as a Discipline

It was not until World War II that project management began to crystallize. The scale of military operations required unprecedented coordination across teams, timelines, and technologies. The Manhattan Project, for example, demanded rigorous planning, secrecy, and cross-functional execution. These pressures gave rise to the formal methods for scheduling, budgeting, and risk management.

By the 1950s and 1960s, organizations like NASA and the U.S. Department of Defense began adopting structured approaches. Techniques like Program Evaluation Review Technique (PERT) and Critical Path Model (CPM) emerged, offering mathematical models to predict timelines and dependencies. These tools laid the groundwork for what would become the discipline of Project Management. Earned Value Management also emerged in this time. But, we will dive more into it in the next section.

So, while the term came later, the practice has always been with us. It evolved from intuition to structure, from art to science. And understanding that evolution helps us see that how today's frameworks—like FinOps—are a part of a much longer story about how humans organize their effort to deliver value.

Earned Value Management Fundamentals

Now, let us discuss the definition of Earned Value Management, its origin and why it became so popular across many industries.

Defining Earned Value Management

Earned Value Management, or EVM, is a method used to measure project performance. It helps the teams understand how much of the work has been completed, how much was planned, and how much it costs to get there. Instead of just tracking time or money separately, **EVM combines scope, schedule, and cost into a single view.**

At its core, EVM asks: are we delivering what we said we would, when we said we would, and for the cost that we had expected? It does this through a few key metrics: Planned Value, Earned Value, and Actual Cost. These metrics reveal whether a project is on track, or drifting off the course.

EVM became popular, because it offers early signals. It does not wait until the end to show the problems. It surfaces them while there is still time to adjust. That is why it is been widely adopted in industries where control and predictability matter, like defense, aerospace, and large-scale engineering.

Even today, as delivery models shift, and cloud operations introduce new dynamics, the core idea behind EVM remains relevant in a FinOps context: measure progress in a way that connects the resource usage to outcome, thereby allowing the understanding of performance in real time.

The Origin of Earned Value Management

Earned Value Management (EVM) originated in the 1960s within the U.S. Department of Defense as a response to the need for a better control over complex, high-budget programs. It evolved from earlier project control methods, and became formalized through the Cost/Schedule Control Systems Criteria (C/SCSC) policy in 1967.

Before the EVM was named, the core idea—comparing planned work to actual progress—was already in use. Efficiency charts and progress tracking methods appeared as early as the 1900s. These tools helped visualize how much work had been completed versus how much was planned, subsequently laying the groundwork for what would become earned value thinking.

The turning point came in 1967, when the U.S. Department of Defense introduced the **Cost/Schedule Control Systems Criteria (C/SCSC)**. This policy was designed to manage large defense contracts more effectively. It did not prescribe specific tools, but outlined the criteria for integrating cost, schedule, and technical performance into a unified management system. The goal was to ensure that the performance measurement covered both budget and timeline, creating a more holistic view of the project health.

Figure 2.4: *Buzz on the Footpad of the LM Eagle at Tranquility Base - Apolo 11 Mission, 1969.* *(Source: Wikimedia Commons contributors, "File:Buzz on the footpad.webp," Wikimedia Commons, https://commons.wikimedia.org/w/index.php?title=File:Buzz_on_the_footpad.webp&oldid=1102326762 (accessed October 31, 2025))*

Initially confined to defense and aerospace, EVM began spreading to other industries in the late 1970s. A pivotal moment came in 1979, when an article introduced earned value concepts to the engineering and architecture sectors. From there, adoption grew steadily, especially among organizations working with government contracts.

By the 1990s, EVM was widely recognized as a best practice in project control. It continued to evolve, incorporating tools like **Earned Schedule (ES)** to address the limitations in time-based forecasting. Today, EVM is considered as one of the most predictive and structured approaches to performance management, though its static assumptions are increasingly challenged by agile, and cloud-native delivery models.

Understanding EVM's origin reveals its intent: to provide early warning signals and actionable insights through an integrated performance data. That legacy remains relevant, even as we adapt its principles to dynamic environments, like FinOps.

The Popularity of EVM

Earned Value Management (EVM) became popular, not because it was perfect, but because it solved a problem that had long plagued project delivery: the inability to see trouble coming before it was too late. In the early days of large-scale engineering and defense projects, teams could track how much they had spent, and how much time had passed, but they lacked a reliable way to measure what had actually been accomplished. EVM filled that gap by introducing a structured method to quantify progress in financial terms, linking scope, schedule, and cost into a single performance narrative.

At its core, EVM answers a deceptively simple question: "Are we getting value for what we have spent so far?" It does this by comparing three key metrics—Planned

Value (what we intended to achieve), Earned Value (what we have actually achieved), and Actual Cost (what we have spent to get there). From these, we derive variances and performance indices that reveal whether we are ahead or behind, under or over budget, and how efficiently we are delivering.

This clarity is what has made the EVM indispensable, especially in high-stakes environments like aerospace, defense, and infrastructure. When the U.S. Department of Defense formalized the Cost/Schedule Control Systems Criteria in the 1960s, it was much more than a tool. EVM became a contractual requirement, and with that, it gained traction across industries that needed to manage complexity with discipline.

But, EVM's popularity was not just about compliance. It offered something rare: early warning. Traditional financial reporting tells you where you have been. EVM tells you where you are headed. That predictive power gave the project managers a fighting chance to intervene before the costs spiraled, or deadlines slipped. It also gave the executives a common language to assess performance across diverse portfolios.

Over time, EVM matured into a global standard. It was adopted by governments, embraced by project management bodies, and embedded into tools and methodologies. Its structured approach appealed to organizations seeking control, accountability, and transparency. Even as delivery models evolved—from waterfall to agile, from on-premise to cloud—the core logic of EVM remained relevant: measure what matters, and measure it early.

Today, EVM stands at a crossroads. Its assumptions about fixed baselines and linear progress are being challenged by dynamic, cloud-native environments. But its principles, especially the integration of cost, schedule, and scope, still offer value. In fact, as FinOps emerges to bring financial rigor to cloud operations, many of the EVM's foundational ideas are being reinterpreted, rather than discarded.

EVM became popular because it gave the organizations a way to see clearly. It remains important because the need for that clarity has not gone away. What is changing is the context. And as we will explore, the next evolution of value measurement will depend not on abandoning EVM, but on adapting its insights to meet the demands of a faster, more fluid world.

Understanding Earned Value Management

Earned Value Management is built on a simple, but a powerful idea: measure progress by comparing what was planned, what was delivered, and what it cost. To do this, EVM relies on a set of core metrics that, when used together, provide a clear picture of project performance. These metrics are signals. They help the teams understand where they stand, where they are heading, and what needs attention.

Let us break down the key components:

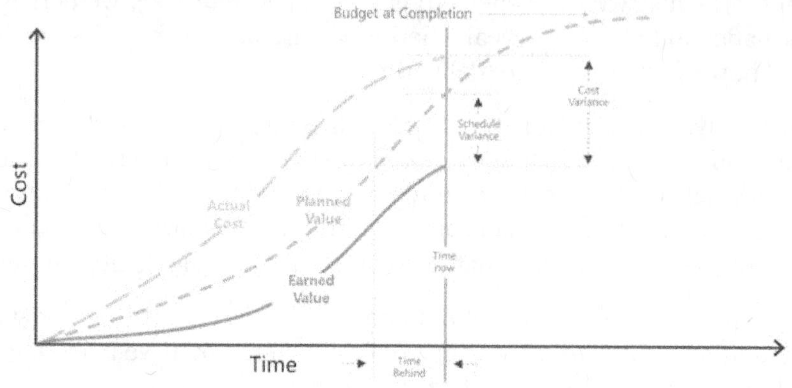

Figure 2.5: *Earned Value Management Key Metrics is a Cumulative Cost over Time Graph*

Planned Value (PV)

Planned Value represents the budgeted cost of work, scheduled to be completed by a specific point in time. It answers the question: *How much value should we have delivered by now, according to the plan?*

PV is calculated based on the project's baseline schedule and budget. It is cumulative, meaning that it grows over time as more work is planned. If a project is halfway through its timeline, and the total budget is $100,000, the PV might be $50,000—assuming that the plan was to complete half of the work by now.

Earned Value (EV)

Earned Value is the budgeted cost of the work that has actually been completed. It tells us: *How much value have we truly delivered so far?*

EV is not based on actual cost—it is based on progress. If 40% of the work is done, and the total budget is $100,000, the EV is $40,000. This metric is critical because it anchors the performance to outcomes, not just effort.

It is important to know that the progress measurement is a point in time. Like a picture of the state of the work completed at a specific moment. Consistency is the key, so that the result has little influence on the timing, when the progress is being measured.

When it comes to a budget with several items, it is recommended that the value is calculated on the percentage of progress on the total accumulated until the measurement moment.

For example, consider a budget of $600 spent linearly throughout 6 months. The Planned Value (PV) is the cumulative amount of budget.

Month	Budget	PV
0	0	0
1	100	100
2	100	200
3	100	300
4	100	400
5	100	500
6	100	600

Table 2.1: *Monthly Budget Example – Budget of $600 Spent Linearly throughout 6 Months*

If everything goes according to the plan, the progress measured at each month will be 100% for each month. In that case, the Earned Value will be equal to Planed Value.

Month	Budget	PV	% Complete (according to plan)	EV (PV * % Complete)
0	0	0	0%	0
1	100	100	100%	100
2	100	200	100%	200
3	100	300	100%	300
4	100	400	100%	400
5	100	500	100%	500
6	100	600	100%	600

Table 2.2: *If the Progress is According to the Plan, Planed Value (PV) is Equal to Earned Value (EV)*

Consider the scenario, where in the first 2 months, the progress goes according to the expectation, but in the third month, just 80% of what was expected is completed. In this case, see that the EV will be less than what is expected.

Month	Budget	PV	% Complete (according to plan)	EV (PV * % Complete)
0	0	0	0%	0
1	100	100	100%	100
2	100	200	100%	200
3	100	300	80%	240
4	100	400		
5	100	500		
6	100	600		

Table 2.3: *Earned Value is Lower Than the Expected (PV)*

So, the most important conclusion is that Earned Value is the product of Planed Value and the percentage of the completed work.

$$PV \times \%Complete = EV$$

Keep this knowledge for now, as in the future chapters, we will learn how to adapt it to a FinOps perspective.

Actual Cost (AC)

Actual Cost is the amount of money that has been spent to complete the work so far. It answers: *How much have we actually spent?*

AC is drawn from the real financial data—timesheets, invoices, procurement records. If the team has completed 40% of the work, but spent $60,000 to get there, the AC is $60,000. Comparing AC to EV reveals the cost efficiency.

Cost Variance (CV)

Cost Variance is the difference between the Earned Value and the Actual Cost. It shows whether the project is under or over budget.

CV = EV – AC

A positive CV means that the project is under budget. A negative CV signals overspending. It is a direct measure of cost performance.

Schedule Variance (SV)

Schedule Variance compares the Earned Value to the Planned Value. It shows whether the project is ahead or behind schedule.

SV = EV – PV

A positive SV means that more work has been completed than planned. A negative SV indicates delays. SV helps the teams in assessing the delivery pace.

Performance Indices

Two ratios offer deeper insight:

- **Cost Performance Index (CPI) = EV / AC:** A CPI above 1 means cost efficiency. Below 1 means overruns.
- **Schedule Performance Index (SPI) = EV / PV:** An SPI above 1 means faster-than-planned progress. Below 1 means delays.

Together, these metrics form the backbone of EVM. They transform the raw data into actionable insight, helping the teams make informed decisions, and course corrections before the problems escalate.

Earned Value Management in Action

Let us walk through a few example scenarios using real numbers to demonstrate how Earned Value Management reveals what traditional budget tracking often misses. These cases will show how EVM surfaces performance issues that remain hidden when we only compare actual spend against budget. By layering in progress and planned outcomes, EVM gives us a more complete and more actionable view of project health.

Underspending is Not a Win

Imagine a team, managing a six-month software rollout with a total budget of $600,000. At the three-month mark, the finance team reports that only $250,000 has been spent. On the surface, this looks like a good news—spending is under control, and the project appears to be on track financially.

But, when the project manager applies Earned Value Management, a different story emerges.

According to the baseline plan, by month three, the team should have completed the work equivalent to $100,000 per month. That sets the **Planned Value (PV)** at $300,000. However, after reviewing deliverables and progress, the team determines that only 60% of the work has actually been completed. That makes the **Earned Value (EV)** $180,000. The **Actual Cost (AC)** remains $250,000.

Now, let us look at the performance indicators:

- **Cost Variance (CV) = EV – AC = $180,000 – $250,000 = –$70,000.** This means that the project is over budget for the value it has delivered.
- **Schedule Variance (SV) = EV – PV = $180,000 – $300,000 = –$120,000.** It indicates that the project is significantly behind schedule. Graphically, you can see that it is approximately 1.5 month behind the schedule.
- **Cost Performance Index (CPI) = EV / AC = 0.72.** Therefore, for every dollar spent, only 72 cents of value has been earned.
- **Schedule Performance Index (SPI) = EV / PV = 0.60,** One can infer that the team is progressing at just 60% of the planned rate.

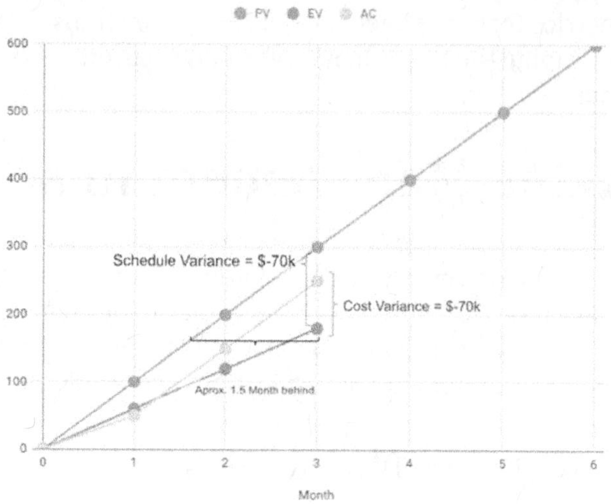

Figure 2.6: EVM *in Action – Despite Spending Less Than the Total Budget, the Project is Both Late and Inefficient*

Despite spending less than the total budget, the project is both late and inefficient. Without EVM, this would have gone unnoticed until much later. With it, the team has a clear signal to investigate the root causes, reallocate resources, and adjust the course before the gap widens.

This is the value of EVM: it measures performance based on the value delivered.

Overspending Signaling Acceleration

Consider a nine-month infrastructure upgrade project with a total budget of $900,000. At month five, the finance team reports that $600,000 has already been spent. On paper, this looks concerning. The project appears to be burning through its budget faster than expected.

But, when the project manager applies Earned Value Management, the picture shifts.

According to the baseline schedule, by the end of month five, the team was expected to complete 100% of the work expected for each month. That sets the **Planned Value (PV)** at $500,000. However, after reviewing deliverables, it is clear that they completed 30% above of what was expected. That makes the **Earned Value (EV)** $650,000. The **Actual Cost (AC)** remains $600,000.

Now, let us look at the performance indicators:

- **Cost Variance (CV) = EV – AC = $650,000 – $600,000 = +$50,000.** This means that the project is ahead of budget in terms of the value delivered.
- **Schedule Variance (SV) = EV – PV = $650,000 – $450,000 = +$200,000.** It indicates that the project is significantly ahead of schedule.

- **Cost Performance Index (CPI) = EV / AC = 1.08.** For every dollar spent, $1.08 of value has been earned.
- **Schedule Performance Index (SPI) = EV / PV = 1.3.** One can infer that the team is progressing at 130% of the planned rate.

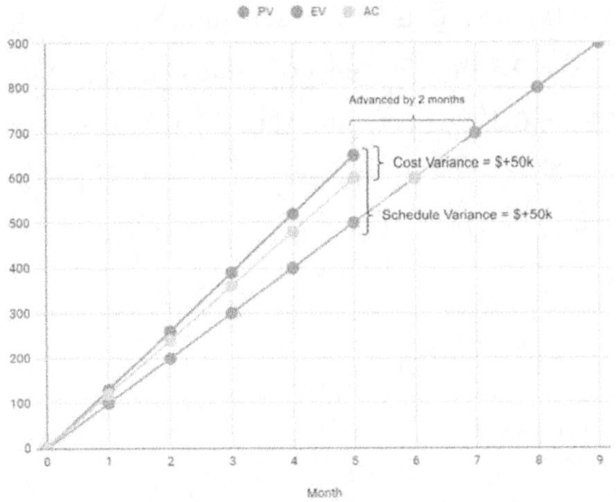

***Figure* 2.7:** EVM *in Action – Despite Spending More Than Half the Budget, the Project is Outperforming Expectations*

Despite spending more than half the budget, the project is outperforming expectations. More work has been completed than planned, and the cost efficiency is strong. Without EVM, this acceleration might have been misread as a budget issue. With it, the team can recognize high performance, and adjust the forecasts accordingly.

This is the nuance EVM provides: it evaluates the value, instead of just tracking the spending.

Activity is Not Progress

A product development team is halfway through a four-month sprint to launch a new feature set. The total budget is $400,000. At the two-month mark, reports show that $200,000 has been spent, and the team has logged significant hours. Meetings have been held, prototypes reviewed, and documentation drafted. From a time and cost perspective, everything seems on track.

But, when the project manager applies Earned Value Management, the numbers tell a different story.

The **Planned Value (PV)** at this point is $200,000—half the total budget, reflecting the expectation that 50% of the work would be completed. However, after reviewing actual deliverables, only 25% of the scope has been achieved. That sets the **Earned Value (EV)** at $100,000. The **Actual Cost (AC)** remains $200,000.

Let us look at the metrics:

- **Cost Variance (CV) = EV – AC = $100,000 – $200,000 = –$100,000.** This shows that the project is significantly over budget for the value delivered.
- **Schedule Variance (SV) = EV - PV = $100,000 - $200,000 = –$100,000,** It indicates that the project is behind schedule.
- **CPI = EV / AC = 0.5** Only 50 cents of value earned per dollar spent.
- **SPI = EV / PV = 0.5.** One can infer that the progress is at half of the expected rate.

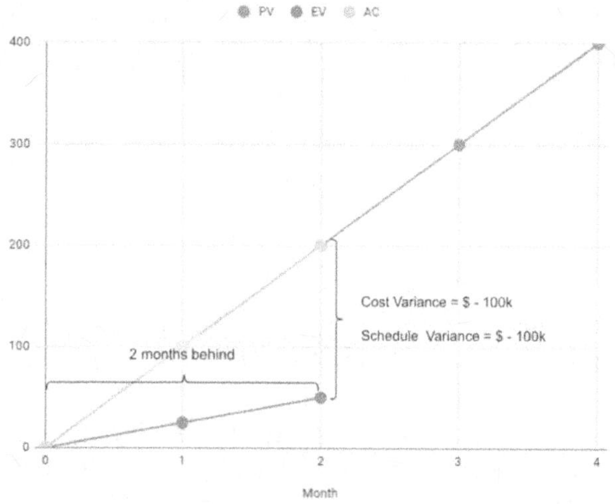

Figure 2.8: *EVM in Action – Common Trap of Mistaking Activity for Progress*

This scenario highlights a common trap: mistaking activity for progress. Without EVM, the team might assume that things are moving forward simply because the resources are engaged. With EVM, it becomes clear that value delivery is lagging, and that corrective action is needed.

Conclusion

Earned Value Management has endured for decades, because it delivers what many frameworks promise, but only few achieve: clarity. By integrating scope, schedule, and cost into a unified view of performance, EVM equips teams to detect misalignment early, intervene with purpose, and communicate progress with precision. It does not just track the effort—it measures outcomes. And in doing so, it transforms raw data into insight.

Throughout this chapter, we have explored the mechanics of EVM, its historical context, and the scenarios that reveal its strength. We have also seen how it surfaces the inefficiencies that traditional budget tracking misses, and how it can validate acceleration even when spending appears high. These examples underscore a central theme: value must be measured in a context. Without that, decisions are reactive, not informed.

Before we begin adapting these principles to cloud-native environments, we will make a brief pause to explore the fundamentals of FinOps. The next chapter will focus on how FinOps reframes financial accountability in dynamic, decentralized systems. It introduces new ways to align spend with business outcomes, optimize usage, and drive decisions in real time.

This grounding in FinOps will be essential. In future chapters, we will bring both the disciplines together—EVM and FinOps—to build a unified approach to value-driven cost management. One that is structured enough to measure, and flexible enough to adapt.

References

- Aidev. (2023, October 27). *The future (and history) of earned value management.* AzTech. Retrieved October 31, 2025, from https://goaztech.com/resources/blog/the-future-and-history-of-earned-value-management/
- Ian. (2025, January 2). The history of project management - and how did it begin? *Management.Org*. Retrieved October 31, 2025, from https://management.org/history-of-project-management
- M, M. (2024, September 3). The history of project management Ancient to modern day. *Project Templates*. Retrieved October 31, 2025, from https://www.projectmanagertemplate.com/post/the-history-of-project-management-ancient-to-modern-day
- Pells, D. (2022, August 7). *The Origins and History of Earned Value Management - PM World Journal*. PM World Journal. Retrieved October 31, 2025, from https://pmworldjournal.com/article/the-origins-and-history-of-earned-value-management
- Six, T. (2021, August 18). *The history of Earned Value Management*. Ten Six. Retrieved October 31, 2025, from https://tensix.com/the-history-of-earned-value-management/

CHAPTER 3
Introduction to FinOps

Introduction

In the rapidly evolving landscape of cloud computing, the need for a disciplined approach to financial management has never been more critical. As organizations transition from traditional Capital Expenditure (CAPEX) models to Operational Expenditure (OPEX) frameworks, the complexity of managing costs, and ensuring financial accountability has increased significantly. This is where FinOps comes into play.

FinOps, short form of Financial Operations, is not merely a set of practices; it is an operational framework, and a cultural shift that integrates financial accountability into the dynamic world of cloud computing. By fostering collaboration across engineering, finance, and business teams, FinOps enables the organizations to make timely, data-driven decisions that balance cost, speed, and quality. The essence of FinOps lies in empowering teams to manage cloud spending efficiently, ensuring that every dollar spent drives the business value.

This chapter will delve into the foundational concepts of FinOps, providing a comprehensive understanding of its importance, and the transformative impact that it can have on your organization. We will explore the definition and principles of FinOps, which serve as the guiding lights for developing effective strategies, and ensuring that actions align with the overall vision. The principles of FinOps, such as collaboration and business value-driven decisions, are crucial for achieving financial transparency, and optimizing cloud expenditures.

Moreover, we will examine the FinOps lifecycle, which encompasses the stages through which organizations mature in their FinOps practices. This lifecycle provides a roadmap for continuous improvement, helping teams to progressively enhance their capabilities, and achieve a greater efficiency in cloud cost management. Key stakeholders and their roles will also be discussed, highlighting the importance of cross-functional collaboration, and the contributions of various teams to the success of FinOps initiatives.

Additionally, this chapter introduces the FinOps maturity model, a framework that assesses an organization's current state, and provides insights into areas for improvement. By understanding where you stand in the maturity model, you can identify actionable steps to advance your FinOps practices, and drive better financial outcomes.

Finally, we will cover the core capabilities of FinOps, which include real-time monitoring, cost optimization, and forecasting. These capabilities are essential for maintaining control over cloud spending, and ensuring that financial decisions are aligned with business objectives.

As we embark on this journey through the world of FinOps, you will gain valuable insights into how to integrate financial operations into your cloud strategy effectively. By embracing FinOps, your organization can achieve a harmonious balance between technological innovation and financial sustainability, paving the way for a long-term success in the digital age.

Structure

In this chapter, we will cover the following topics:

- Definition of FinOps
- Principles of FinOps
- The FinOps Lifecycle: Inform, Optimize, and Operate
- Main FinOps Personas, Their Roles, Contributions and Expectations
- FinOps Domains and Capabilities
- The FinOps Maturity: Crawl, Walk and Run

Definition of FinOps

FinOps, short form of Financial Operations, is an operational framework, and a cultural practice that maximizes the business value of cloud computing. It enables timely, data-driven decision-making, and creates financial accountability through collaboration between engineering, finance, and business teams. At its core, FinOps is about bringing financial accountability to the variable spend model of cloud, empowering the teams to make informed trade-offs between speed, cost, and quality.

Principles of FinOps

Principles are the essential starting point. Instead of jumping straight to actions, people often overlook them. However, when developing a strategy, principles serve as a guiding light. They help determine, if your actions are on the right track. Even after many years of experience, I still revisit the principles from time to time. This helps me remember them, and ensures that my ideas and projects align with the overall vision they provide.

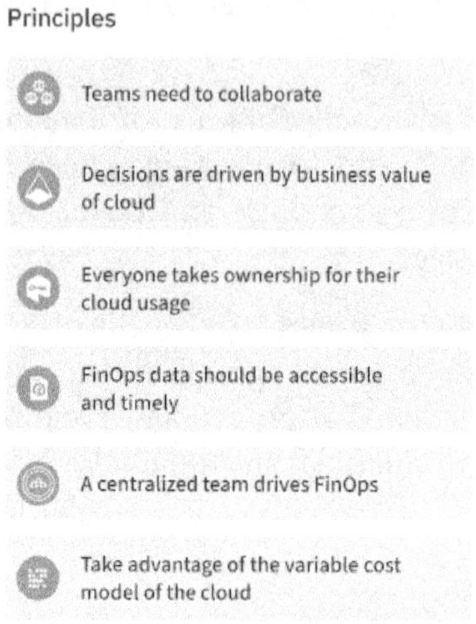

Figure 3.1: *FinOps Principles by FinOps Foundation*

Teams Need to Collaborate

Collaboration is the cornerstone of FinOps. It requires finance, technology, product, and business teams to work together in near real-time. This principle ensures that all stakeholders are aligned, and can make informed decisions quickly.

Example: A global e-commerce company implemented FinOps by creating cross-functional teams that included members from finance, engineering, and product management. These teams held regular meetings to review cloud spending and identify cost-saving opportunities. This collaborative approach led to a 20% reduction in cloud costs within six months.

Decisions are Driven by Business Value

FinOps emphasizes that decisions should be based on business value rather than just cost. This means evaluating the impact of cloud spending on business outcomes, and prioritizing the investments that drive the most value.

Example: A media streaming service used FinOps to analyze the cost and performance of its cloud infrastructure. By focusing on the business value, they identified that investing in higher-performance instances for their recommendation engine would improve the user experience and retention, thereby leading to an increased revenue. This strategic decision, driven by the business value, resulted in a 15% increase in user engagement.

Everyone Takes Ownership of Their Cloud Usage

In FinOps, accountability is decentralized. Engineers and product teams are responsible for managing their cloud costs from design to operations. This principle ensures that those who are closest to the cloud resources are also responsible for optimizing their usage.

Example: A financial services firm adopted FinOps by implementing a tagging strategy that allowed them to allocate the cloud costs to specific teams and projects. Each team received a monthly report detailing their cloud usage and costs. This transparency encouraged the teams to take ownership of their cloud spending, leading to more efficient resource utilization and a 10% reduction in overall cloud costs.

FinOps Data Should be Accessible and Timely

Real-time visibility into cloud spending is crucial for an effective FinOps. Teams need access to accurate and up-to-date data to make informed decisions, and optimize cloud usage.

Example: A healthcare provider implemented a FinOps platform that provided real-time dashboards and alerts for cloud spending. This immediate visibility allowed them to quickly identify and address cost anomalies, such as unexpected spikes in usage. As a result, they were able to reduce their cloud costs by 12% within the first quarter of implementation.

A Centralized Team Drives FinOps

While everyone is responsible for their cloud usage, a centralized FinOps team is essential for driving the best practices, and ensuring consistency across the organization. This team acts as a hub of expertise and support for other teams.

Example: A large retail company established a centralized FinOps team that developed and enforced cloud cost management policies. This team provided training and resources to other departments, helping them implement FinOps practices. The centralized approach led to a more cohesive strategy, and a 25% reduction in cloud spending over a year.

Take Advantage of the Variable Cost Model of the Cloud

The cloud's variable cost model allows organizations to pay only for what they use. FinOps encourages leveraging this model through just-in-time prediction, planning, and purchasing.

Example: A software development company used FinOps to optimize their use of Reserved Instances and Savings Plans. By analyzing their usage patterns and predicting future needs, they were able to purchase the right amount of reserved capacity at discounted rates. This proactive approach resulted in a 30% reduction in their cloud costs.

The FinOps Lifecycle: Inform, Optimize, and Operate

Although, FinOps Foundation call them *Phases*, I believe that the term *Lifecycle* is more appropriate. The FinOps lifecycle is a continuous process, designed to manage and optimize cloud financial operations effectively. It consists of three iterative phases: Inform, Optimize, and Operate. Each phase plays a crucial role in ensuring efficient and cost-effective cloud resource management. Let us explore each phase in detail, along with real-life examples and relevant Microsoft Azure features.

Figure 3.2: *FinOps Phases by FinOps Foundation*

Inform

The Inform phase is all about gaining visibility into cloud spending and usage. This phase involves collecting and analyzing data to understand where and how cloud resources are being utilized. Accurate allocation of cloud spend based on tags, accounts, or business rules enables a precise reporting and better decision-making.

Real-Life Example: A global retail company implemented the Inform phase by using detailed tagging strategies to track cloud costs across different departments and projects. By leveraging tools like Azure Cost Management and Azure Advisor, they were able to gain insights into their cloud spending patterns. This visibility allowed them to identify the areas of high expenditure, and allocate costs accurately, leading to a more informed budgeting and forecasting.

Azure Features

- **Azure Cost Management:** Provides comprehensive tools to monitor, allocate, and optimize cloud costs. It helps with tracking spending, setting budgets, and forecasting future costs.

- **Azure Advisor:** Offers personalized recommendations to optimize cloud resources for cost, performance, security, and reliability.
- **Azure Pricing Calculator:** Estimates the costs of various Azure services, helping teams to plan and budget effectively.

Optimize

The Optimize phase focuses on improving cloud efficiency by identifying and implementing cost-saving opportunities. This involves rightsizing underutilized resources, managing workloads, and automating the elimination of waste. Optimization also includes leveraging pricing models like Reserved Instances and Savings Plans to reduce costs.

Real-Life Example: A software development company used the Optimize phase to analyze their cloud usage, and identify underutilized virtual machines. By using Azure's recommendations, they resized or decommissioned these resources, resulting in significant cost savings. Additionally, they adopted Azure Reserved Instances for predictable workloads, which provided substantial discounts compared to pay-as-you-go pricing.

Azure Features

- **Azure Reservations:** Allows organizations to reserve virtual machines and other resources in advance at a discounted rate.
- **Azure Savings Plans:** Provides flexible pricing options for consistent cloud usage, offering significant cost savings.
- **Azure Automation:** Automates repetitive tasks and processes, helping to eliminate waste and improve efficiency.

Operate

The Operate phase is about maintaining and enhancing the efficiency of cloud operations. This involves continuous monitoring, anomaly detection, and implementing the best practices for cost management. The goal is to ensure that the cloud resources are used efficiently, and that any issues are promptly addressed.

Real-Life Example: A healthcare provider implemented the Operate phase by setting up continuous monitoring and alerting their cloud infrastructure. Using Azure Monitor and Azure Security Center, they were able to detect and respond to anomalies in real-time. This proactive approach helped them in maintaining optimal performance and security, while keeping the costs under control.

Azure Features

- **Azure Monitor:** Provides full-stack monitoring and diagnostics to ensure the health and performance of cloud resources.

- **Azure Security Center:** Enhances security posture by providing unified security management, and advanced threat protection.
- **Azure Policy:** Helps enforce organizational standards and assess compliance at scale, ensuring that the resources are optimized and compliant.

Main FinOps Personas, Their Roles, Contributions and Expectations

FinOps is a collective game. It is important that each player does its part, so that a good cloud financial management is performed. As the position's name may vary from organization to organization, reason the FinOps framework uses the term *personas*. These personas play critical roles in the successful implementation of FinOps within an organization. By understanding their unique contributions and expectations, businesses can foster a collaborative environment that drives financial accountability and optimized cloud spending.

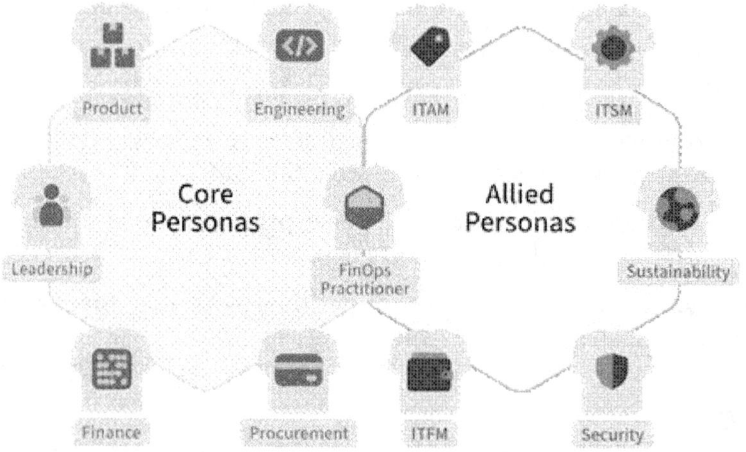

Figure 3.3: *FinOps Personas by FinOps Foundation*

The Leadership

- **Role:** The Leadership or, as I prefer to call, the Executive Sponsor is typically a senior leader, who champions the FinOps initiative within the organization. They secure the necessary resources and support, ensuring alignment with the organization's strategic goals.
- **Contribution:** By leveraging their influence, the Executive Sponsor helps bridge the gaps between departments, ensuring collaboration and communication. They advocate for the FinOps principles, and provide the financial backing and political support needed to drive the initiative forward.

- **Expectations:** They expect measurable outcomes, such as cost savings, improved financial accountability, and enhanced transparency. They look for regular updates on progress, challenges, and successes to report back to other senior stakeholders.

The FinOps Practitioner

- **Role:** This person is the hands-on expert responsible for the day-to-day implementation of FinOps practices. They serve as the relay that connects all the other personas, by driving the FinOps practice into the organization with a strong emphasis on culture, cost and value awareness, standardization, and support.
- **Contribution:** The FinOps Practitioner plays a pivotal role in identifying cost-saving opportunities and implementing best practices. They monitor cloud usage, create reports, and provide recommendations to various teams to optimize cloud expenses.
- **Expectations:** They expect access to comprehensive data and tools to perform their job effectively. They also look for support from other teams to implement their recommendations, and achieve the desired cost efficiencies.

The Finance Team

- **Role:** The Finance Team manages the organization's budget, forecasts spending, and ensures financial accountability. They work with the FinOps team to understand cloud costs and their impact on the overall budget.
- **Contribution:** By providing financial insights and analysis, the Finance Team helps the organization make informed decisions about cloud spending. They develop and maintain financial models that incorporate cloud costs, and ensure compliance with accounting standards.
- **Expectations:** They expect timely and accurate information on cloud spending and potential cost-saving opportunities. They also look for clear communication from the FinOps team regarding financial objectives and expectations.

The Engineering Team

- **Role:** The Engineering Team builds and maintains the applications and services that run on the cloud. They are one of the key consumers of the cloud resources, and work closely with the FinOps team to optimize usage.
- **Contribution:** By implementing the recommendations from the FinOps team, the Engineering Team ensures that their applications are cost-efficient and scalable. They play a pivotal role in monitoring, and adjusting the cloud resources to meet budgetary constraints.

- **Expectations:** They expect practical and actionable recommendations from the FinOps team. They also look for the tools and processes that make it easier to monitor, and optimize cloud usage without disrupting their development workflow.

The Product Owner

- **Role:** The Product Owner is responsible for the strategic vision and roadmap of a product or service. They ensure that the product meets the customer needs, while staying within any budgetary constraints.
- **Contribution:** By prioritizing features and allocating resources, the Product Owner ensures that the product delivers a value to the customers without exceeding financial limits. They work with the FinOps team to balance cost, performance, and customer satisfaction.
- **Expectations:** They expect clear and consistent communication about cloud costs and their impact on the product's financial performance. They also look for a support in the understanding the financial implications of their decisions.

The Procurement Team

- **Role:** The Procurement Team negotiates contracts and manages vendor relationships. They work with the FinOps team to ensure that the cloud service agreements are cost-effective, and are aligning with the organization's financial goals.
- **Contribution:** By securing favorable terms and conditions in cloud service contracts, the Procurement Team helps the organization control costs and optimize spending. They also ensure compliance with contractual obligations, and manage renewals and negotiations.
- **Expectations:** They expect a detailed information about cloud usage patterns and spending trends. They also look for support in negotiating terms that align with the organization’s financial objectives.

The FinOps Allied Personas

In March 2024, on the FinOps Foundation Framework review, the incorporation of three new Allied Personas, and the renaming of ITAM and Sustainability were announced. The FinOps allied personas—IT Asset Management (ITAM), IT Service Management (ITSM), Sustainability, Security, and IT Financial Management (ITFM)—each plays a key role in optimizing financial operations within an organization.

- **ITAM** ensures an efficient use of IT assets, minimizing costs and maximizing returns on investments. Proper asset management can avoid unnecessary purchases, and ensure compliance with software licenses.
- **ITSM** focuses on delivering high-quality IT services, improving operational efficiencies, and reducing downtime. This, in turn, supports business goals by maintaining a robust and reliable IT infrastructure.
- **Sustainability** aims to reduce the environmental impact of IT operations, promoting energy-efficient practices, and a responsible disposal of electronic waste. This aligns IT initiatives with broader corporate sustainability goals, potentially reducing costs through energy savings.
- **Security** ensures that the financial data and IT operations are protected from threats, reducing the risk of costly breaches, and maintaining trust with stakeholders. A secure IT environment supports seamless and safe financial operations.
- **ITFM** provides transparency and control over IT spending, allowing organizations to make informed financial decisions. This involves budgeting, forecasting, and optimizing IT expenditures to align with business objectives.

Together, these personas enhance the strategic value of IT, balancing cost, performance, and risk to achieve optimal financial performance and drive business success.

FinOps Domains and Capabilities

The core Domains of the FinOps Framework outline the essential business outcomes that a FinOps practice is expected to deliver. Each Domain is supported by a collection of Capabilities, that are specific organizational actions that enable teams to reach those outcomes in a practical, measurable way. Rather than adopting every Capability at once, organizations should focus on developing the ones that generate meaningful value for their context, aligning their choices with current needs and their stage of FinOps Maturity.

Taken together, the Domains and their Capabilities form an interconnected operating model that guides how FinOps is executed across industries, organizational structures, team sizes, and maturity levels. They reinforce one another, creating a cohesive system that supports sustainable financial accountability, operational excellence, and continuous value realization. The next figure illustrates the FinOps Domains and Capabilities that make up the framework.

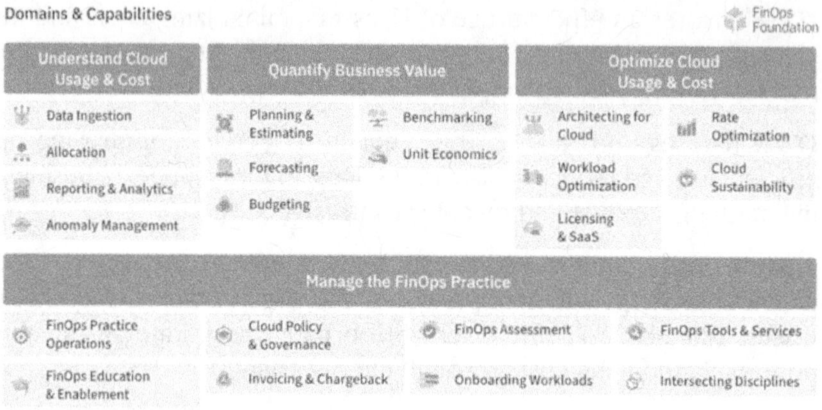

Figure 3.4: *FinOps Domains and Capabilities by FinOps Foundation*

FinOps Domains

FinOps Domains are broad categories that encompass various activities and responsibilities within the FinOps framework. Think of them as the pillars that hold up the entire structure of financial operations in cloud computing. Each domain covers a specific area of focus, ensuring a comprehensive approach to managing cloud costs.

FinOps Capabilities

FinOps Capabilities are the specific skills, practices, and tools within each domain that enable the organizations to achieve their FinOps objectives. These are the actionable elements that teams use to manage, optimize, and report on cloud spending.

Here is how they connect:

- **Domains** are the overarching areas of focus, like "Understand Cloud Usage and Cost".
- **Capabilities** are the specific methods and tools used within those domains, like "Data Ingestion" and "Reporting and Analytics".

Together, FinOps Domains and Capabilities help the organizations create a structured and an effective approach to cloud financial management.

Let us dive deeper into the FinOps domains and their capabilities, along with the examples of Azure features that can help in each domain.

Understand Cloud Usage and Cost

This domain focuses on gaining a comprehensive understanding of an organization's cloud usage and costs. It involves gathering and analyzing data to provide insights into how the cloud resources are utilized and the associated costs.

Capabilities:

- **Data Ingestion:** Collecting and processing data from various sources to create a comprehensive view of cloud usage and costs.
- **Allocation:** Assigning costs to different teams, projects, or departments using accounts, tags, and labels.
- **Reporting and Analytics:** Creating reports and dashboards to visualize cloud usage and costs, helping stakeholders make informed decisions.
- **Anomaly Management:** Detecting and managing unexpected spikes in cloud costs to minimize their impact on the business.

Azure Features:

- **Azure Cost Management + Billing:** Provides tools for tracking and managing cloud spending, including cost analysis, budgeting, and reporting.
- **Azure Resource Manager (ARM):** Allows for tagging the resources to allocate costs accurately.
- **Power BI:** Integrates with Azure to create visual reports and dashboards for better insights into cloud usage and costs.
- **Azure Advisor:** Offers recommendations to optimize cloud usage and reduce costs.

Quantify Business Value

This domain aims to connect cloud usage and costs with the business value they generate. It helps ensure that the value delivered by cloud investments is transparent, and aligns with the organizational goals.

Capabilities:

- **Planning and Estimating:** Forecasting future cloud costs and usage based on historical data and business plans.
- **Budgeting:** Setting and managing budgets for cloud spending to ensure financial accountability.
- **Benchmarking:** Comparing cloud costs and performance metrics with industry standards and other organizations.
- **Unit Economics:** Analyzing the financial performance of individual units or projects to understand their contribution to the overall business value.
- **Forecasting:** Formulating a forecast of the projected expenses and benefits of cloud systems by employing statistical techniques, analyzing past spending trends, planned modifications, and pertinent data points.

Azure Features:

- **Azure Pricing Calculator:** Helps estimate costs for various Azure services and plan budgets accordingly.
- **Azure Total Cost of Ownership (TCO) Calculator:** Assists in understanding the long-term costs of using Azure services.
- **Azure Cost Management + Billing:** Provides budgeting tools and cost forecasting to align cloud spending with business goals.
- **Azure Monitor:** Offers performance monitoring and insights to quantify the business value of cloud investments.

Optimize Cloud Usage and Cost

This domain focuses on optimizing cloud resource usage and costs to ensure that the resources are used efficiently and cost-effectively.

Capabilities:

- **Architecting for Cloud:** Designing cloud architectures that balance performance, cost, and sustainability.
- **Rate Optimization:** Negotiating and managing cloud service rates to get the best possible pricing.
- **Workload Optimization:** Ensuring that the cloud workloads are running efficiently and only when needed.
- **Cloud Sustainability:** Considering the environmental impact of cloud usage and implementing sustainable practices.
- **Licensing and SaaS:** Analyzing and improving how software licenses and SaaS investments affect cloud costs and value by comprehending vendor terms, usage rights, and pricing, planning for optimal deployment.

Azure Features:

- **Azure Hybrid Benefit:** Provides cost savings by using on-premises licenses with Azure services.
- **Azure Reserved Virtual Machine Instances:** Offers discounted pricing for committing to using Azure VMs for a one or three-year term.
- **Azure Savings Plans:** Allows for flexible pricing and savings on Azure services.
- **Azure Advisor:** Provides recommendations to optimize cloud usage and reduce costs.

Manage the FinOps Practice

This domain involves establishing and maintaining a continuous FinOps practice within the organization. It focuses on improving processes, tools, and collaboration to support effective cloud management.

Capabilities:

- **FinOps Education and Enablement:** Providing training and resources to help all stakeholders understand and adopt FinOps practices.
- **FinOps Practice Operations:** Managing the day-to-day operations of the FinOps practice, including monitoring, reporting, and continuous improvement.
- **Cloud Policy and Governance:** Establishing policies and governance mechanisms to ensure compliance with financial and regulatory requirements.
- **FinOps Assessment:** Evaluating the effectiveness of the FinOps practice and identifying areas for improvement.
- **FinOps Tools and Services:** Offering the organization with a common set of tools and services according to the needs of each FinOps persona.
- **Onboarding Workloads:** Managing cloud workloads to ensure a clear visibility of costs and usage, meet operational goals, and maintain cost efficiency.
- **Invoicing and Chargeback:** Creating tailored reports, cloud invoice reconciliation processes, and chargeback models with Finance, Product, and Engineering teams to ensure that the cloud cost data and reporting aligns with the budgets and accounting needs.
- **Intersecting Disciplines:** Collaborating with allied disciplines like ITAM, ITFM, Sustainability, and Security to align their broader responsibilities with the organization's cloud strategy through FinOps.

Azure Features:

- **Azure Policy:** Helps set and enforce policies for resource governance and compliance.
- **Azure Governance:** Provides tools for managing and governing cloud resources effectively.
- **Azure Security Center:** Offers security recommendations and compliance monitoring to ensure best practices are followed.
- **Azure Training and Certification:** Provides resources for learning and certification to boost productivity and FinOps knowledge.

The FinOps Maturity: Crawl, Walk and Run

FinOps Maturity refers to the level of sophistication and effectiveness with which an organization implements and practices FinOps principles and processes. It is often described using a "Crawl, Walk, Run" model, where organizations start with the basic practices (Crawl), move to more structured and repeatable processes (Walk), and finally achieve optimized and mature FinOps practices (Run).

Crawl Maturity

Crawl Maturity in FinOps is the initial stage of maturity, where an organization is just beginning to understand and manage its cloud costs. At this stage, the focus is on basic practices and gaining initial insights into cloud spending. The organization may not have sophisticated tools or processes in place, and actions are often reactive rather than proactive.

Key Characteristics of Crawl Maturity:

- **Basic Reporting and Tooling:** Limited reporting capabilities and basic tools are used to gather data on cloud usage and costs.
- **Basic KPIs:** Simple Key Performance Indicators (KPIs) are set to measure success, but they may not cover all aspects of cloud spending.
- **Basic Processes and Policies:** Fundamental processes and policies are defined, but they are not yet fully implemented, or followed by all teams.
- **Understanding, but Limited Adoption:** The concept of FinOps is understood within the organization, but not all major teams are actively following the practices.
- **Low Hanging Fruit:** Efforts are focused on addressing the most obvious and easily achievable cost-saving opportunities.

Real Case Example:

Imagine a mid-sized software development company that has recently migrated some of its applications to the cloud. The company notices that its cloud spending is higher than expected, and decides to implement the basic FinOps practices to gain control over its costs.

At the Crawl stage, the company starts by:

- **Setting up the basic cost tracking:** Using simple tools to monitor cloud usage and costs.

- **Creating basic reports:** Generating monthly reports to identify major cost drivers.
- **Defining simple KPIs:** Establishing KPIs such as total cloud spend and cost per user.
- **Implementing basic policies:** Introducing policies to turn off unused resources and enforce cost-saving measures.

The company's finance team collaborates with the IT department to gather data and create initial reports. They focus on addressing the most obvious cost-saving opportunities, such as shutting down unused instances and optimizing resource allocation.

While the company is still in the initial stages of its FinOps journey, these initial steps help lay the foundation for more advanced practices in the future. As the company gains more insights and confidence, it can move on to the next stages of the FinOps Maturity Model: Walk and Run.

Walk Maturity

Walk Maturity in FinOps represents the intermediate stage, where an organization has moved beyond the basic practices and begins to develop more structured and repeatable processes. At this stage, FinOps practices are becoming more ingrained in the organization's operations, and there is a greater emphasis on collaboration and proactive management.

Key Characteristics of Walk Maturity:

- **Enhanced Reporting and Tooling:** More sophisticated tools and comprehensive reporting capabilities are in place to provide deeper insights into cloud costs and usage.
- **Advanced KPIs:** Detailed Key Performance Indicators (KPIs) are established to measure success across various aspects of cloud spending.
- **Defined Processes and Policies:** Well-defined processes and policies are in place and consistently followed by all relevant teams.
- **Cross-Functional Collaboration:** Increased collaboration between finance, engineering, IT, and other departments to optimize cloud costs.
- **Proactive Cost Management:** Emphasis on proactive management of cloud costs, including forecasting and optimization efforts.

Real Case Example:

Consider a large e-commerce company that has been using cloud services extensively for its online platform. Initially, they struggled with managing cloud costs, leading to the implementation of basic FinOps practices. After gaining initial insights, and addressing the most obvious cost-saving opportunities, they move to the Walk stage.

At the Walk stage, the company undertakes the following actions:

- **Implementing Enhanced Reporting:** They adopt more advanced reporting tools like Power BI and Azure Cost Management + Billing to provide detailed insights into cloud usage and costs. Reports are generated on a weekly basis and shared with the key stakeholders.
- **Establishing Advanced KPIs:** The company sets up the detailed KPIs, such as cost per transaction, cost per customer, and cost per application. These KPIs are tracked and analyzed regularly to measure the effectiveness of their cloud spending.
- **Defining and Following Processes:** The organization defines clear processes for provisioning and deprovisioning resources, enforcing tagging policies, and conducting regular cost reviews. These processes are documented and communicated to all relevant teams.
- **Fostering Cross-Functional Collaboration:** The finance team collaborates closely with engineering and IT departments to identify cost-saving opportunities and optimize resource usage. Regular meetings are held to discuss cloud spending and share best practices.
- **Proactive Cost Management:** The company focuses on proactive cost management by forecasting future cloud usage and costs, based on historical data and business plans. They implement strategies, such as reserved instances and spot instances, to optimize spending.

One specific initiative that they have undertaken is optimizing their use of Virtual Machines (VMs). By analyzing usage patterns and performance metrics, they identify the underutilized VMs, and consolidate workloads onto fewer instances. This results in significant cost savings while maintaining performance and reliability.

Additionally, they negotiate better pricing with their cloud service provider by leveraging their increased understanding of usage patterns and future needs. They also implement automated scripts to shut down non-production environments outside of business hours, further reducing the costs.

Through these efforts, the company successfully manages its cloud costs, ensuring financial accountability and optimizing resource usage. The Walk stage serves as a crucial stepping stone towards achieving full FinOps maturity, paving the way for more advanced and sophisticated practices in the future.

Run Maturity

Run Maturity in FinOps is the advanced stage where an organization has fully integrated FinOps practices into its operations. At this level, FinOps is ingrained in the company culture, with robust processes, tools, and automation enabling proactive and strategic cloud cost management. The organization operates with a high degree of efficiency and collaboration, and continuous improvement is a key focus.

Key Characteristics of Run Maturity:

- **Advanced Reporting and Tooling:** Utilizing sophisticated tools and automation for comprehensive insights and real-time reporting on cloud costs and usage.
- **Strategic KPIs:** Implementing complex KPIs that drive strategic decision-making and align with business objectives.
- **Mature Processes and Policies:** Established, documented, and widely adopted processes and policies that govern cloud cost management across the organization.
- **Deep Collaboration:** Seamless collaboration between finance, engineering, IT, and other departments, with cloud cost management being a shared responsibility.
- **Continuous Improvement:** A focus on refining and improving processes, tools, and practices to optimize cloud costs continually.

Real Case Example:

Let us take the example of a global financial services firm that has achieved Run Maturity in its FinOps practices.

At this stage, the firm has implemented the following actions:

- **Advanced Reporting and Tooling:** The firm uses advanced tools like Azure Cost Management + Billing, Power BI, and custom-built dashboards that provide real-time insights into cloud spending. They have automated alerts for anomalies, and utilized machine learning algorithms to predict the future costs and usage patterns.
- **Strategic KPIs:** The firm tracks complex KPIs, such as cost per transaction, cost per customer, and cost per application, which are integrated into the overall business performance metrics. These KPIs are reviewed regularly by the senior management to remain informed of the strategic decisions.
- **Mature Processes and Policies:** Well-documented and widely adopted processes and policies ensure that the cloud cost management practices are followed across the organization. Policies are enforced using Azure Policy and Compliance tools, ensuring adherence to the best practices.
- **Deep Collaboration:** There is a seamless collaboration between finance, engineering, IT, and procurement teams. Regular cross-functional meetings are held to discuss cloud spending, share insights, and identify opportunities for optimization. Cloud cost management is seen as a shared responsibility across the organization.

- **Continuous Improvement (CI):** The firm has a dedicated team that focuses on a continuous improvement of FinOps practices. This team regularly evaluates the effectiveness of processes and tools, identifies areas for improvement, and implements changes. They also stay updated with the latest industry trends and the best practices to ensure that the firm remains at the forefront of cloud cost management.

Additionally, the firm negotiates enterprise agreements with their cloud service providers, leveraging their understanding of usage patterns and future needs to secure favorable terms. They also implement a chargeback model, where each department is billed for their actual cloud usage, promoting accountability and efficient resource use.

Through these efforts, the firm successfully manages its cloud costs, ensuring financial accountability, optimizing resource usage, and aligning cloud spending with business goals. The Run stage represents the pinnacle of FinOps maturity, where the organization operates with a high degree of efficiency, and continuously seeks to improve its practices.

FinOps Maturity: Side-by-Side Comparison

FinOps maturity is easier to understand, when the stages can be compared directly. Each level reflects a different relationship between visibility, accountability, and operational discipline. The following table places the Crawl, Walk, and Run stages side by side, so that you can see how practices evolve, how responsibilities shift, and how cloud cost management becomes progressively more strategic.

Maturity Level	Description	Key Characteristics	RealWorld Behavior	Cloud/FinOps Impact
Crawl	Initial stage focused on visibility and basic control.	Basic reporting, simple KPIs, early policies, limited adoption, reactive actions.	Teams track spend monthly, shut down unused resources, and address obvious inefficiencies.	Visibility improves, but decisions remain slow and mostly tactical.
Walk	Intermediate stage with structured, repeatable processes.	Enhanced reporting, advanced KPIs, defined processes, crossfunctional collaboration, proactive cost management.	Weekly reporting, tagging enforcement, forecasting, VM rightsizing, and negotiated pricing.	Cloud spend becomes predictable, and teams begin optimizing based on usage patterns.

Maturity Level	Description	Key Characteristics	RealWorld Behavior	Cloud/FinOps Impact
Run	Advanced stage with integrated, automated, and strategic FinOps.	Realtime insights, strategic KPIs, mature governance, deep collaboration, continuous improvement.	Automated optimization, enterprise agreements, chargeback models, MLbased forecasting.	Cloud becomes a managed investment with measurable business outcomes and shared accountability.

***Table 3.1:** FinOps Maturity Side by Side Comparison*

Maturity Continuous Improvement

FinOps maturity is not a finish line. The idea, often expressed as "there are no runners", reflects the reality that no organization operates at a full Run maturity across every capability. Cloud environments evolve too quickly, business priorities shift, and different teams mature at different speeds. An organization may intentionally invest in advancing one capability to Run, while keeping another at Walk, because that balance delivers the right outcomes for that moment. Maturity in FinOps is, therefore. a continuous improvement effort, where progress is measured by how effectively teams adapt, learn, and refine their practices, rather than by reaching a permanent end state.

Assessing Maturity for Continuous Improvement

Here are some topics to consider, when assessing the FinOps maturity level of a department or organization.

- **Continuous Improvement:** Organizations should regularly evaluate and refine their FinOps practices. This involves staying updated with the latest tools, technologies, and the best practices in cloud cost management.
- **Cross-Functional Collaboration:** Ensuring that all relevant teams (finance, engineering, IT, procurement, and the like) are actively involved in FinOps processes. Collaboration and communication are the key in maintaining an elevated level of maturity.
- **Adaptability:** Being flexible and open to change is crucial. Organizations should be ready to pivot their strategies based on new insights, market trends, and technological advancements.
- **Skill Development:** Investing in continuous training and development for FinOps practitioners. This includes attending conferences like FinOps X, participating in workshops, and obtaining certifications.

- **Benchmarking:** Regularly comparing your FinOps practices with industry standards and the best practices. This helps identify areas for improvement, and ensures that the organization remains competitive.
- **Automation and Tooling:** Leveraging advanced tools and automation to streamline FinOps processes. This includes using AI and machine learning to predict costs, detect anomalies, and optimize resource usage.
- **Feedback Loops:** Establishing mechanisms for gathering feedback from all stakeholders involved in FinOps. This feedback can be used to make informed decisions, and drive continuous improvement.

By adopting this mindset, organizations create space for continuous learning and steady improvement, ensuring that their FinOps capabilities stay relevant and effective, as cloud environments and business need to evolve.

Conclusion

FinOps brings financial clarity to an environment defined by speed, elasticity, and constant change. Throughout this chapter, we established the foundations that make this possible: a shared definition of FinOps, the principles that guide decision-making, the lifecycle that structures day-to-day practice, and the personas and capabilities that turn the framework into an operating model. These elements form the baseline for any organization seeking to align cloud usage with business value.

What becomes clear is that FinOps is not a finance initiative or an engineering initiative. It is a collaborative discipline that depends on shared ownership. Engineers need timely data to make efficient architectural choices. Finance needs transparency to forecast and govern spend. Product teams need to understand how cloud decisions influence customer value. The FinOps principles exist to keep these groups aligned, especially when cloud behavior shifts faster than traditional governance models can respond.

The lifecycle reinforces this dynamic. Inform, Optimize, and Operate are not the sequential steps, but continuous motions that help organizations adapt to new workloads, new pricing models, and new business priorities. The maturity model adds another layer of realism: progress is uneven by design. Teams advance capability by capability, improving where it matters most rather than chasing a theoretical end state. This is why continuous improvement sits at the heart of FinOps. The goal is not perfection—it is responsiveness.

In the next chapter, we will explore the link between the two key concepts: FinOps as a cloud cost management framework and Earned Value Management, which is used to assess value. The main goal of FinOps is to maximize business value, while Earned Value shows us how to measure it. By combining these approaches, we create FinOps

Earned Value Management—a method for measuring and managing costs in the era of cloud technology. This is what we shall explore next.

References

- Oliveira, A. C. (2025). Ultimate FinOps for Azure. AVA Orange.
- FinOps Foundation. (n.d.-a). Adopting FinOps - Getting started. Retrieved October 21, 2024, from https://www.finops.org/wg/adopting-finops/
- FinOps Foundation. (n.d.-b). FinOps personas. Retrieved October 21, 2024, from https://www.finops.org/framework/personas/
- FinOps Foundation. (n.d.-c). Leadership persona. Retrieved October 21, 2024, from https://www.finops.org/framework/persona/leadership/
- Markanastasakis, V. & FinOps Foundation. (n.d.). Key 2024 Changes to the FinOps Framework: Evolving the Framework with the Practice of FinOps. Retrieved October 21, 2024, from https://www.finops.org/insights/2024-finops-framework/
- Martin, R. & FinOps Foundation. (n.d.). "There are no runners" underlines the point that getting to Run is not the goal, and it's not the end of the line. Retrieved October 21, 2024, from https://www.finops.org/insights/no-runners/
- The history of Microsoft Azure. (n.d.). TECHCOMMUNITY.MICROSOFT.COM. Retrieved October 21, 2024, from https://techcommunity.microsoft.com/t5/educator-developer-blog/the-history-of-microsoft-azure/ba-p/3574204

CHAPTER 4
The FinOps EVM Framework

Introduction

At this stage of our journey, we have reviewed the definition of Earned Value, its historical roots, and how it became a cornerstone of project control. Earned Value shifted the focus from a simple comparison of actual spend against the budgeted cost , to a more meaningful measure of outcomes delivered. We also examined the FinOps framework, which has risen in importance during the cloud era, as organizations seek to maintain visibility and discipline over dynamic, and often unpredictable costs. FinOps provides a structure that demonstrates how finance, engineering, and business teams must collaborate to ensure that cloud investments generate the expected value for the enterprise.

This chapter represents a pivotal moment in the book. Here, the two frameworks converge to form a new construct: the FinOps EVM Framework. The purpose of this framework is to translate the key Earned Value datapoints, such as Percent Complete, Actual Cost, and Planned Cost, into the language of cloud operations. It also requires us to address fundamental distinctions, such as the difference between the finite duration of a project and the ongoing nature of an operation. While some cloud initiatives are structured as projects with defined start and end dates, many others operate continuously, with no predetermined conclusion. Recognizing this distinction is critical for applying EVM principles in a cloud context.

In the pages ahead, we will explore the essential concepts of the FinOps EVM Framework and provide detailed guidance on how to calculate and interpret them. Practical exercises will be included to reinforce understanding, and to help readers apply these ideas in real-world scenarios. By engaging with these exercises, readers will not only grasp the mechanics of the framework, but also develop the ability to connect financial accountability with operational delivery. With this foundation established, we are ready to move into the details.

Structure

In this chapter, the following topics will be covered:

- Positioning EVM within the FinOps Framework
- Recognizing the Differences
- Applying EVM Concepts
- Earned Value, Percent Complete, and Unit Economics
- Calculating the FinOps Earned Value Management
- Estimating FinOps EVM Accurately
- Understanding EVM Cost Performance Indicator
- Applying FinOps EVM CPI to Cloud FinOps
- Challenges and Considerations on CPI

Positioning EVM within the FinOps Framework

Let us begin by considering the broader context. FinOps is an expansive discipline, and understanding where the FinOps EVM Framework fits within it, is essential for an effective cloud financial management.

In the previous chapter, we introduced FinOps Domains and Capabilities, which help structure this field. The FinOps EVM technique is best positioned within the Quantify Business Value domain, where it supports organizations in measuring, forecasting, and maximizing the value derived from cloud investments.

The succeeding figure presents the FinOps Framework from the FinOps Foundation, outlining the principles, domains, personas, phases, and maturity elements that shape a complete cloud financial management practice, highlighting the Quantify Business Value Domain and its capabilities.

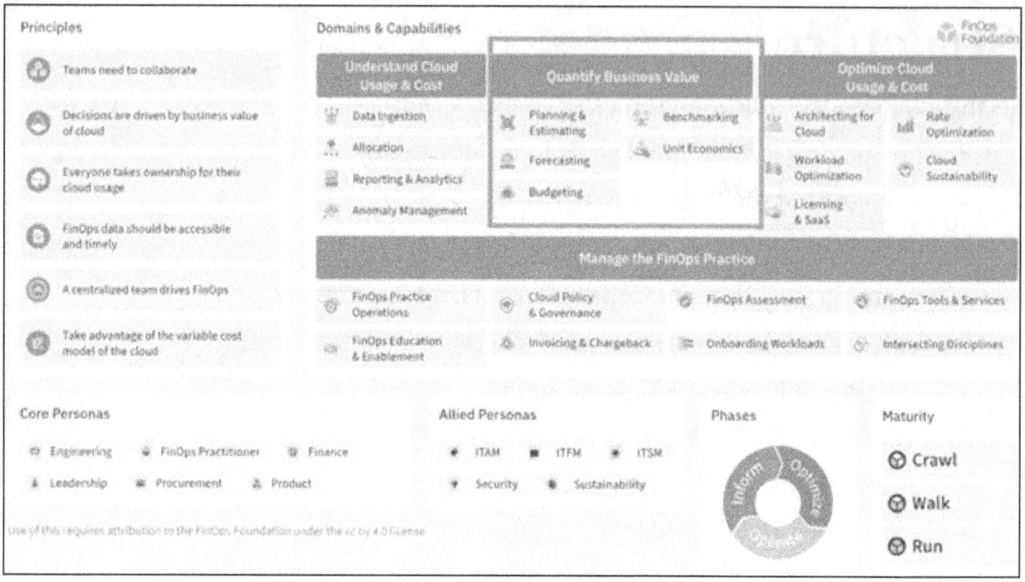

Figure 4.1: *The FinOps Framework from FinOps Foundation*

If we dig a little deeper into this domain, we will find the following definition.

The Capabilities in this Domain will help the organization:

- Plan, estimate, and forecast cloud needs using relevant cloud cost, impact, and usage data
- Enable teams to budget consistently and decrease probability of budgetary overrun
- Define techniques and models to establish benchmarks tied to business value
- Develop metrics that reveal the business value of cloud based on objective measurements

Figure 4.2: *FinOps Quantify Business Value Domain from FinOps Foundation*

As stated in the previous figure, the definitions of this capability fits very well with what the FinOps EVM Framework can provide. The combination of Earned Value Management and FinOps offers significant advantages for the broader 'Quantify Business Value' domain.

Recognizing the Differences

Earned Value Management and FinOps share a common goal of connecting financial accountability with delivery outcomes, yet they operate in distinct contexts. EVM was designed as a project management technique, built to measure progress against a defined scope, schedule, and budget. FinOps, on the other hand, emerged to address the realities of cloud operations, where spending is continuous, elastic, and often tied directly to business activity, rather than a fixed project plan. Understanding these differences is essential before attempting to merge the two into a unified framework.

- **Time Span**: EVM typically operates within project timelines, whereas FinOps spans an entire year or budget cycle.
- **Percent Complete**: In EVM, percent complete reflects project progress. In FinOps, it relates to planned versus actual unit economics (such as cost per order).

Applying EVM Concepts

Now, let us check how EVM concepts align with the FinOps context.

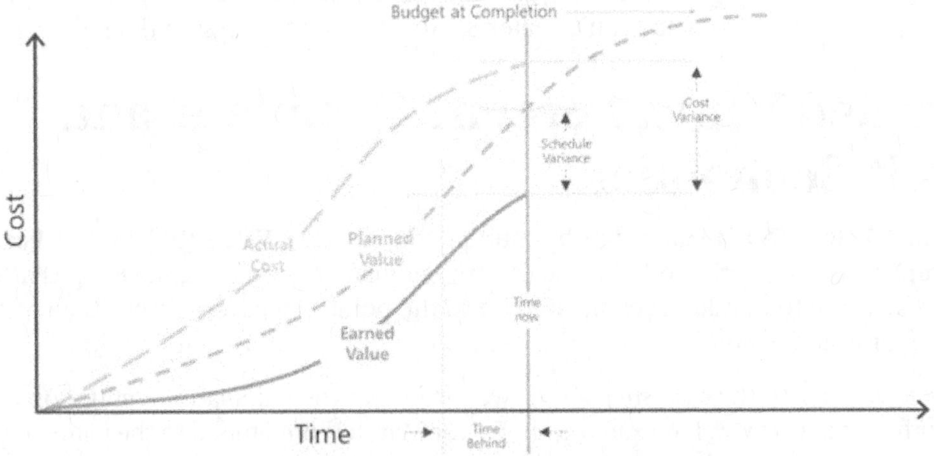

***Figure 4.3:** Earned Value Management*
Key Metrics in a Cumulative Cost Overtime Graph

- **Planned Value (PV)**: In FinOps, PV represents the budgeted cost for cloud resources over the year. It aligns with the annual budget plan.
- **Earned Value (EV)**: EV corresponds to the actual value of cloud services consumed. Tracking EV helps measure progress against the budget.
- **Actual Cost (AC)**: AC reflects the actual cloud spending. Comparing AC with EV provides insights into cost efficiency.
- **Cost Performance Index (CPI)**: CPI indicates whether cloud spending is on track. A CPI < 1 suggests overspending. The formula is CPI = EV / AC.
- **Schedule Performance Index (SPI)**: SPI assesses the pace of cloud resource consumption. An SPI < 1 indicates inefficiencies. The formula is SPI = EV / PV.

Assumptions

For an effective FinOps EVM calculation, we must assume that the following artifacts are present.

- Well-defined and understood **Unit Economics**. This is one of the Capabilities within the **'Quantify Business Value'** domain. We assume that there is a Unit Economics target for the budgeting period. For example, the X cost per order target for the year. Unit Economics will be explored in detail on *Chapter 7, Determining Unit Economics.*

- An established **Budget** for the budgeting period. More specifically, a plan of how much you think you are going to spend on each time division within your budget cycle. It is recommended that you have a monthly number, if the budgeting cycle is yearly, to say the least. This budget or Plan Value (PV) is an output of the **Budgeting** and **Planning and Estimating** capabilities. The Budget topic will be explored in details on *Chapter 8, The Budgeting Process with FinOps* EVM.

Earned Value, Percent Complete, and Unit Economics

Earned Value (EV) is calculated by multiplying **Planned Value (PV)** by the **Percent Complete** of the work. Both EV and PV are cumulative measures, meaning that they represent the total value accumulated up to the point of analysis, rather than just the value for a single month.

When we refer to the *assessing period*, we mean that the cumulative amount up to the month is under review. For example, the PV for March is not limited to the planned value of March alone. Instead, it represents the sum of the planned values for January, February, and March combined. In the same way, EV for March reflects the cumulative earned value for all work completed from the beginning of the year through the end of March.

This cumulative approach is essential, because it allows FinOps practitioners to see the full trajectory of progress and spending over time. Rather than focusing on isolated monthly snapshots, cumulative values provide a continuous picture of how the initiative is performing against expectations. This perspective makes it possible to identify trends, variances, and potential risks earlier, enabling corrective actions before issues escalate.

$$EV = PV \ x \ \%Complete$$

Figure 4.4: *Earned Value Formula*

For FinOps, Percent Complete is the relation between the Unit Economic, in the assessing period with the target Unit Economic. For example, let us say that in March, our cumulative cost per order is $0.54, and our target cost per order is $0.50. The Percent Complete will be 92.6%.

$$\%Complete = \frac{Unit\ Economic_{Target}}{Unit\ Economic_{Month}}$$

Figure 4.5: *Percent Complete Formula*

Calculating the FinOps Earned Value Management

Let us use a simple example to demonstrate how this can be calculated. Consider a budgeting cycle of a year, starting in January and finishing in December. For simplicity, consider that the monthly spend is estimated at $100 flat. PV is the cumulative amount at any given month.

Month	Budget	PV	% Complete	EV	Actual	AC	CPI	Forecast
0	0	0						
1	100	100						
2	100	200						
3	100	300						
4	100	400						
5	100	500						
6	100	600						
7	100	700						
8	100	800						
9	100	900						
10	100	1000						
11	100	1100						
12	100	1200						

Table 4.1: *Planned Value (PV) is a Cumulative Sum of the Budget by Month*

See how the Planned Valued is graphically represented on the following sentence. As mentioned, it resulted in a flat line.

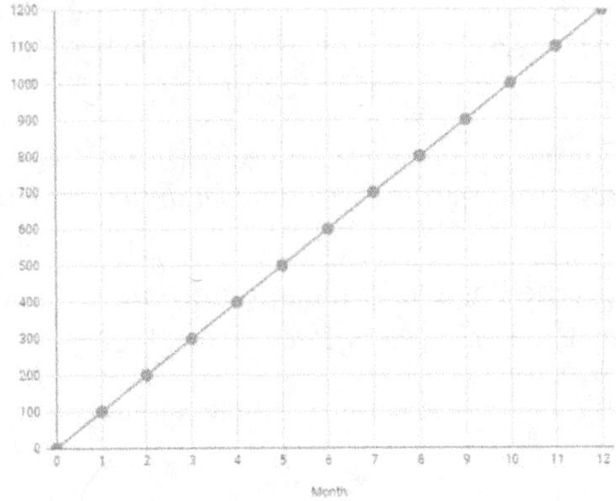

Figure 4.6: *Graphical Representation of the Planned Value*

Scenario 1: Under Budget

Consider that we are assessing the month 5 (May), and that the calculated figures for %Complete, Actual Cost, and cumulative Actual Cost (AC) are as follows:

PV x %Complete = EV

Month	Budget	PV	% Complete	EV	Actual	AC	CPI	Forecast
0	0	0	0%	0	0	0		
1	100	100	130%	130	80	80		
2	100	200	130%	260	70	150		
3	100	300	150%	450	80	230		
4	100	400	140%	560	85	315		
5	100	500	145%	725	85	400		
6	100	600						
7	100	700						
8	100	800						
9	100	900						
10	100	1000						
11	100	1100						
12	100	1200						

Table 4.2: *Scenario 1 – Under Budget*

Let us put these numbers in a graph and discuss them a little further.

PV x %Complete = EV

Month	Budget	PV	% Complete	EV	Actual	AC	CPI	Forecast
0	0	0	0%	0	0	0		
1	100	100	130%	130	80	80	1.63	
2	100	200	130%	260	70	150	1.73	
3	100	300	150%	450	80	230	1.96	
4	100	400	140%	560	85	315	1.78	
5	100	500	145%	725	85	400	1.81	
6	100	600						
7	100	700						
8	100	800						
9	100	900						
10	100	1000						
11	100	1100						
12	100	1200						

Table 4.3: *Scenario 1 – Under Budget with CPI Calculated*

On the graph, we now add the Earned Value and Actual Cost according to this scenario, highlighting even clearer the variance between the two.

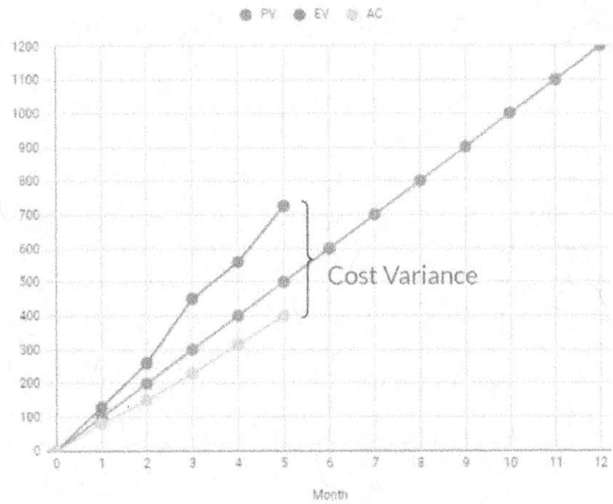

Figure 4.7: *Cost Variance for Scenario 1*

The cost variance is the difference between the Earned Value and the Actual Cost. This is the real value that we have earned up, until that point in time.

$$CV = EV - AC$$

Figure 4.8: *Cost Variance Formula*

Cost Variance, in this example, equals \$325. If Earned Value were not calculated, we would only have the normal comparison of Actuals versus Plan, which would be \$100. It is a good result, but not as good as the real situation. Earned Value takes into consideration the business result by accounting for expected and real Unit Economics.

Scenario 2: Over Budget

Now, let us consider that, although PV and AC are the same, %Complete went differently, as unit economics were not according to what was expected.

PV x %Complete = EV

Month	Budget	PV	% Complete	EV	Actual	AC	CPI
0	0	0	0%	0	0	0	
1	100	100	45%	45	80	80	0.56
2	100	200	50%	100	70	150	0.67
3	100	300	60%	180	80	230	0.78
4	100	400	55%	220	85	315	0.70
5	100	500	50%	250	85	400	0.63
6	100	600					
7	100	700					
8	100	800					
9	100	900					
10	100	1000					
11	100	1100					
12	100	1200					

Table 4.4: *Scenario 2 – Over Budget with CPI Calculated until May*

Considering the same Planned Value, and let us plot the Earned Value figures into the graph.

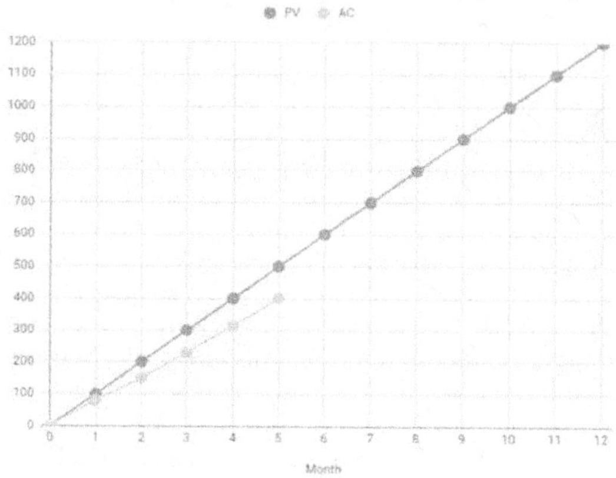

Figure 4.9: *Monthly Progression until May, and Cost Variance*

If only Actuals and Plan were considered, we could be deceived by the apparent positive result of $25 under. But in reality, when we compare Actuals (AC) to Earned Value, we will see that we are actually $150 over. In other words, there is a negative Cost Variance of -$150.

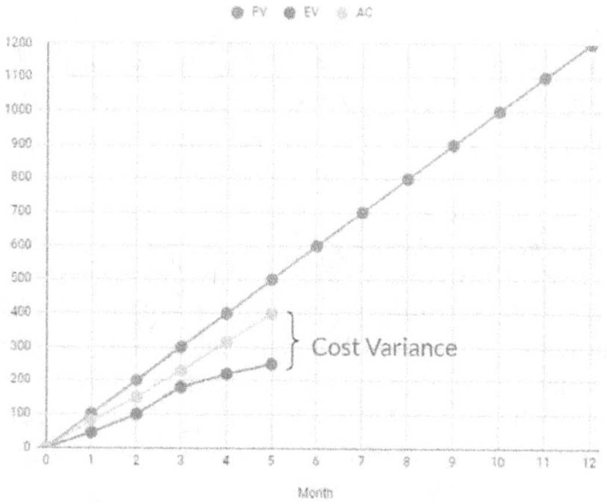

Figure 4.10: *Cost Variance for Scenario 2*

This scenario concludes that, although we are spending less than planned, we are not reaching the expected business value, due to a negative cost variance.

Estimating FinOps EVM Accurately

Accurate estimation of **Earned Value (EV)** is essential for an effective **Earned Value Management (EVM)**. Let us break down the steps to estimate EV accurately:

Determine Percent Complete

- This is the most important part. The percent complete will be tied to Unit Economics.
- A target Unit Economic should be determined in advance. Normally, it can be done as a part of the budgeting exercise, and should be reviewed on a periodic basis.
- Assess the Unit Economic for the reporting period. For more advanced teams, determine the Unit Economics specifically for the team. Determine what percentage compared with the target established for the team/product/area/and so on. This step provides the foundation for calculating EV.

$$\%Complete = \frac{Unit\ Economic_{Target}}{Unit\ Economic_{Month}}$$

Figure 4.11: *Percent Complete Formula for FinOps EVM*

Planned Value (PV)

- PV represents the planned budget for the work completed up to a specific point in time. It is the value of the work that was scheduled to be done.
- In the FinOps context, it is simply the budget amount for any given specific day, on the lowest level available.

Earned Value (EV)

- EV measures the actual value of what has been delivered from the products and services on the cloud. It reflects the progress achieved.
- Earned Value (EV) is the result of Planned Value (PV) times %Complete. Remember that both EV and PV are cumulative for the assessing period. By assessing period, we mean "the cumulative amount until the month we are doing the analysis". For example, PV of March is the cumulative amount of the first 3 months of the year.

$$EV = PV\ x\ \%Complete$$

Figure 4.12: *Earned Value Formula*

Actual Cost (AC)

- AC represents the actual cost incurred for the assessing period. Obtain this information from cloud billing data.
- AC is the total cost spent up to the current point in time.

- Make sure that the AC comes from data that is correctly mapped within your reporting system. Also, make sure that the period assessed contains the entire Actual Cost, as some costs may take a few days to show on reports.

Cost Variance (CV)

- CV shows whether the project is under or over budget.
- Calculate CV using the formula: CV = EV – AC

Cost Performance Indicator (CPI)

Cost Performance Indicator (CPI) is obtained by dividing Earned Value (EV) by Actual Cost (AC).

$$CPI = \frac{EV}{AC}$$

Figure 4.13: *Cost Performance Indicator Formula*

If we apply this formula for the two scenarios, here is what we get:

$$CPI = \frac{\$725}{\$400} \qquad CPI = \frac{\$250}{\$400}$$

$$CPI = 1.81 \qquad CPI = 0.63$$

Scenario 1 *Scenario 2*

Figure 4.14: *CPI for Scenarios 1 and 2*

- CPI is higher than 1; we are spending less to achieve the business results.
- CPI is lower than 1; we are spending more, and missing the target.
- CPI is equal to 1; we are progressing according to the plan.

It turns out that CPI becomes a good indicator, as with just one number, we are able to know if our cloud expenditure is delivering the value expected.

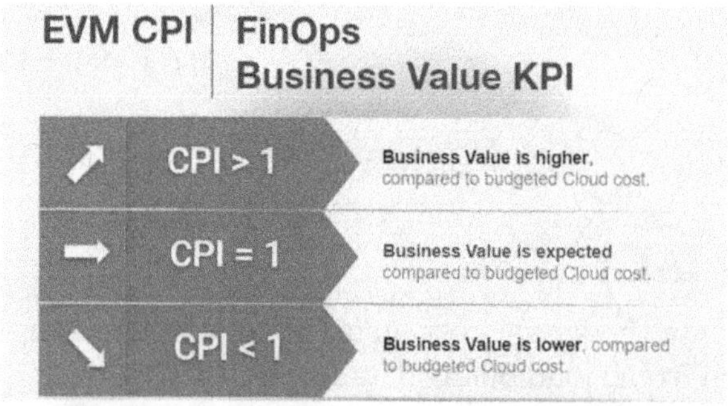

Figure 4.15: *Quick Card to Help Interpret the CPI Result*

When executives finally grasp the concept of FinOps, EVM CPI, and truly understand its implications, they gain the power to instantly gauge the success or failure of a project, or an initiative in terms of delivering the Business Value. The ability to swiftly evaluate current cloud spending is invaluable. The mere existence of this KPI, and its accurate calculation, signifies that the fundamental processes for managing cloud costs are, at the very least, in place to offer this concise measurement that empowers well-informed decisions.

Other EVM Indicators

- Besides CV and CPI, consider other indicators:
  - **Cost Performance Index (CPI)**: CPI = EV / AC.
  - **Estimate at Completion (EAC)**: EAC estimates the total cost of the budgeting period based on the current performance.
  - **Estimate to Complete (ETC)**: ETC estimates the remaining cost needed to complete the budgeting period.
  - **Budget at Completion (BAC):** Simply the total cost of the budget period.
  - **To-Complete Performance Index (TCPI)**: TCPI = (BAC – EV) / (BAC – AC).
  - **Schedule Variance (SV):** SV = EV – PV. It is the cost of the actual schedule (delayed or ahead of schedule).

Applying FinOps EVM CPI to Cloud FinOps

There are two main areas where FinOps EVM can be applied: Cost Optimization and Business Value Management. Let us look at each one of them:

Cloud Cost Optimization

In the context of cloud computing, EVM CPI becomes a powerful tool for **Financial Operations (FinOps)** leaders. Here is why:

- **Cost Efficiency**: EVM CPI helps organizations assess whether their cloud spending aligns with the value delivered. A high EVM CPI indicates an efficient utilization of the cloud resources, while a low EVM CPI signals a potential waste or overspending.
- **Resource Allocation**: By tracking EVM CPI, leaders can allocate resources effectively. If a specific cloud service or workload consistently shows a low EVM CPI, it warrants investigation. Perhaps, there is an opportunity to optimize resource allocation, or choose a more cost-effective solution.

Cloud Business Value Measurement

- **Business Alignment**: EVM CPI directly ties financial performance to business outcomes. Leaders can evaluate whether cloud investments are translating into tangible business value. For example, if a new feature deployment has a high EVM CPI, it suggests that the investment is paying off.
- **Decision Making**: EVM CPI informs strategic decisions. Leaders can prioritize projects, based on their EVM CPI scores. Initiatives with a positive EVM CPI may receive additional funding, while those with a negative EVM CPI may require adjustments or revaluation.

Challenges and Considerations on CPI

Understanding CPI in FinOps EVM requires a careful attention to data accuracy and contextual interpretation, ensuring meaningful insights for decision-making.

Data Accuracy

- Accurate data is essential for calculating EVM CPI. Leaders must ensure that cost and performance data are up-to-date and reliable. Here, the FinOps team has an important role to play, in order to ensure that the processes and practices are properly followed.

Contextual Interpretation

- EVM CPI should be interpreted in context. A low EVM CPI does not automatically indicate failure; it might be acceptable, if the project is at an early stage, or if certain costs are front-loaded.

Conclusion

Although the application of Earned Value Management (EVM) to FinOps may appear novel, the underlying technique has been established for many years. Concepts such as Actual Cost (AC), Earned Value (EV), and Planned Value (PV) may not directly correspond to the terminology commonly used in day-to-day cloud cost management. However, adherence to these established terms provides a significant advantage: it allows practitioners to leverage the extensive body of knowledge already available in the form of articles, research papers, training materials, and professional discussions that have accumulated around EVM over decades.

The strength of the FinOps EVM approach lies in its ability to condense complex financial and operational realities into a small set of indicators. These indicators reveal the relationship between cost and expected business outcomes, expressed in monetary terms that are accessible to both technical and financial stakeholders. Among them, the Cost Performance Indicator (CPI) stands out as a particularly effective measure. CPI consolidates actual expenditure, planned expectations, and business results into a single figure, offering a rapid assessment of performance. It is important to emphasize that CPI is not a definitive judgment, but rather an indicator—a tool designed to prompt discussion, highlight variances, and guide corrective action.

Adopting EVM principles within FinOps requires a certain level of organizational maturity. Capabilities such as planning and estimating, budgeting, and unit economics must be sufficiently developed to provide the necessary inputs for accurate reporting and analytics. From an optimistic perspective, the integration of EVM into FinOps can be seen as a natural progression in the maturity journey of cloud financial management. As organizations evolve, FinOps EVM enables senior leaders and practitioners across the "Quantify Business Value" domain to align on shared metrics, communicate with clarity, and act proactively in pursuit of business objectives.

In the next chapter, we will learn how to calculate the core FinOps EVM indicators. We will revisit the foundational metrics introduced here—AC, PV, EV, and CPI—and see how they serve as inputs to additional indicators that expand our analytical capabilities. This progression will help us measure value with more precision, and support a more disciplined approach in managing cloud performance and financial outcomes.

Exercises

The following exercises provide an opportunity to apply the concepts introduced in this chapter. Solutions are available at the end of the chapter.

Exercise 1:

Context: A company planned to process **100,000 customer orders in Q1** with a target **cost per order of $0.50**. By the end of the quarter, the company actually processed **95,000 orders**, and the total cloud spend reported was **$60,000**.

Task:

1. Calculate the **Planned Value (PV)** for Q1.
2. Calculate the **Actual Cost (AC)** for Q1.
3. Calculate the **Earned Value (EV)** based on the actual number of orders processed.
4. Provide an analysis of the current situation, considering whether the company is overbudget or underbudget, and explain what the calculated values reveal about efficiency and performance.

Exercise 2:

Context: A product team forecasted **80,000 API calls in April** with a target **cost per call of $0.10**. By the end of the month, the team actually delivered **82,000 API calls**, and the total cloud spend reported was **$6,500**.

Task:

1. Calculate the **Planned Value (PV)** for April.
2. Calculate the **Actual Cost (AC)** for April.
3. Calculate the **Earned Value (EV)** based on the actual number of API calls delivered.
4. Provide an analysis of the current situation, considering whether the team is overbudget or under budget, and explain what the calculated values reveal about efficiency and performance.

Exercise 3:

Context: A company budgeted **$120,000** for cloud spend in the first half of the year. The expected unit economics were **$0.40 per transaction**. By the end of June, the actual unit economics were **$0.48 per transaction**, and the actual spend reported was **$130,000**.

Task:

1. Calculate the **Planned Value (PV)** based on the budget.
2. Identify the **Actual Cost (AC)** from reported spend.
3. Calculate the **Percent Complete**, defined here as Unit Economic Target : Actual Unit Economic.
4. Calculate the **Earned Value (EV)** using EV = PV × Percent Complete.
5. Calculate the **Cost Variance (CV)** using CV = EV – AC.
6. Provide an analysis of the situation, including CPI and Cost Variance, and interpret the results.

Exercise 4:

Context: A company budgeted **$100,000** for cloud spend in Q2. The expected unit economics were **$0.25 per API call**. By the end of the quarter, the actual unit economics were **$0.30 per API call**, and the actual spend reported was **$95,000**.

Task:

1. Calculate the **Planned Value (PV)** based on the budget.
2. Identify the **Actual Cost (AC)** from reported spend.
3. Calculate the **Percent Complete**, defined as Unit Economic Target : Actual Unit Economic.
4. Calculate the **Earned Value (EV)** using EV = PV × Percent Complete.
5. Calculate the **Cost Performance Indicator (CPI)** and **Cost Variance (CV = EV – AC)**.

6. Provide an analysis of the situation, explaining why this is worse than a simple PV versus AC comparison.

Exercise 5: Apparent Overspend but True Efficiency

Context: A company budgeted **$150,000** for cloud spend in Q3. The expected Unit Economics was defined as **$0.50 per transaction**. By the end of the quarter, the actual unit economics were measured at **$0.45 per transaction**, and the actual spend reported was **$160,000**. The company processed **360,000 transactions** during this period.

At first glance, the actual spending is higher than the planned budget, suggesting an overspend. However, Earned Value analysis reveals a different outcome.

Task:

1. Calculate the **Planned Value (PV)** based on the budget.
2. Identify the **Actual Cost (AC)** from reported spend.
3. Calculate the **Percent Complete**, defined as Unit Economic Target : Actual Unit Economic.
4. Calculate the **Earned Value (EV)** using EV = PV × Percent Complete.
5. Calculate the **Cost Performance Indicator (CPI)** and **Cost Variance (CV = EV – AC).**
6. Provide an analysis of the situation, explaining why this is better than expected.

Exercise Solutions

Let us check the responses for the proposed exercises.

Exercise 1 Solution:

Planned Value (PV): 100,000 orders × $0.50 = **$50,000**

- **Actual Cost (AC):** Reported cloud spend = **$60,000**
- **Earned Value (EV):** 95,000 orders × $0.50 = **$47,500**
- **Cost Performance Indicator (CPI):** EV : AC = 47,500 : 60,000 = **0.79**

Analysis: The CPI is below 1, which indicates an **over-budget situation**. The company spent more than planned while delivering fewer orders than expected. This reflects an inefficiency in cloud usage, and highlights the need for corrective actions, such as workload optimization, architectural adjustments, or improved forecasting.

Exercise 2 Solution:

- **Planned Value (PV):** 80,000 calls × $0.10 = **$8,000**

- **Actual Cost (AC):** Reported cloud spend = **$6,500**
- **Earned Value (EV):** 82,000 calls × $0.10 = **$8,200**
- **Cost Performance Indicator (CPI):** EV : AC = 8,200 : 6,500 = **1.26**

Analysis: The CPI is above 1, which indicates an **underbudget situation**. The team delivered more API calls than planned, while spending less than forecasted. This reflects efficiency in cloud usage, and suggests that the optimization strategies or favorable workload patterns contributed to the improved performance. The challenge is to determine whether this efficiency can be sustained over time, and to identify the practices that led to the positive outcome.

Exercise 3 Solution:

- Planned Value (PV): 120,000
- Actual Cost (AC): 130,000
- Percent Complete: 0.40 : 0.48 = 0.83 (83%)
- Earned Value (EV): 120,000 × 0.83 = 99,600
- Cost Performance Indicator (CPI): 99,600 : 130,000 = 0.77
- Cost Variance (CV): EV – AC = 99,600 – 130,000 = –30,400

Analysis: CPI of 0.77 indicates an overbudget situation with reduced efficiency in unit economics. Comparing PV to AC alone suggests a **$10,000** overspend, but CV reveals a **$30,400** shortfall in earned value against plan. The variance is larger when business value is considered, since higher-than-target cost per transaction lowers percent complete and compresses EV. The organization is paying more, while converting spending into outcomes less effectively. Corrective actions should target efficiency drivers in architecture, scaling, pricing, and workload patterns to improve unit economics, and close the EV gap.

Exercise 4 Solution:

- Planned Value (PV): 100,000
- Actual Cost (AC): 95,000
- Percent Complete: 0.25 : 0.30 = 0.83 (83%)
- Earned Value (EV): 100,000 × 0.83 = 83,000
- Cost Performance Indicator (CPI): 83,000 : 95,000 = 0.87
- Cost Variance (CV = EV – AC): 83,000 – 95,000 = –12,000

Analysis: AC is lower than PV, which suggests a favorable spend at first glance. EV is lower than both PV and AC, which signals reduced value delivery and inefficiency. The CPI of 0.87 confirms weak cost performance, and the negative CV of –12,000 indicates an overbudget condition relative to earned value. The situation is worse than expected when the business value is considered, since spending did not translate into outcomes at the planned efficiency. Corrective actions should investigate unit economics drivers, workload design, scaling policies, and pricing levers to restore the cost effectiveness.

Exercise 5 Solution:

- Planned Value (PV): 150,000
- Actual Cost (AC): 160,000
- Percent Complete: 0.50 : 0.45 = 1.11 (111%)
- Earned Value (EV): 150,000 × 1.11 = 166,500
- Cost Performance Indicator (CPI): 166,500 : 160,000 = 1.04
- Cost Variance (CV = EV – AC): 166,500 – 160,000 = +6,500

Analysis: Although, AC is higher than PV, it suggests an overspending when viewed in isolation, EV is higher than both PV and AC. This indicates that the company delivered more business value than planned, at a lower unit cost per transaction. The CPI of 1.04 confirms efficiency, and the positive CV of +6,500 shows that outcomes exceeded expectations relative to spending. In other words, the situation is actually **under budget and better than expected** when business value is considered. This demonstrates how FinOps EVM provides a more accurate picture than simple budget comparisons, highlighting efficiency gains that traditional cost tracking would miss.

Reference

- Oliveira, A. O. (2024, November 7). A *Comprehensive Guide to FINOPs Earned Value Management*. ZEPHYR GLOBE. Retrieved December 8, 2025, from https://zephyrglobe.com/2024/11/07/a-comprehensive-guide-to-finops-earned-value-management/

Chapter 5
Calculating FinOps EVM Indicators

Introduction

FinOps Earned Value Management reaches a new level of clarity, once the practitioners move beyond the foundational indicators, and start working with the full suite of EVM metrics. The previous chapter established the essential building blocks: Earned Value, Actual Cost, Planned Value, Cost Variance, and the Cost Performance Index. These metrics form the core of any EVM system, and they give FinOps teams the first reliable signals about whether the cloud spend is aligned with expectations. They also reveal how effectively engineering teams are converting cloud investment into measurable progress.

This chapter expands the analytical toolkit. Traditional EVM includes a broader set of indicators that help forecast outcomes, evaluate schedule performance, and anticipate financial risk. When translated into the FinOps domain, these metrics become powerful instruments for predicting future cloud costs, assessing the pace of cloud adoption, and identifying the financial impact of architectural or operational decisions. They also support more mature conversations with engineering, product, and executive stakeholders, by grounding the discussions in quantifiable trends, rather than intuition.

You will explore metrics, such as Schedule Variance, Schedule Performance Index, Estimate at Completion, Estimate to Complete, Variance at Completion, and To-Complete Performance Index. Each one offers a different perspective on performance and forecast accuracy. The chapter explains how these indicators are calculated, how they behave in traditional project management, and how they can be adapted to cloud-driven environments, where spend is continuous, variable, and influenced by both technical and business decisions.

To reinforce learning, the chapter includes practical exercises that simulate real FinOps scenarios. These activities help readers apply the formulas, interpret the results, and understand how EVM metrics guide decision-making in day-to-day cloud operations.

The goal is to equip the practitioners with a complete, actionable framework for measuring financial performance across the cloud lifecycle.

Structure

In this chapter, the following topics will be covered:

- Overview of FinOps EVM Metrics
- EVM Metrics: Classification
- Input Metrics
- Output Metrics: Current Status
- Key Takeaways from Current-Status Output Metrics
- Output Metrics: Forecast
- Key Takeaways from Forecast Output Metrics

Overview of FinOps EVM Metrics

FinOps Earned Value Management relies on a set of interconnected metrics that describe the performance from different angles. Some metrics serve as inputs, forming the raw material for all calculations. Others are outputs that reveal the current state of financial performance, or project progress. A third group looks ahead, offering forecasts that help FinOps teams anticipate future spending, evaluate expected outcomes, and guide corrective actions. Understanding how these metrics relate to one another is essential for building a reliable EVM practice in cloud-driven environments.

This section organizes the full EVM metric suite into a simple structure: input metrics, current-status output metrics, and forecast output metrics. Each metric is listed with a concise definition, and a clear indication of how it translates into FinOps practice. This classification helps the readers navigate the growing set of indicators, and prepares them for the detailed explanations and exercises that follow.

EVM Metrics: Classification

EVM metrics can be classified as Input and Output metrics. Let us see each one of them in summary.

Input Metrics

These metrics are the foundation for all EVM calculations.

- **Planned Value (PV):** The authorized budget for the work planned to be completed by a given date. In FinOps, PV represents the expected cloud spend for planned engineering or platform activities.

- **Earned Value (EV):** The budgeted value of the work actually completed. In FinOps, EV reflects the value of cloud-enabled progress delivered so far, based on Unit Economics, such as the number of events processed, active users served, or requests handled.
- **Actual Cost (AC):** The real cost incurred for the work performed. In FinOps, AC is the actual cloud spent recorded in billing data.
- **Budget at Completion (BAC):** The sum of all budgets established for the work to be performed.

Output Metrics: Current Status

These metrics describe how things are going right now.

- **Cost Variance (CV):** This is EV minus AC. It indicates whether cloud spend is above or below expectations.
- **Cost Performance Index (CPI):** This is EV divided by AC. It shows cost efficiency in converting cloud spend into progress.
- **Schedule Variance (SV):** This is EV minus PV. It measures whether progress is ahead or behind the planned pace.
- **Schedule Performance Index (SPI):** This is EV divided by PV. It indicates the rate at which value is being delivered compared to the plan.

Output Metrics: Forecast

These metrics project future outcomes based on current performance.

- **Estimate at Completion (EAC):** Forecasted total cost at the end of the initiative. In FinOps, EAC predicts total cloud spending based on current trends.
- **Estimate to Complete (ETC):** Expected cost required to finish the remaining work. In FinOps, ETC estimates future cloud spend needed to complete the initiative.
- **Variance at Completion (VAC):** Budget at Completion minus EAC. Shows whether the initiative is expected to finish under or over the planned cloud budget.
- **To-Complete Performance Index (TCPI):** The efficiency required from now on to meet a target (BAC or EAC). In FinOps, TCPI indicates the cost discipline needed to stay within the budget.

As we head to the next sections, we will detail each metric, outline the method of calculation and provide the context for its application within FinOps. Each metric will be examined in turn to highlight how it can be used to monitor and forecast, and why not say, optimize cloud spend. With these metrics in hand, senior leaders, directors and engineering managers will be able to make informed decisions about what to prioritize their optimization efforts based on value. With all that said, let us head to it.

Input Metrics

The aforementioned metrics are repeated here, just so that we have all the FinOps EVM metrics consolidated in just one place. We will discuss BAC, that was the only one, which was not mentioned previously, but has a strong connection with Planned Value.

Input metrics are the foundation of every Earned Value Management calculation. They represent the raw data that feeds all performance and forecasting indicators. In FinOps, these inputs come from a mix of cloud billing, engineering progress tracking, and financial planning. Understanding them deeply is essential, because every output metric depends on their accuracy and consistency.

The succeeding figure highlights the core input metrics used in Earned Value Management, showing how AC, PV, and EV originate raw data sources, as examples.

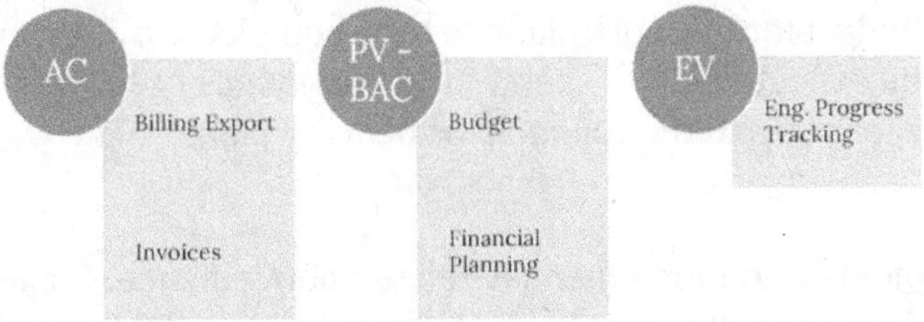

***Figure 5.1:** FinOps EVM Core Input Metrics and Their Raw Sources*

In the following sections, you will find the four core input metrics: **Actual Cost (AC), Planned Value (PV), Earned Value (EV), and Budget at Completion (BAC)**. They were extensively discussed in *Chapter* 4, with The FinOps EVM Framework.

Each one plays a distinct role in describing the cost, progress, and expectations in cloud-driven environments.

Actual Cost

Abbreviation: AC

Definition

The total cost incurred for the work performed, and resource used up to a specific point in time. In FinOps, AC represents the real cloud spend captured in billing data for the initiative, workload, or project.

How it is used

AC is the anchor for all cost-related performance metrics. It allows FinOps teams to compare the actual cloud spend with planned spend and with the value delivered. It is also the primary input for cost efficiency indicators, such as Cost Variance and the Cost Performance Index.

Equation

$$AC = \textit{Sum of actual cloud costs incurred to date}$$

Interpretation

AC shows how much has been spent so far. A rising AC without a corresponding increase in EV signals an inefficiency or unexpected consumption. A stable AC aligned with EV indicates a healthy cost control.

Planned Value

Abbreviation: PV

Definition

The authorized budget for the work planned to be completed by a given date. In FinOps, PV represents the expected cloud spend for the amount of progress that should have been achieved, according to the roadmap or delivery plan.

How it is used

PV establishes the baseline for schedule-related performance. It allows the teams to determine whether the progress is happening at the expected pace. PV also supports forecasting by showing how much spend should have occurred by now, if the plan was being followed.

Equation

$$PV = \textit{Sum of what was planned to date}$$

Interpretation

PV reflects what "should" have happened by this point. If EV is lower than PV, the initiative is behind schedule. If EV is higher than PV, progress is ahead of the planned pace.

Earned Value

Abbreviation: EV

Definition

The budgeted value of the work actually completed to date. In FinOps, EV represents the value of cloud-enabled progress delivered so far, and is expressed in budget terms rather than cost terms.

How it is used

EV is the central metric of FinOps EVM, because it connects the progress with financial expectations. It allows FinOps teams to quantify how much value has been delivered relative to both planned spend and actual spend. EV is used in every major performance indicator, including CV, CPI, SV, and SPI.

Equation

$$EV = \textit{Actual percentage of work completed} \times PV$$

Interpretation

EV shows how much value has been earned. If EV grows steadily in line with AC, the initiative is converting cloud spend into progress efficiently. If EV lags behind AC, the initiative is consuming cloud resources without delivering proportional value.

Budget at Completion

Abbreviation: BAC

Definition

The total authorized budget for the entire initiative or project. In FinOps, BAC represents the expected total cloud spend allocated for delivering the full scope of work within a budget cycle, that normally is defined in a yearly basis.

How it is used

BAC is the reference point for all planning and forecasting. It defines the financial boundary within which the initiative is expected to operate. BAC is used to calculate PV, EV, Variance at Completion, and the To-Complete Performance Index.

Equation

$$BAC = \textit{Total planned cloud budget for the initiative}$$

Interpretation

BAC sets the financial target. If forecasts such as EAC exceed BAC, the initiative is projected to overspend. If the EAC stays below BAC, the initiative is on track to finish within the allocated cloud budget.

Exercise: Identifying Input Metrics in a Cloud Scenario

A platform team is migrating a set of internal services to a managed Kubernetes environment. The FinOps team is tracking the progress using Earned Value Management. The initiative has a total approved cloud budget of **€240,000**, planned to be spent evenly across 10 sprints. The delivery plan follows the same structure:

progress was also expected to advance in equal increments throughout those 10 sprints.

By the end of Sprint 4, the team planned to complete 40 percent of the migration work. Actual engineering progress shows that 35 percent of the work is complete. Cloud billing data for the same period shows €92,000 of actual spending.

Using this information, identify the four input metrics: **AC, PV, EV, and BAC.**

Answer Key

It is normal for these metrics to feel abstract at first. With practice, the patterns become easier to recognize, because each metric answers a different question about cost, progress, or expectations. The following table shows how the values map to the four input metrics.

Metric	Amount	Why
BAC	€ 240,000	This is the total approved cloud budget for the entire migration initiative.
AC	€ 92,000	This is the actual cloud spend recorded in billing data up to the end of Sprint 4.
PV	€ 96,000	Sum of what was planned to date was 40 percent, so PV equals 0.40 × €240,000.
EV	€ 84,000	Actual progress was 35 percent, so EV equals 0.35 × €240,000.

Table 5.1: *Exercise - Identifying Input Metrics in a Cloud Scenario*

Exercise: Identifying Input Metrics in an Operational, Unit-Economics Scenario

A SaaS platform runs a real-time analytics service that processes customer events. The FinOps team uses Unit Economics to measure value creation. The service has a total budget of **€480,000** for the current fiscal year. Due to some front loaded cost, it is expected that 60% is spent during the first half to the year (H1). By the end of Q2, the team planned to process **1.2 billion events**, which corresponds to **50 percent** of the annual value target. Actual processing shows **1.05 billion events**, which represents **43.75 percent** of the annual target. Cloud billing data for the same period shows **€218,000** of actual spending.

Using this information, identify the four input metrics: **AC, PV, EV, and BAC.**

Answer Key

It often feels tricky to map the EVM inputs to operational environments, because the value is continuous, and tied to usage. With practice, the patterns become easier to spot because Unit Economics gives a clear way to express progress in budget terms. The succeeding table shows how each metric is derived.

Metric	Amount	Why
BAC	€ 480,000	This is the total annual cloud budget allocated for running the analytics service.
AC	€ 218,000	This is the actual cloud spend recorded in billing data up to the end of Q2.
PV	€ 288,000	H1 is the same as end of Q2. Total for H1 Planned Value is 60% of BAC. Cumulative Plan equal 0.60 × €480,000
EV	€ 210,000	Actual progress was 43.75 percent of annual value, so EV equals 0.4375 × €480,000.

Table 5.2: *Exercise – Identifying Input Metrics in an Operational, Unit Economics Scenario*

Key Takeaways from Input Metrics

Input metrics form the backbone of Earned Value Management in FinOps. They define how cost, progress, and expectations are measured, and how they influence every performance and forecasting calculation that follows. The following points highlight the most important lessons from this section, and reinforce the practical considerations that FinOps teams must keep in mind.

- **Input Metrics Shape Every EVM Calculation:** AC, PV, EV, and BAC are the raw ingredients for all output metrics. Any inaccuracy in these inputs will cascade through the entire EVM system. Reliable data collection, consistent definitions, and clear ownership are essential for trustworthy results.
- **Unit Economics Must be a Part of Planning and Budgeting:** Unit Economics provides the structure that allows EV and PV to be expressed in meaningful terms. When a value is tied to units, such as processed events, active users, or deployed features, EVM becomes far more accurate. This only works when Unit Economics is defined early, validated with engineering and product teams, and integrated into the budgeting process. Poorly designed Unit Economics leads to misleading EV and PV values, which weakens the entire EVM framework.
- **Unit Economics Requires a Thoughtful Design:** Choosing the wrong unit of value can distort performance signals. Teams must consider whether the chosen unit reflects customer value, engineering effort, and cloud consumption patterns. A well-designed unit becomes a stable anchor for EV and PV. A weak one creates noise and confusion.
- **Alignment with Finance is Essential:** Finance teams often operate on billing dates, while engineering and FinOps teams frequently work with usage

dates. This difference can create mismatches in AC, if not addressed early. Clear alignment on which the date convention is used for EVM, prevents reconciliation issues, and avoids unnecessary disputes during reviews.

- **Upfront Expenses Must be Included in the Actual Cost:** Cloud environments often involve upfront commitments such as reserved instances, savings plans, or prepaid credits. These expenses must be incorporated into AC because they represent real financial outflow. The method of allocation should be transparent and agreed upon, especially when the upfront cost benefits multiple teams or workloads.

- **BAC Must Reflect a Realistic Scope and Cloud Dynamics:** BAC is not a static number. Cloud environments evolve, architectures change, and consumption patterns shift. BAC should be reviewed periodically to ensure that it still reflects the expected scope and financial boundaries of the initiative. A rigid BAC leads to a misleading PV and EV calculations.

- **PV and EV Depend on Clear Definitions of Progress:** Progress measurements must be objective and consistent. Whether progress is measured through story points, milestones, or unit-based value, the method must be understood by all stakeholders. Ambiguity in progress measurement leads to unreliable EV and PV values.

- **AC Must be Traceable and Reproducible:** FinOps teams must be able to explain how the AC was calculated, which accounts were included, and how the shared costs were allocated. Transparency builds trust, and ensures that the EVM outputs are accepted by engineering, product, and finance stakeholders.

- **Input Metrics Require Cross-Functional Collaboration:** No single team owns all the data needed for EVM. Engineering provides progress, Finance provides budget and accounting rules, and FinOps provides cost data and allocation logic. Collaboration ensures that the input metrics are accurate, and aligned with the organizational expectations.

- **Strong Input Metrics Enable Reliable Forecasting:** Forecast metrics such as EAC, ETC, and VAC are only as good as the inputs that feed them. When AC, PV, EV, and BAC are well-defined and consistently applied, forecasting becomes a powerful tool for anticipating cloud spend, and guiding strategic decisions.

As soon as the input metrics are clear, the next step is to understand what they reveal about the present moment. FinOps teams rely on a set of output indicators that translate the raw cost and progress data into meaningful signals about the performance. These metrics show whether cloud spend is aligned with expectations, whether the value is being delivered at the right pace, and whether the initiative is operating within healthy financial boundaries. They form the real-time dashboard of Earned Value Management. The upcoming section explores these current-status metrics in detail, and explains how they help the practitioners interpret what is happening right now, in their cloud environments.

Output Metrics: Current Status

Current-status output metrics translate the input values into meaningful signals about how an initiative is performing right now. They help FinOps practitioners understand whether cloud spend is aligned with expectations, whether value is being delivered efficiently, and whether progress is unfolding at the planned pace. These indicators form the operational heartbeat of Earned Value Management. They allow teams to detect deviations early, guide conversations with engineering and product stakeholders, and support timely corrective actions.

This section explores the four core current-status metrics: **Cost Variance (CV), Cost Performance Index (CPI), Schedule Variance (SV), and Schedule Performance Index (SPI)**. Each one provides a different perspective on performance, and together they offer a balanced view of cost efficiency and delivery pace.

Cost Variance

Abbreviation: CV

Definition

Cost Variance, as covered in *Chapter* 4, measures the difference between the value earned and the actual cost incurred. It shows whether the initiative is spending more or less than expected for the amount of progress achieved.

How it is used

FinOps teams use CV to identify cost overruns or cost savings in real time. A positive CV indicates that the initiative is delivering the value at a lower cost than planned. A negative CV signals that cloud spending is exceeding the value delivered so far. CV is often used in executive reviews to highlight the financial performance, and justify corrective actions.

Equation

$$CV = EV - AC$$

Interpretation

- **Positive CV:** Spending is efficient relative to the value delivered.
- **Zero CV:** Spending is aligned with the expectations.
- **Negative CV:** Spending is higher than the value delivered, which may indicate an inefficiency, unexpected consumption, or architectural issues.

Cost Performance Index

Abbreviation: CPI

Definition

The Cost Performance Index expresses cost efficiency as a ratio. It shows how much value is being earned for each euro spent. This is covered in detail in *Chapter* 4.

How it is used

CPI is one of the most influential metrics in FinOps EVM. It provides a clear, normalized indicator of cost efficiency that can be compared across teams, workloads, or time periods. CPI is also used in forecasting metrics, such as Estimate at Completion.

Equation

$$CPI = \frac{EV}{AC}$$

Interpretation

- **CPI greater than 1:** The initiative is earning more value than the cost incurred.
- **CPI equal to 1:** Value earned matches the cost incurred.
- **CPI less than 1:** The initiative is earning less value than the cost incurred, which signals an inefficiency or unexpected cloud consumption.

Schedule Variance

Abbreviation: SV

Definition

Schedule Variance measures the difference between the value earned and the value planned. It indicates whether the initiative is ahead of or behind the planned pace of progress.

How it is used

SV helps FinOps teams understand the delivery performance in relation to the roadmap. It is especially useful in cloud migrations, modernization programs, and platform initiatives, where the progress can be quantified through milestones, story points, or unit-based value.

From an operation standpoint, it indicates how soon, or later the business unit will achieve the expected value , according to what was planned on Unit Economics terms.

SV highlights whether delays are emerging, and whether they may influence future cloud spend.

Equation

$$SV = EV - PV$$

Interpretation

- **Positive SV:** Progress is ahead of the plan.
- **Zero SV:** Progress is aligned with the plan.
- **Negative SV:** Progress is behind the plan, which may lead to an increased future cloud spend or extended timelines.

Schedule Performance Index

Abbreviation: SPI

Definition

The Schedule Performance Index expresses schedule efficiency as a ratio. It shows the rate at which the value is being delivered compared to the planned rate.

How it is used

SPI provides a normalized view of schedule performance. It is useful for identifying delivery bottlenecks, assessing the impact of delays, and supporting discussions with engineering teams. SPI also influences forecasting metrics, because schedule delays often translate into extended cloud consumption.

Equation

$$SPI = \frac{EV}{PV}$$

Interpretation

- **SPI greater than 1:** Value is being delivered faster than planned.
- **SPI equal to 1:** Delivery pace matches the plan.
- **SPI less than 1:** Delivery is slower than planned, which may increase future cloud costs, or delay expected outcomes.

Exercise: Applying Current-Status Output Metrics in a Cloud Operations Scenario

A corporation runs several internal products on a shared cloud platform. One of the products, **InsightHub**, is a data-analytics service used across the company. The FinOps team tracks its operational performance using EVM.

For the current quarter:

- Budget at Completion (BAC): €300,000

- Planned Value (PV): €150,000 (the team planned to deliver 50 percent of the quarterly analytics improvements).
- Earned Value (EV): €135,000 (actual improvements delivered correspond to 45 percent of the planned value).
- Actual Cost (AC): €160,000 (actual cloud spend from usage-based billing and committed-use amortization).

Using this information, calculate **CV, CPI, SV, and SPI**, and interpret what each one means for a cloud service already in full operation.

Answer and Explanation

Here are the results, each followed by a clear explanation that links the cloud scenario to the EVM concept.

1. **Cost Variance (CV)**

   Equation:

   $$CV = EV - AC$$

   Calculation:

   CV = €135,000 – €160,000 = –€25,000

   Explanation:

   InsightHub has delivered €135,000 worth of value, but has spent €160,000 to achieve it. The negative CV shows that the service is consuming more cloud resources than the value delivered so far. In cloud terms, this may reflect inefficient queries, oversized clusters, or unexpected data-processing spikes. CV translates these operational issues into a financial signal.

2. **Cost Performance Index (CPI)**

   Equation:

   $$CPI = \frac{EV}{AC}$$

   Calculation:

   CPI = 135,000 : 160,000 = **0.84**

   Explanation:

   A CPI of 0.84 means that for every €1 spent on cloud resources, InsightHub is generating €0.84 of planned value. This indicates cost inefficiency. In cloud operations, this often points to suboptimal autoscaling, under-utilized compute, or workloads that were not tuned for the expected performance. CPI expresses this inefficiency as a simple ratio.

3. **Schedule Variance (SV)**

   Equation:

   $$SV = EV - PV$$

   Calculation:

   SV = €135,000 – €150,000 = –€15,000

   Explanation:

   InsightHub planned to deliver 50 percent of its quarterly improvements, but has only delivered 45 percent. The negative SV shows that the team is behind the schedule. In cloud operations, this may reflect delays in feature rollouts, slower-than-expected data-pipeline refactoring, or postponed performance optimizations. SV converts these delivery delays into a measurable variance.

4. **Schedule Performance Index (SPI)**

   Equation:

   $$SPI = \frac{EV}{PV}$$

   Calculation:

   SPI = 135,000 : 150,000 = **0.90**

   Explanation:

   An SPI of 0.90 means that the team is delivering the value at 90 percent of the planned pace. In operational cloud environments, this often happens when engineering teams prioritize incident response, platform stability, or unplanned work. SPI shows how these operational realities affect the delivery rate of planned improvements.

Key Takeaways from Current-Status Output Metrics

Current-status metrics give FinOps teams a real-time view of how cloud initiatives are performing. They reveal whether value delivery is aligned with expectations and whether cloud spend is being converted into meaningful progress. These indicators help teams detect issues early and support informed conversations with engineering, product, and finance stakeholders. The following points highlight the most important lessons from this section.

CV and CPI Reveal Cost Efficiency in Real Time

Cost Variance and the Cost Performance Index show whether the cloud spend is producing the expected value. They help identify the inefficiencies, such as oversized compute, poorly tuned workloads, or unexpected consumption patterns. These metrics turn operational cloud issues into financial signals that leadership can understand.

SV and SPI Expose Delivery Pace, and Its Financial Impact

Schedule Variance and the Schedule Performance Index show whether the progress is unfolding at the planned pace. In cloud environments, delays often translate into extended consumption, longer use of temporary environments, or postponed decommissioning. SV and SPI help quantify the financial impact of delivery slowdowns.

Cloud Operations Create Continuous Variability

Unlike traditional projects, cloud workloads run continuously and respond to real-time demand. This variability affects AC, EV, and PV, which in turn influences CV, CPI, SV, and SPI. FinOps teams must account for this dynamic nature, when interpreting the current-status metrics.

Engineering Decisions Directly Influence Performance Metrics

Autoscaling rules, data-processing patterns, architectural choices, and deployment frequency all shape the values of CV, CPI, SV, and SPI. These metrics are not abstract indicators. They reflect real engineering behavior and operational decisions.

Negative Variances are Early Warning Signals

A negative CV or SV often appears before major financial or delivery problems become visible. These metrics help FinOps teams detect issues early, long before they escalate into budget overruns or missed milestones.

Ratios Provide a Normalized View across Teams

CPI and SPI allow comparisons across workloads, teams, or business units. This is especially valuable in large organizations with diverse cloud environments. Ratios help identify which teams are delivering value efficiently, and which ones need support.

Current-Status Metrics Support Better Stakeholder Conversations

These metrics help FinOps practitioners communicate with engineering and product teams using shared, objective indicators. They also help finance teams understand how operational realities influence cloud spend. This shared language strengthens the alignment across the organization.

Accurate Input Metrics are Essential for Reliable Output Metrics

CV, CPI, SV, and SPI depend entirely on the accuracy of AC, PV, and EV. Any inconsistency in progress measurement, cost allocation, or budgeting will distort the current-status indicators. Strong input discipline leads to trustworthy output signals.

Current-Status Metrics Prepare the Ground for Forecasting

These indicators are the foundation for the next stage of EVM. Forecast metrics such as EAC, ETC, VAC, and TCPI rely heavily on CPI and SPI. Understanding the current performance is essential before projecting future outcomes.

Output Metrics: Forecast

Forecast metrics help FinOps practitioners anticipate where cloud initiatives are heading. They take the current performance signals from CV, CPI, SV, and SPI and project them into the future. These indicators are essential for understanding whether an initiative will stay within the budget, how much additional cloud spend may be required, and what level of efficiency is needed to reach financial targets. Forecast metrics support strategic decision-making by transforming present-day performance into forward-looking insights.

This section explores the four core forecast metrics: **Estimate at Completion (EAC), Estimate to Complete (ETC), Variance at Completion (VAC), and To-Complete Performance Index (TCPI)**. Together, they form the predictive engine of Earned Value Management in cloud environments.

Estimate at Completion

Abbreviation: EAC

EAC is one of the most flexible and powerful metrics in Earned Value Management. Because cloud environments behave differently from that of the traditional project settings, FinOps practitioners benefit from understanding every variation of EAC, and when each one is appropriate. Different formulas reflect different assumptions about future performance, cost efficiency, and operational stability.

Here are the primary EAC variations used in practice, along with their formulas, assumptions, and FinOps-specific interpretations.

1. **EAC Based on Current Cost Efficiency (Most Common in FinOps)**

   Formula

   $$EAC = \frac{BAC}{CPI}$$

   When to use it

   This is the default formula for cloud environments. It assumes that **current cost efficiency (CPI)** will continue for the rest of the initiative.

   Assumption

   Future performance will mirror the current performance.

   FinOps interpretation

   Useful, when cloud workloads show stable patterns of inefficiency or efficiency. For example, if a service is consistently over-provisioned or poorly tuned, CPI reflects that reality, and EAC projects it forward.

2. **EAC Based on Actual Cost, Plus the Remaining Work at Planned Efficiency**

   Formula

   $$EAC = AC + (BAC - EV)$$

   When to use it

   Use this when the **past performance is not representative** of future performance. This often happens after a major optimization effort, architectural redesign, or cost-saving initiative.

   Assumption

   Future work will be completed at the **original planned efficiency**, not the current CPI.

   FinOps interpretation

   Useful when engineering teams have fixed inefficiencies, such as:

   - Rightsizing clusters
   - Optimizing queries
   - Reducing data retention
   - Eliminating unnecessary workloads

This formula resets the expectations to the original plan.

3. **EAC Based on Actual Cost, Plus the Remaining Work at Current Efficiency**

   Formula

$$EAC = AC + \frac{BAC - EV}{CPI}$$

   When to use it

   Use this when **past inefficiencies are expected to continue**, but you want to anchor the calculation in actual cost, rather than a full CPI-based projection.

   Assumption

   Remaining work will continue at the current CPI, but AC is already sunk and should not be recalculated.

   FinOps interpretation

   Useful when:

   - Workloads are consistently inefficient.
   - Demand patterns are stable.
   - No major optimization is planned.

   This formula is more conservative than the BAC/CPI version, because it separates the past and future performance.

4. **EAC Based on Combined Cost and Schedule Performance**

   Formula

$$EAC = AC + \frac{BAC - EV}{CPI \times SPI}$$

   When to use it

   Use this when **both, the cost and schedule performance are influencing the future spend**. This is common in cloud initiatives, where delays increase consumption.

   Assumption

   Future performance will reflect both cost efficiency (CPI) and delivery pace (SPI).

   FinOps interpretation

   Useful when schedule delays increase cloud spend, such as:

   - Extended use of temporary environments
   - Prolonged data-migration windows

- Delayed decommissioning of legacy systems
- Longer-than-expected testing cycles

This formula is the most pessimistic one, and often produces the highest EAC.

5. **EAC Based on Manual Forecasting (Expert Judgment)**

Formula

$$EAC = AC + \textit{New Forecast for Remaining Work}$$

When to use it

Use this when **neither CPI nor SPI reflect reality**, often due to major changes in scope, architecture, or business priorities.

Assumption

Future performance must be estimated manually.

FinOps interpretation

Common in situations such as:

- Sudden traffic surges
- New compliance requirements
- Major architectural redesign
- Migration to a new cloud service
- Unexpected vendor price changes

This version relies on engineering and FinOps collaboration to produce a realistic forecast.

6. **EAC Based on Revised BAC (Re-Baselined Budget)**

Formula

$$EAC = \textit{Revised } BAC$$

When to use it

Use this when the **budget itself has changed** due to new scope or strategic decisions.

Assumption

The original BAC is no longer valid.

FinOps interpretation

Common in large enterprises where:

- New features are added.
- Business units expand usage.

- Cloud adoption accelerates.
- Regulatory requirements increase the workload.

This is not a calculation, but a formal reset of expectations.

Summary Table of EAC Variations

EAC Variation	Formula	Best Used When
Based on CPI	BAC : CPI	Current efficiency expected to continue
AC + Remaining Work at Planned Rate	AC + (BAC – EV)	Future work expected to follow original plan
AC + Remaining Work at Current CPI	AC + (BAC – EV) : CPI	Inefficiencies expected to continue
Combined CPI and SPI	AC + (BAC – EV) : (CPI × SPI)	Both cost and schedule issues affect future spend
Manual Forecast	AC + New Forecast	Major changes make CPI/SPI unreliable
Re-baselined Budget	Revised BAC	Scope or budget has officially changed

Table 5.3: *Summary Table of EAC Variations*

Estimate to Complete

Abbreviation: ETC

Definition

Estimate to Complete represents the expected cost required to finish the remaining work. It isolates the future portion of the spending forecast. ETC is derived from EAC and AC, making it a forward-looking indicator of how much additional cloud spend will be needed.

How it is used

ETC helps FinOps teams plan future budgets, evaluate the financial impact of delays, and determine whether the upcoming work requires optimization. It is especially useful in long-running cloud initiatives, where consumption patterns evolve over time.

Equation

$$ETC = EAC - AC$$

Interpretation

- **High ETC:** Significant work remains, or current inefficiencies will continue to drive spend.
- **Low ETC:** Most of the value has already been delivered, or the initiative is nearing completion.

ETC helps teams understand the financial runway ahead and prepare for upcoming cloud costs.

Variance at Completion

Abbreviation: VAC

Definition

Variance at Completion measures the difference between the original budget and the forecasted total cost. It shows whether the initiative is expected to finish under or over the approved cloud budget.

How it is used

VAC is used in executive reporting, quarterly planning, and budget reviews. It provides a simple, direct indicator of financial health. FinOps teams rely on VAC to highlight risks early, and justify optimization efforts.

Equation

$$VAC = BAC - EAC$$

Interpretation

- **Positive VAC:** The initiative is expected to finish under budget.
- **Zero VAC:** The initiative is expected to finish exactly on budget.
- **Negative VAC:** The initiative is expected to exceed the budget.

VAC is one of the clearest indicators of whether financial expectations will be met.

To-Complete Performance Index

Abbreviation: TCPI

Definition

TCPI answers a very different question from CPI. CPI tells you **how efficiently you have been performing so far**. TCPI tells you **how efficiently you must perform from now on** to hit a financial target.

Think of CPI as a rear-view mirror and TCPI as the windshield.

How it is used

TCPI measures the **required cost efficiency for the remaining work**. It shows the performance level needed to meet either:

- The original budget (BAC), or
- the revised forecast (EAC).

This makes TCPI a forward-looking indicator. It tells you whether recovery is possible under realistic cloud-consumption patterns.

Why TCPI Exists

Cloud initiatives often drift away from their budget due to scaling, data growth, or operational inefficiencies. CPI alone cannot tell you whether the initiative can still be brought back on track. TCPI fills that gap by quantifying the efficiency required to recover.

If CPI shows what happened, TCPI shows what must happen next.

Equations

To meet the original budget (BAC):

$$TCPI_{BAC} = \frac{BAC - EV}{BAC - AC}$$

To meet the revised forecast (EAC):

$$TCPI_{EAC} = \frac{BAC - EV}{EAC - AC}$$

Interpretation

- **TCPI greater than 1:** The team must operate more efficiently than it has done so far. In cloud terms, this means an aggressive optimization, rightsizing, or architectural changes.
- **TCPI equal to 1:** Current efficiency is enough to meet the target.
- **TCPI less than 1:** The target can be met even with lower efficiency. This is rare in cloud operations, unless early work was unusually efficient.

The Difference between CPI and TCPI

Here is the simplest and most practical way to explain the difference:

Metric	What it Measures	Time Orientation	Key Question
CPI	Actual cost efficiency so far	Past and present	"How efficiently have we been converting cloud spend into value?"
TCPI	Required cost efficiency going forward	Future	"How efficiently must we operate from now on to meet the target?"

Table 5.4: *Difference between CPI and TCPI*

In other words:

- **CPI = Performance achieved**

- **TCPI = Performance required**

This distinction is essential in FinOps, because cloud environments are dynamic. Past efficiency does not guarantee future efficiency, and TCPI helps quantify the gap between the two.

A Cloud-Specific Example

If CPI is **0.85**, the team has been inefficient so far. If TCPI is **1.10**, the team must operate at **110 percent efficiency** relative to the plan to recover.

This tells leadership two things:

1. The current trajectory is not enough.
2. The required improvement may or may not be realistic, depending on the workload.

TCPI becomes a decision-making tool: Should we optimize, redesign, or accept that the budget will be exceeded?

Exercise: Forecasting Cloud Spend Using EVM Metrics in a SaaS Company

A SaaS company operates **StreamFlow**, a real-time data-processing platform that ingests customer telemetry. The platform runs continuously, and scales with demand. The FinOps team uses EVM to forecast the financial outcomes for the current quarter.

Here is the current data:

- **Budget at Completion (BAC):** €600,000
- **Actual Cost (AC):** €310,000
- **Earned Value (EV):** €270,000
- **Cost Performance Index (CPI):** EV : AC = 0.87

Using this information, calculate the four forecast metrics:

- **Estimate at Completion (EAC)**
- **Estimate to Complete (ETC)**
- **Variance at Completion (VAC)**
- **To-Complete Performance Index (TCPI)**

Interpret what each result means for a cloud service, which is already in full operation.

Answer and Explanation

Here are the results, followed by explanations that connect cloud-operations behavior to EVM forecasting.

1. **Estimate at Completion (EAC)**

   Equation:

   $$EAC = \frac{BAC}{CPI}$$

   Calculation:

   EAC = 600,000 : 0.87 = **€689,655**

   Explanation:

   StreamFlow is projected to finish the quarter with a total cloud spend of about €690k. The low CPI indicates inefficiencies, such as high ingestion volume, suboptimal autoscaling, or expensive data-processing patterns. EAC translates these operational realities into a forecasted overspend.

2. **Estimate to Complete (ETC)**

   Equation:

   $$ETC = EAC - AC$$

   Calculation:

   ETC = 689,655 – 310,000 = **€379,655**

   Explanation:

   StreamFlow is expected to spend an additional €380k to complete the quarter. This reflects the cost of continuing operations under current efficiency levels. In cloud terms, this may involve a sustained high compute usage, large data-transfer volumes, or ongoing reliance on premium storage tiers.

3. **Variance at Completion (VAC)**

   Equation:

   $$VAC = BAC - EAC$$

   Calculation:

   VAC = 600,000 – 689,655 = **–€89,655**

   Explanation:

   The initiative is forecasted to exceed its quarterly cloud budget by nearly €90k. This negative VAC is a clear signal that corrective actions may be needed, such as rightsizing clusters, optimizing pipelines, or adjusting ingestion patterns.

4. **To-Complete Performance Index (TCPI)**

   Equation:

   $$TCPI = \frac{BAC - EV}{BAC - AC}$$

Calculation:

TCPI = (600,000 – 270,000) : (600,000 – 310,000)

TCPI = 330,000 : 290,000

TCPI = 1.14

Explanation:

A TCPI of 1.14 means StreamFlow must operate with significantly higher cost efficiency for the rest of the quarter to meet the original budget. In cloud operations, this may require aggressive optimization, workload tuning, or architectural adjustments. TCPI quantifies how much improvement is needed to recover financially.

Exercise: Forecasting Cloud Spend in a Large Enterprise Environment

A global corporation operates dozens of internal services on a shared cloud platform. One of these services, **CoreLedger**, handles financial reconciliation across business units. It runs continuously, processes large data volumes, and relies on a mix of serverless functions, managed databases, and containerized workloads.

The FinOps team is evaluating CoreLedger's quarterly performance using EVM. Here is the current data:

- **Budget at Completion (BAC):** €1,200,000
- **Actual Cost (AC):** €540,000
- **Earned Value (EV):** €480,000
- **Cost Performance Index (CPI):** EV : AC = 0.89

Using this information, calculate the four forecast metrics:

- **Estimate at Completion (EAC)**
- **Estimate to Complete (ETC)**
- **Variance at Completion (VAC)**
- **To-Complete Performance Index (TCPI)**

Interpret what each result means for a large corporation running internal cloud services.

Answer and Explanation

Here are the results, followed by the explanations that connect enterprise cloud operations to EVM forecasting.

1. **Estimate at Completion (EAC)**

   Equation:

   $$EAC = \frac{BAC}{CPI}$$

   Calculation:

   EAC = 1,200,000 : 0.89 = **€1,348,315**

   Explanation:

   CoreLedger is projected to finish the quarter with a total cloud spend of about €1.35 million. The CPI of 0.89 indicates inefficiencies, such as heavy database usage, high-frequency serverless invocations, or container clusters running above expected capacity. EAC converts these operational patterns into a financial forecast.

2. **Estimate to Complete (ETC)**

   Equation:

   $$ETC = EAC - AC$$

   Calculation:

   ETC = 1,348,315 – 540,000 = **€808,315**

   Explanation:

   The service is expected to consume an additional €808k to complete the quarter. In a large enterprise, this may reflect sustained data-processing loads, compliance-driven retention requirements, or shared-platform overhead. ETC highlights the financial runway still ahead.

3. **Variance at Completion (VAC)**

   Equation:

   $$VAC = BAC - EAC$$

   Calculation:

   VAC = 1,200,000 – 1,348,315 = **–€148,315**

   Explanation:

   CoreLedger is forecasted to exceed its quarterly cloud budget by roughly €148k. This negative VAC is a clear signal that the service is trending above expectations. In enterprise environments, this often triggers discussions about optimization, architectural adjustments, or budget reallocation across business units.

4. **To-Complete Performance Index (TCPI)**

   Equation:

$$TCPI = \frac{BAC - EV}{BAC - AC}$$

   Calculation:

   TCPI = (1,200,000 – 480,000) : (1,200,000 – 540,000)

   TCPI = 720,000 : 660,000 = **1.09**

   Explanation:

   A TCPI of 1.09 means CoreLedger must operate with noticeably higher cost efficiency for the rest of the quarter to meet the original budget. In a large corporation, this may require coordinated action across platform teams, database administrators, and application owners. TCPI quantifies the level of improvement needed to recover financially.

Key Takeaways from Forecast Output Metrics

Forecast metrics transform the current performance into forward-looking insights. They help FinOps practitioners anticipate financial outcomes, evaluate the impact of operational decisions, and guide leadership conversations about future cloud spend. These indicators are essential for organizations that rely on continuous cloud operations, where consumption patterns shift rapidly, and budgets must adapt to real-time behavior.

Forecast Metrics Turn Today's Performance into Tomorrow's Financial Outlook: EAC, ETC, VAC, and TCPI extend the meaning of CV, CPI, SV, and SPI into the future. They show where the initiative is heading, if the current patterns continue. This predictive capability is crucial in cloud environments, where spend can accelerate quickly due to scaling, data growth, or architectural changes.

- **EAC is the Most Critical Forecasting Signal:** Estimate at Completion gives leadership a clear view of the expected final cloud spend. It highlights whether the initiative is trending toward overspend or underspend. cloud operations, EAC often becomes the primary reference for quarterly or annual budget adjustments.
- **ETC Helps Teams Understand the Remaining Financial Runway:** Estimate to Complete isolates the future portion of the forecast. It helps FinOps teams plan upcoming budgets, anticipate spikes in consumption, and prepare for the financial impact of new features, scaling events, or compliance requirements.
- **VAC Shows Whether the Initiative Will Meet Its Budget:** Variance at Completion provides a simple, direct indicator of financial health. A negative VAC signals that

the initiative is expected to exceed its budget, which often triggers optimization efforts, architectural reviews, or discussions about budget reallocation.

- **TCPI Quantifies the Efficiency Required to Recover:** The To-Complete Performance Index shows the level of cost efficiency needed to meet a financial target. It is especially valuable, when an initiative is already trending above budget. TCPI helps teams understand whether recovery is realistic under the current cloud-consumption patterns.
- **Forecast Metrics Depend on Accurate Current-Status Metrics:** EAC, ETC, VAC, and TCPI rely heavily on CPI and EV. Any inaccuracies in input or current-status metrics will distort the forecast. Strong discipline in AC, PV, EV, and CPI leads to reliable predictions.
- **Cloud Variability Makes Forecasting Essential:** Cloud environments scale dynamically. Demand spikes, data growth, and architectural changes can rapidly alter consumption. Forecast metrics help organizations stay ahead of these shifts by projecting their financial impact before they materialize.
- **Forecast Metrics Strengthen Strategic Decision-Making**: These indicators support conversations about resource allocation, optimization priorities, and long-term planning. They help leadership understand the financial trajectory of cloud initiatives, and make informed decisions about investment, scaling, or redesign.
- **Forecasting Encourages Proactive FinOps Behavior:** Instead of reacting to overspend after it happens, forecast metrics empower teams to take early action. They highlight risks before they become budget issues, and help the teams adjust the course, while there is still time to influence outcomes.

Conclusion

Earned Value Management brings structure, clarity, and discipline to the financial and operational realities of running workloads in the cloud. Throughout this chapter, we explored how the core input metrics establish the foundation for understanding cost, progress, and expectations. AC, PV, EV, and BAC give FinOps practitioners a shared language to describe what has happened so far and what should have happened by this point. When these inputs are well-defined and grounded in thoughtful Unit Economics, they become powerful tools for interpreting cloud behavior.

We then examined the current-status output metrics that reveal how efficiently cloud resources are being used and how closely delivery aligns with the plan. CV and CPI expose cost efficiency, while SV and SPI highlight delivery pace. These indicators help teams detect early signs of drift, whether caused by scaling patterns, engineering decisions, or operational constraints. They turn cloud consumption into actionable insights that support better conversations across engineering, product, and finance.

Finally, we explored the forecast metrics that project today's performance into tomorrow's financial outcomes. EAC, ETC, VAC, and TCPI help organizations anticipate overspend, understand the remaining financial runway, and evaluate whether recovery is realistic. These metrics transform EVM from a reporting tool into a forward-looking decision framework. They allow teams to plan proactively, adjust course early, and align cloud strategy with business expectations.

Together, these metrics form a complete system for understanding cloud performance across past, present, and future. They give organizations the ability to measure value delivery, evaluate efficiency, and forecast financial outcomes with confidence. Yet the accuracy of every calculation depends on the quality of the underlying data. Cloud environments generate vast amounts of billing, usage, and operational signals, and EVM relies on these signals being clean, consistent, and well-structured.

This brings us to the next chapter. Now that we understand the mechanics of EVM, we turn our attention to the data plumbing required to make these metrics reliable. We will explore how to collect, normalize, and align cloud data so that EVM calculations reflect reality rather than noise. Accurate data is the backbone of trustworthy EVM, and the next chapter shows how to build that backbone with intention and precision.

References

- PMI (2020). The standard for earned value management. Project Management Institute.
- EVM Formulas. (n.d.). CIEs' Project Management Training. Retrieved December 20, 2025, from https://c-pmt.weebly.com/uploads/4/0/1/7/4017805/033-evm_formula.pdf
- Hartney, J. (2025, June 26). The earned value formulas. Project Engineer. Retrieved December 20, 2025, from https://www.projectengineer.net/the-earned-value-formulas
- Lukas, J. A. (2012). How to make earned value work on your project. Paper presented at PMI® Global Congress 2012—North America, Vancouver, British Columbia, Canada. Newtown Square, PA: Project Management Institute. Retrieved December 21, 2025, from https://www.pmi.org/learning/library/make-earned-value-work-project-6001
- Sokolova, V., & Sokolova, V. (2025, November 20). Earned Value Management (EVM): key metrics, benefits, and how to calculate it. Epicflow. Retrieved December 20, 2025, from https://www.epicflow.com/blog/earned-value-management/
- Vasiliauskas, V. (2025, September 12). Earned Value Management: Formulas, Examples & Best Tools. Teamhood. Retrieved December 20, 2025, from https://teamhood.com/project-management-resources/earned-value-management/

CHAPTER 6

Data, Tooling, and Automation

Introduction

The previous chapters established the foundations of Earned Value Management in a FinOps context. The concepts, formulas, and decision making patterns are already familiar to you. With this groundwork in place, the focus now, shifts to the practical side of EVM. This chapter explains how to obtain the data that feeds AC, PV, and EV, how to structure it, and how to prepare the environment that supports the ongoing measurement.

Cloud financial management depends on accurate and timely information. Actual Cost requires a clear understanding of how each cloud provider exposes billing data, and how cost types influence the interpretation of spend. Planned Value depends on the budgeting processes owned by Finance, and on the ability to translate those numbers into a time-phased baseline that aligns with the cadence of cloud consumption. Earned Value requires a definition of economic units, and a reliable source of usage or product data that reflects the progress in a measurable way.

The goal of this chapter is to guide you through the practical steps needed to collect and organize these inputs. The sections that follow describe how to extract AC from Azure, AWS, GCP, and FOCUS, how to work with Finance to obtain PV, and how to define and source the unit data required for EV. The chapter concludes with a guidance on automation and data quality, so that the EVM cycle can operate consistently over time.

By the end of this chapter, you will understand how to build the data foundation that supports EVM in real cloud environments, and how to prepare these inputs for use in the workflows, introduced earlier in the book.

Structure

In this chapter, the following topics will be covered:

- Obtaining the Actual Cost
- Obtaining AC from Azure
- Obtaining AC from AWS
- Obtaining AC from GCP
- Obtaining AC from FOCUS
- What Planned Value Represents in Practice
- Obtaining PV from Finance
- Obtaining Unit Data
- Designing the EVM Data Pipeline

Obtaining the Actual Cost (AC)

Actual Cost is the first data pillar you work with, when applying EVM in cloud environments. Cloud billing is detailed, dynamic, and often fragmented across accounts, subscriptions, and services. To use AC effectively, you need a clear method for locating the right data, extracting it in a consistent format, and understanding how each provider classifies the cost types. This section guides you through that process. You will learn where AC data lives in Azure, AWS, GCP, and FOCUS, how to extract it step by step, and how to interpret the cost categories that influence your EVM calculations. The goal is to give you a repeatable approach that produces reliable AC data, regardless of the provider or tooling you use.

Actual Cost in Cloud Billing

Actual Cost reflects the financial impact of your cloud usage for a defined period. Cloud billing includes several charge types, and understanding how each one behaves, helps you build a consistent AC view.

- **Usage-based charges:** These represent the direct consumption of cloud resources. They form the core of AC, because they reflect what your workload actually used.
- **Purchases and commitments:** Items such as reservations, savings plans, or committed use discounts appear as upfront or recurring charges. Depending on your accounting approach, you may include them as full charges, or amortize them across the commitment term.

- **Adjustments, credits, and refunds:** Providers issue corrections or benefits that modify the previous charges. You need to decide whether these entries belong in your AC view, since they influence how AC aligns with PV and EV.
- **Taxes and fees:** Some organizations include them for completeness, while others remove them to focus on operational consumption. The key is to apply the same rule across all providers.
- **Provider-specific cost categories:** Each cloud platform uses its own terminology. Understanding these categories helps you classify costs consistently when preparing AC for EVM.

Decisions Needed before Extracting AC Data

Before you begin pulling the AC data, you need to make a few structural decisions that shape the consistency of your results.

- **Define the measurement scope:** Choose whether you will extract AC at the subscription, account, project, or workload level.
- **Select the time granularity:** Monthly periods are common for EVM, but you may choose weekly or daily intervals, depending on your internal processes.
- **Choose invoiced or amortized values:** Invoiced values reflect the bill as issued. Amortized values distribute commitment-related costs across the period of use. Pick one approach, and apply it consistently.
- **Decide the level of detail:** You may extract raw line items, or summarized views. The choice depends on how you plan to allocate and analyze AC.
- **Confirm tagging or labeling standards:** Reliable metadata is essential for allocating AC to projects or products. Validate that your tagging or labeling strategy supports your EVM structure.
- **Establish consistency rules across providers:** Aligning these decisions early, ensures that your AC extraction process remains stable across Azure, AWS, GCP, and FOCUS.

Obtaining AC from Azure

Azure offers several ways to access Actual Cost data, and each option supports a different level of detail. Your goal is to extract consistent, time-aligned information that reflects the financial impact of your cloud usage. Azure Cost Management is the primary interface for this work. It provides visual reports, downloadable tables, and automated exports. When you need programmatic access, or integration with your data pipeline, the Cost Management API is the natural extension. For screenshots, you can rely on the Azure portal itself or Microsoft Learn, which maintains up-to-date UI examples.

Finding AC Data in Azure

- **Azure Portal:** Cost Management is available at the subscription, resource group, or management group level.
- **Cost Analysis:** The main interface for filtering, grouping, and exploring cost data.
- **Cost Management Exports:** Automated delivery of daily or monthly cost data to a storage account.
- **Cost Management API:** Programmatic access for automation and integration.
- **Microsoft Learn Documentation:** A reliable source for screenshots and UI references.

Step by Step: Extracting AC from Azure Cost Management

To extract the Actual Cost from Azure Cost Management, start by navigating to the Cost Management console in your subscription. Cloud providers update their interfaces frequently, so the layout or visuals you see may differ slightly from the examples shown here.

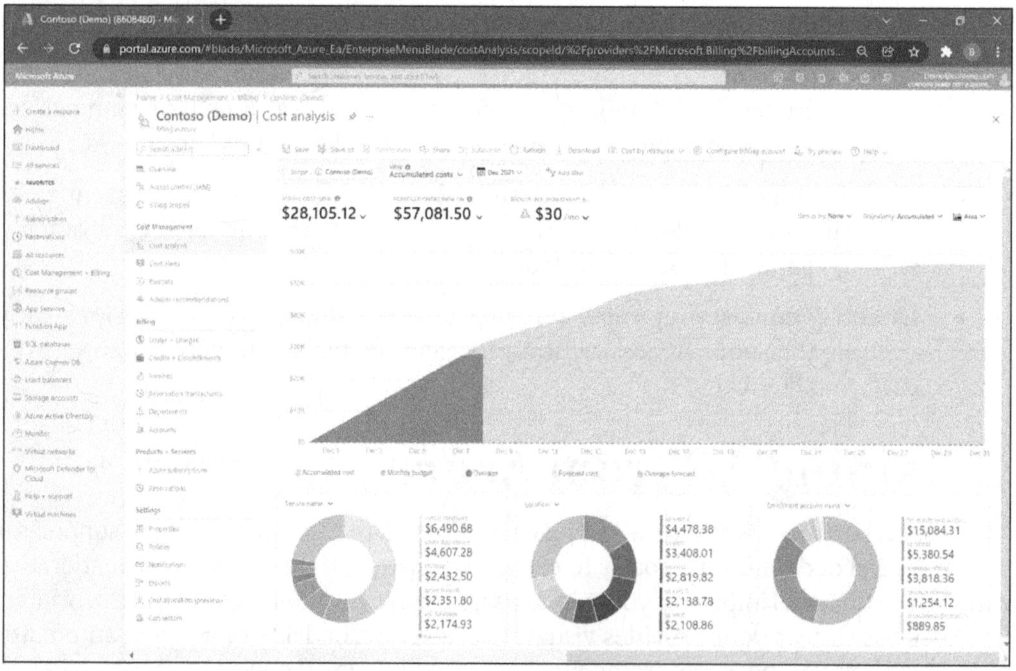

Figure 6.1: Azure Cost Management

- **Select the correct scope:** Choose the subscription, resource group, or management group based on your EVM structure.
- **Open Cost Analysis:** Set the period you want to measure, and apply the filters that match your project or workload.
- Choose the Actual Cost or Amortized Cost metric. For more details on what to choose, see the section "Azure Cost Types and EVM AC" in the subsequent section.
- **Download the data:** Export the table view as CSV for validation or manual analysis.
- **Configure automated exports:** Set up recurring exports to a storage account for consistent ingestion into your EVM pipeline.

Azure Cost Types and EVM AC

Azure provides two main cost perspectives: Actual Cost and Amortized Cost. Understanding how each one behaves is essential for choosing the right approach for EVM.

Actual Cost in Azure

Actual Cost reflects charges exactly as they appear on your invoice, with one important exception: **Azure Cost Management does not include taxes**. Taxes appear only on invoices and billing profile pages, not in Cost Analysis or cost exports.

- **Usage charges:** Recorded on the day resources are consumed.
- **Upfront purchases:** Reservations and Savings Plans appear as full charges in the purchase month.
- **Credits and adjustments:** Reflected immediately, which can create spikes or dips.
- **No taxes in Cost Management:** Taxes are excluded from Cost Analysis and exports.

Actual Cost is easy to reconcile with Finance, because it mirrors the invoice structure, aside from taxes. The challenge is that the commitment purchases can distort period-to-period comparisons.

Amortized Cost in Azure

Amortized Cost spreads the value of reservations and Savings Plans across the period in which the benefits are consumed. This creates a smoother view of ongoing cloud usage.

- **Reservation amortization:** One- or three-year commitments are divided across each month of the term.
- **Savings Plan amortization:** Commitment value is distributed across the period of use.
- **Alignment with consumption:** Costs map more closely to the workloads that benefit from the commitment.
- **Reduced volatility:** Eliminates large spikes caused by upfront purchases.

Amortized Cost often provides a more realistic operational view, especially when commitments play a significant role in your cloud strategy.

Impact on Earned Value

Your choice between the Actual Cost and the Amortized Cost influences how AC aligns with PV and EV.

- **Commitment purchases:** Actual Cost may show a large spike in the purchase month. Amortized Cost smooths this effect, and aligns better with the value delivered over time.
- **Taxes:** Since taxes do not appear in Cost Management, including them would require manual reconciliation. Many teams exclude taxes from EVM to keep AC focused on the operational consumption.
- **Credits:** Credits reduce AC in the period they are applied. You need to decide whether they should influence EVM, or be excluded for analytical consistency.

Consistency is the key. Once you choose Actual Cost or Amortized Cost for EVM, apply the same approach across all providers and reporting periods.

Obtaining AC from AWS

AWS provides one of the most detailed billing datasets among cloud providers. You can access Actual Cost through Cost Explorer, the Billing console, and the Cost and Usage Report. Each tool exposes cost types that influence how you interpret AC for EVM. AWS offers more cost type variations than Azure or GCP, so understanding these definitions is essential before you extract the data. For screenshots, you can rely on the AWS Billing console, or the AWS documentation pages that show the Cost Explorer Interface.

Finding AC in AWS

- **Cost Explorer**: The primary interface for exploring, filtering, and grouping cost data.

- **Cost and Usage Report (CUR)**: The most detailed dataset, delivered to S3, and often queried through Athena.
- **Billing Console**: High-level views of charges, credits, and invoices.
- **AWS Budgets**: Not an AC source, but useful for cross-checking PV alignment.
- **AWS Documentation**: The best place to find UI screenshots and cost type definitions.

Step by Step: Extracting AC from Cost Explorer and CUR

To extract the Actual Cost in AWS, start by opening the AWS Billing and Cost Management console, and navigating to Cost Explorer. AWS updates its interface regularly, so the layout or visuals you see may differ slightly from the examples provided here.

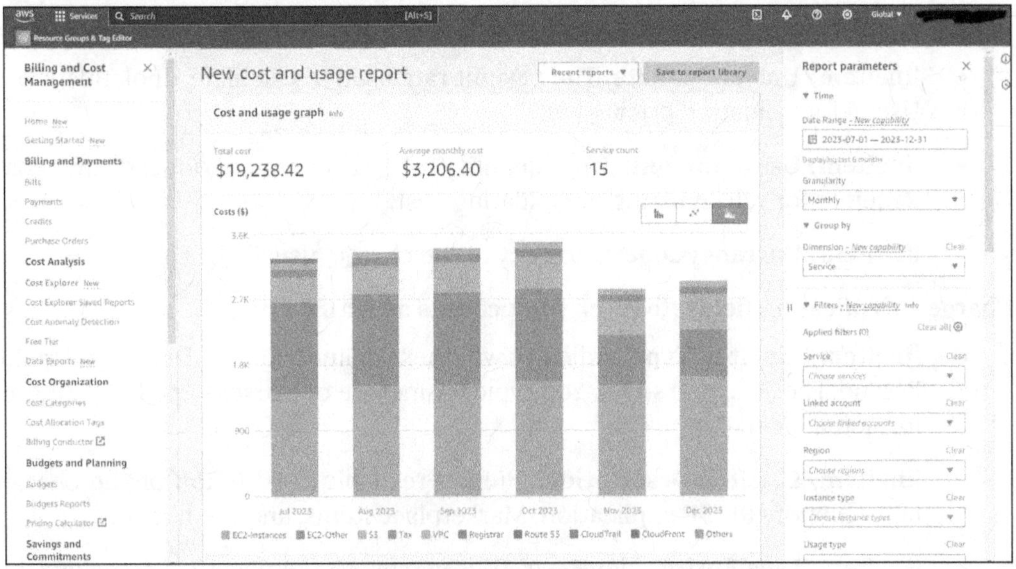

Figure 6.2: AWS Cost Explorer

- **Select the correct account or organization**: Choose the payer account, if you want a consolidated view.
- **Open Cost Explorer**: Set the time range, and ensure that the "Cost" metric is selected.
- **Choose the cost type**: AWS allows you to switch between Unblended, Blended, Amortized, and Net Amortized.
- **Apply filters and groupings**: Use tags, services, usage types, or linked accounts to match your EVM structure.

- **Download the data**: Export the table view as CSV for validation.
- **Use the CUR for detailed analysis**: Configure the CUR to deliver daily or hourly line items to S3 for ingestion into your EVM pipeline.

Important CUR Fields for Actual cost

The **Actual Cost** in AWS FinOps terms comes directly from the **unblended, undiscounted, non-amortized cost columns** in the AWS Cost and Usage Report (CUR). The CUR exposes several fields that are essential for reconstructing Actual Cost with precision.

Here is a structured list of the most relevant fields, grouped by purpose, with citations from AWS documentation.

Core cost fields (directly tied to the Actual Cost)

- **lineItem/UnblendedCost**: The raw cost for the usage, without blended allocation or amortization. This is the closest representation of Actual Cost.
- **lineItem/UnblendedRate**: The perunit rate used to calculate UnblendedCost. Useful for validating pricing.
- **lineItem/UsageAmount**: The quantity of usage that produced the cost. Required for recalculating or validating cost.
- **lineItem/CurrencyCode**: Currency of the charge (usually USD).

Charge classification fields (to filter what counts as Actual Cost)

- **lineItem/LineItemType**: Indicates whether the line is Usage, Discount, Credit, Refund, Fee, Tax, and so on. You typically include only *Usage* and *RecurringFee* for Actual Cost.
- **lineItem/LineItemDescription**: Human-readable description of the charge; helps identify RI/SP application, Marketplace items, and the like.
- **lineItem/LegalEntity**: Identifies AWS versus Marketplace seller; useful for separating thirdparty costs.

Pricing and discountrelated fields (to exclude from the Actual Cost)

These fields help you *remove* amortization, blended allocation, or discount artifacts:

- **lineItem/BlendedCost**: Not used for Actual Cost; included here, because you must avoid it.
- **lineItem/BlendedRate**: Same reason as mentioned previously; blended allocation is not Actual Cost.

Allocation and metadata fields (useful for attribution, not cost calculation)

These fields do not change the Actual Cost, but are essential for allocating it:

- `resourceTags/*`: Cost allocation tags (appear only when enabled).

Summary: Minimum fields required to compute Actual Cost

If you want the **strict minimum** to compute Actual Cost per line item:

Field	Purpose
lineItem/UnblendedCost	The Actual Cost itself
lineItem/UsageAmount	Validates cost and supports unit economics
lineItem/UnblendedRate	Reconstructs cost if needed
lineItem/LineItemType	Filters out credits/discounts/refunds
product/ProductName	Identifies the AWS service
product/UsageType	Identifies the usage dimension

Table 6.1: *Minimum CUR Fields for AC*

AWS Cost Types and Their EVM Implications

AWS provides several cost types. Each one reflects a different interpretation of spending. Following are the definitions, based on the AWS documentation.

Unblended Cost

Unblended Cost represents the actual rate charged for each individual resource. It reflects the price after discounts that apply directly to that resource, such as Reserved Instance or Savings Plan discounts.

- **EVM implication**: Best for workload level AC, because it reflects the true cost of each resource.

Net Unblended Cost

Net Unblended Cost is Unblended Cost minus credits, refunds, and promotions.

- **EVM implication**: Useful when you want the AC to reflect the financial impact after credits.

Blended Cost

Blended Cost is an average rate applied across the accounts in an AWS Organization, when consolidated billing is enabled. It blends the rates of On Demand and Reserved Instance usage across accounts.

- **EVM implication**: Not recommended for EVM, because it hides the real cost of individual workloads.

Amortized Cost

Amortized Cost spreads the upfront and recurring charges of Reserved Instances and Savings Plans across the period in which the benefits are consumed.

- **EVM implication**: Provides a smoother and more accurate representation of ongoing cloud consumption.

Net Amortized Cost

Net Amortized Cost is Amortized Cost minus credits, refunds, and promotions.

- **EVM implication**: Useful when you want amortized values, but also want credits reflected in AC.

Taxes

Taxes do not appear in Cost Explorer or CUR. They appear only on invoices.

- **EVM implication**: Most teams exclude taxes from EVM, because they do not reflect the operational consumption.

Credits

Credits reduce costs in the period in which they are applied. They appear in Net Unblended and Net Amortized views.

In CUR, Credits appear as line items with specific lineItem/LineItemType values, such as:

- Credit
- Refund
- EdpDiscount
- PromotionalCredits

These reduce the effective cost for the period in which they are applied.

- **EVM implication**: You need to decide whether credits should influence AC, or be excluded for analytical consistency.

Obtaining AC from GCP

Google Cloud exposes Actual Cost data primarily through the Billing Export to BigQuery. Unlike AWS and Azure, GCP does not offer multiple cost-type perspectives, such as blended, unblended, or amortized. Instead, GCP provides a single, detailed billing dataset, where each line item includes a field called **`cost_type`**, which identifies the nature of the charge. This structure keeps the model simple, but requires you to understand how discounts, credits, and taxes appear in the exports. For screenshots, you can rely on the Google Cloud Console or the Google Cloud Billing documentation, which provides examples of the Billing Export interface and schema.

Finding AC Data in GCP

- **Billing Export to BigQuery**: The authoritative source for detailed cost data.
- **Cloud Billing Reports**: A visual interface for exploring spend trends.
- **Billing Account Overview**: High-level totals, including taxes.
- **Google Cloud Documentation**: The best source for UI references and schema details.

Step by Step: Extracting AC from Billing Reports and BigQuery

AC from Billing Reports

Cloud Billing Reports in Google Cloud Console give you a visual way to explore Actual Cost, before you move to BigQuery. They help you validate scopes, labels, and cost patterns, and they are useful for confirming that your EVM structure aligns with how GCP organizes the billing data.

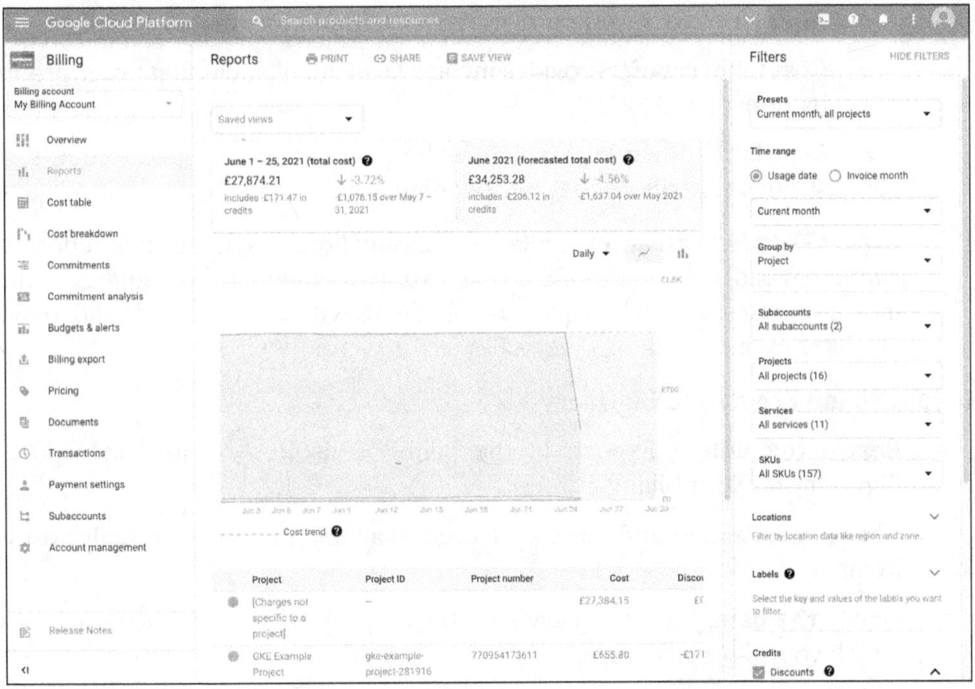

Figure 6.3: *Google Cloud Platform Cost Report*

- **Open the Billing Reports Page:** In the Google Cloud Console, go to your Cloud Billing account and select the Reports page. This view shows usage cost trends for the selected billing account.

- **Confirm the Correct Permissions:** Ensure that your user has a billing role that allows cost visibility, such as Billing Account Viewer or Billing Account Costs Manager.
- **Select the Billing Account and Time Range:** At the top of the Reports page, choose the correct billing account, and set the time range. You can view historical usage cost data back to January 2017, and invoice month data back to January 2019.
- **Adjust the Report Settings:** Use the controls to configure the report:
  - **Time range and granularity**: Choose daily or monthly views depending on your EVM cadence.
  - **Group by**: Summarize costs by project, service, SKU, or location.
  - **Filters**: Narrow the view using project, service, or label filters to match your EVM scope.
- **Use the Available Report Types:** The Reports area includes multiple views that support AC validation:
  - **Billing report**: Shows usage cost trends and forecasts.
  - **Cost table report**: Provides invoice level detail, including taxes, grouped by project and SKU.
  - **Cost breakdown report**: Shows how on demand costs, discounts, and savings contribute to total spending.
- **Export Data for Validation or Reconciliation:** From the Cost table report, you can download the data as CSV. This export includes invoice aligned values, including taxes, which helps you reconcile AC with Finance, and validate what you later extract from BigQuery.

AC from Billing Export and BigQuery

- **Enable the Billing Export**: In the Billing Console, activate the export to BigQuery for your billing account.
- **Choose the dataset and table**: GCP creates a table that receives daily cost line items.
- **Query the data**: Use BigQuery to filter by project, service, SKU, or label to match your EVM structure.
- **Select the correct fields**: Include usage amounts, pricing fields, and the cost type column.
- **Automate ingestion**: Integrate BigQuery queries into your EVM pipeline for consistent AC updates.

How to Query Cost Data in BigQuery

The Google Cloud Billing export sends your detailed cost and usage data into a BigQuery dataset. Once the export is enabled, you can query it using standard SQL. The key fields you use for EVM alignment are:

- `project.id`
- `service.description`
- `sku.description`
- `labels.key / labels.value`
- `cost` and `usage.amount`
- `usage_start_time / usage_end_time`

Here is a clean example of how you would filter by these dimensions.

SQL

```
SELECT
  project.id AS project_id,
  service.description AS service,
  sku.description AS sku,
  labels,
  usage_start_time,
  cost
FROM
  `my_billing_export.gcp_billing_export_v1_XXXXXX`
WHERE
  project.id = 'my-migration-project'
  AND service.description = 'Compute Engine'
  AND sku.description LIKE '%N2 Standard%'
  AND labels.environment = 'production'
  AND usage_start_time BETWEEN '2024-01-01' AND '2024-01-31'
ORDER BY
  usage_start_time;
```

GCP Cost Types and Their EVM Implications

GCP uses the **`cost_type`** field to classify each line item. The values are simple and consistent across all services.

- **regular**: Standard usage-based cost after applying pricing and automatic discounts.
- **tax**: Taxes applied to the billing account. These appear in the exports, unlike AWS and Azure.

- **adjustment**: Manual corrections, or billing changes applied by Google Cloud.
- **`rounding_error`**: Small corrections due to currency rounding.

GCP also includes credits as separate line items. These may represent promotional credits, committed use discounts, or negotiated benefits. They reduce costs in the period in which they are applied.

Impact on Earned Value

GCP's cost model influences how you prepare AC for EVM.

- **No amortized view**: GCP does not amortize Committed Use Discounts. If you want a smoothed cost profile, you must implement amortization manually.
- **Taxes included**: Taxes appear in the exports. You need to decide whether to include them in AC, or exclude them to keep the focus on operational consumption.
- **Credits as line items**: Credits reduce AC immediately. You must decide whether they should influence EVM, or be removed for analytical consistency.
- **Consistent cost structure**: The absence of multiple cost types simplifies extraction, but requires careful interpretation of discounts and credits.

Obtaining AC from FOCUS

FinOps Open Cost and Usage Specification (FOCUS) is not a cloud provider. It is a **standardized billing data schema**, designed to unify how cost and usage information is represented across AWS, Azure, GCP, SaaS vendors, and on-premises systems. Instead of extracting AC directly from a provider interface, you work with a **FOCUS-formatted dataset** produced by a vendor, or by your own transformation pipeline. The goal is to give you a consistent, provider-agnostic structure that simplifies EVM calculations, and eliminates the inconsistencies that normally appear when comparing billing data across platforms. The FOCUS specification defines required fields, cost categories, allocation metadata, and contract commitment structures, giving you a predictable foundation for AC extraction and analysis.

FOCUS is maintained by the FinOps Foundation, and evolves through formal versioned releases. The specification defines how cost and usage rows must be structured; how shared costs should be allocated, and how contract commitments should be represented. This makes FOCUS especially valuable for EVM, because it provides a stable, normalized dataset that aligns with the financial and operational views you need for AC, PV, and EV. The version 1.3 introduce improvements, such as dedicated commitment datasets, allocation transparency, and data completeness indicators, all of which strengthen the reliability of your AC pipeline.

A central feature of FOCUS is its **four cost types**. These cost types allow you to interpret the same usage event through different financial lenses—list price, contracted price, effective operational cost, or final billed amount. Understanding these cost types is essential before deciding which one to use as AC in your EVM pipeline.

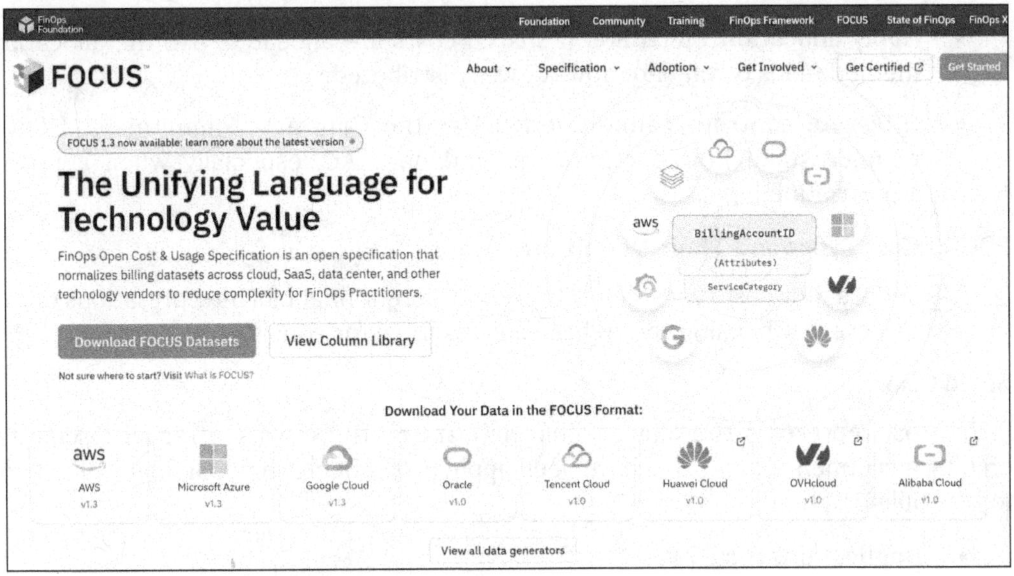

Figure 6.4: *FinOps Foundation FOCUS Version 1.3*

Finding AC in FOCUS

- **FOCUS cost and usage dataset:** The main table containing normalized cost and usage rows across providers.
- **Contract commitment dataset:** A supplemental dataset that isolates reservation and commitment terms.
- **Allocation metadata fields:** Columns that show how shared or distributed costs were split across workloads.
- **Provider and host provider identifiers:** Fields that distinguish the service provider from the underlying platform.
- **Completeness and recency indicators:** Metadata that signals whether the dataset is final or still subject to revision.

Step by Step: Extracting AC from a FOCUS Dataset

- **Obtain the FOCUS-formatted dataset:** This may come from a cloud provider, a FinOps platform, or your internal transformation pipeline.
- **Identify the cost and usage table:** This is the core dataset, where each row represents a costed usage event or charge.

- **Filter by billing period:** Select the month or period that aligns with your EVM reporting cycle.
- **Select the relevant cost fields:** Use the standardized FOCUS columns, such as charge amount, usage amount, currency, and cost category.
- **Apply allocation metadata:** If shared costs are allocated, use the allocation method fields to validate how AC was distributed.
- **Integrate contract commitments:** Use the Contract Commitment dataset to understand how commitments influence AC, especially when applying amortization logic.

FOCUS Cost Types and Their Definitions

FOCUS defines four cost types that represent different financial interpretations of the same usage event. Choosing the right one is essential for consistent EVM reporting.

Billed Cost

Billed Cost represents the amount that appears on the invoice after all discounts, credits, adjustments, and taxes have been applied. It reflects the final financial impact for the billing period.

- **Implications for EVM**
  - **Aligned with finance**, because it matches the invoice.
  - **Includes credits and adjustments**, which may introduce volatility.
  - **Includes taxes**, depending on the provider.
  - Best when EVM must reconcile directly with financial accounting.

Contracted Cost

Contracted Cost reflects the price agreed in a contract or commitment, such as a reservation, savings plan, committed use discount, or enterprise agreement. It excludes list price and focuses on the negotiated rate.

- **Implications for EVM**
  - **Stable and predictable**, ideal for long-term planning.
  - **Useful for PV**, since it aligns with contractual expectations.
  - **Excludes credits and adjustments**, so AC may diverge from Finance.
  - Best when you want AC to reflect the economic reality of commitments.

Effective Cost

Effective Cost represents the cost after applying all discounts and commitment benefits, but **before** applying credits, adjustments or taxes. It reflects the operational cost of running workloads with all negotiated savings applied.

- **Implications for EVM**
  - Most aligned with operational consumption.
  - Smooths commitment effects, when amortization is applied.
  - Excludes credits and taxes, reducing financial noise.
  - Often the best choice for AC when measuring cost performance.

List Cost

List Cost represents the undiscounted price of the resource or service. It ignores commitments, negotiated discounts, and credits.

- **Implications for EVM**
  - **Useful for benchmarking** and efficiency analysis.
  - **Not suitable as AC**, since it does not reflect the real financial impact.
  - Helpful for PV modeling when comparing planned versus actual efficiency.
  - Best used as a reference, not as the AC value in EVM.

Impact on Earned Value

Choosing the right FOCUS cost type determines how AC aligns with PV and EV.

- **Billed Cost** is ideal when EVM must reconcile with Finance.
- **Effective Cost** is ideal when EVM must reflect operational performance.
- **Contracted Cost** is ideal when EVM must align with long-term commitments.
- **List Cost** is ideal for benchmarking, not AC.

Consistency is essential. Once you choose a cost type for AC, apply it across all providers, and all reporting periods.

Planned Value in Practice

Planned Value (PV) is entirely dependent on two Finance-owned capabilities: **Budgeting** and **Unit Economics**. These disciplines define how much an organization expects to spend, how that spend is distributed over time, and how it relates to the value produced by each workload, product or project. Both of the topics will be explored in depth, in their own dedicated chapters later in the book. For now, we will stay with the essential concepts needed to make sense of PV, within the Earned Value framework.

PV represents the **time-phased budget baseline** for a given scope. It answers a simple but foundational question: "*How much cost did we plan to incur by this point in time?*" In traditional project management, this baseline is usually fixed at the start of the project. In cloud environments, PV still plays the same role, but the way it is constructed depends heavily on how Finance models budgets, and how Unit Economics define the cost structure of the workloads.

PV as the Time-Phased Budget Baseline

- **PV reflects the planned cost for each period:** PV distributes the total approved budget across the months, weeks, or days of the project or workload lifecycle. This creates a baseline against which the AC and EV can be compared.
- **PV establishes the financial expectation curve:** It defines the expected spending trajectory, allowing you to see whether the actual consumption is ahead, behind, or aligned with the plan.
- **PV is fixed at the moment the baseline is approved:** Once the budget is time-phased, it becomes the reference point for performance measurement. Any changes must follow formal versioning rules, which we will cover later.
- **PV enables meaningful variance analysis:** Without a time-phased baseline, AC and EV have no context. PV provides that context by defining what "should have happened" financially by now.

Dependence of PV on Finance-Owned Processes

- **Budgeting defines the total amount available:** Finance determines how much money is allocated to each product, project, or organizational unit. PV cannot exist without this starting point.
- **Unit economics define how costs scale:** Finance and FinOps collaborate to understand cost drivers, cost per unit, and expected consumption patterns. These assumptions shape how the budget is distributed over time.
- **Financial governance controls when PV can change:** Budget revisions, re-forecasts, and reallocations follow Finance processes. PV must respect these rules to remain auditable and aligned with corporate governance.
- **PV must align with financial reporting cycles:** Monthly, quarterly, or annual cycles influence how PV is structured and maintained. This ensures that EVM outputs can be reconciled with Finance.

Obtaining PV from Finance

Planned Value does not originate in Engineering or FinOps. It is a **Finance Artifact**, shaped by budgeting cycles, forecasting processes, and the financial structure of the organization. Because of this, PV usually lives inside Finance-owned systems and workflows, rather than cloud or technical platforms. Understanding where PV resides helps you integrate EVM with the broader financial governance of the company.

Common Places Where PV Lives inside Finance

- **Enterprise Resource Planning (ERP) systems:** ERPs such as SAP S/4HANA, Oracle Financials, or Microsoft Dynamics store the organization's official budgets and cost center allocations. These systems often hold the *approved annual budget* for each department, project, or product. PV is typically derived from these budget entries and then time-phased for EVM.
- **Corporate Performance Management (CPM) platforms:** Tools such as Anaplan, Workday Adaptive Planning, or Oracle EPM are used for budgeting, forecasting, and scenario modeling. Finance teams often build **monthly or quarterly budget distributions** in these platforms, making them a natural source for PV.
- **Financial Planning & Analysis (FP&A) spreadsheets:** In many organizations, especially those still maturing their financial processes, budgets, and forecasts are maintained in structured spreadsheets. These files often contain **time-phased budget curves**, which can be directly translated into PV.
- **Project Portfolio Management (PPM) systems:** Platforms such as Clarity PPM, Planview, or Jira Align store project budgets and funding approvals. When cloud spend is tied to a project, PV may come directly from the **project budget baseline**, stored in these systems.
- **Cost center budgets in Finance data warehouses:** Larger organizations centralize financial data in warehouses or data lakes. PV can be extracted from **budget fact tables**, which store monthly or quarterly allocations for each cost center or product line.

Finance as The Source of Truth for PV

- Finance owns the **budgeting process**, so that PV must align with the official budget source of truth.
- Finance controls **forecasting and re-forecasting**, which influence how PV changes over time.
- Finance systems enforce **governance and auditability**, ensuring that PV is traceable and approved.
- These systems already contain the **time-phased structure** needed to build PV curves.

Examples of How PV Appears in Practice

- A product team has a €1.2M annual cloud budget stored in SAP. Finance distributes it as €100k per month in Adaptive Planning. This monthly distribution becomes the PV baseline.

- A project receives €300k of funding in Planview. The project manager phases it across six months. That phasing becomes the PV curve for EVM.
- A cost center has a €500k annual budget in Oracle EPM. FP&A allocates 40% to Q1, 30% to Q2, 20% to Q3 and 10% to Q4. Those quarterly values are converted into monthly PV for EVM.

This is the landscape where PV originates. In the next subsection, we can walk through **how to translate these Finance artifacts into a time-phased PV baseline**, suitable for EVM.

Translating Annual Budgets into Time-Phased PV

Annual budgets are the starting point for Planned Value, but they are not directly usable for Earned Value. Finance typically approves budgets at an annual or quarterly level, while EVM requires a **time-phased baseline** that shows how much cost was planned for each month or week. Translating the annual budget into PV is therefore a joint effort: Finance provides the total amount and the financial rules, while FinOps and Engineering determine how that amount should be distributed across the lifecycle of the workloads.

Why FinOps Must Create a Controllable Version of the Budget

Finance owns the budget, but **Engineering does not control every component of cloud spend**. Taxes, credits, fees, and commitment purchases (such as Reservations, Savings Plans or CUDs) are financial artifacts that do not reflect engineering decisions. If these items remain inside the PV baseline, they distort the comparison between PV and AC.

For this reason, FinOps teams must create a **FinOps-ready version of the budget** that includes only the portion of spend that Engineering can influence. This ensures that PV reflects operational expectations rather than financial noise.

Steps to Translate Annual Budgets into Time-Phased PV

- **Start with the Finance-approved annual budget:** This is the authoritative amount allocated to the product, project, or cost center. It is the upper limit of what PV can represent.
- **Remove non-controllable components:** Engineering cannot influence items such as:
    - Taxes
    - Credits (promotional, negotiated, or programmatic)
    - Fees (support plans, marketplace surcharges, billing adjustments)
    - Upfront purchases of Reservations, Savings Plans, or CUDs: These items must be excluded or handled separately, so that PV reflects only the costs which Engineering can manage.

- **Align the budget with the chosen cost type:** This is critical. If AC is measured using **Effective Cost**, PV must also be built using Effective Cost assumptions. If AC uses **Billed Cost**, PV must reflect the same structure. If you are unsure about the implications of each cost type, revisit the **Actual Cost section**, where the cost-type differences are explained in detail. PV and AC must speak the same financial language; otherwise, variance analysis becomes meaningless.
- **Distribute the controllable budget across the time periods:** The distribution method depends on the workload's expected behavior:
    - **Flat distribution**, for stable, predictable workloads.
    - **Seasonal distribution**, for workloads with known peaks.
    - **Ramp-up distribution**, for new products or migrations.
    - **Consumption-based distribution**, when Unit Economics define cost per unit. The goal is to create a realistic spending curve that reflects how the workload is expected to evolve.
- **Validate the distribution with engineering:** Engineering teams understand the expected consumption patterns. Their input ensures that PV reflects operational reality, rather than purely financial assumptions.
- **Lock the baseline:** Once the time-phased PV is approved, it becomes the baseline for EVM. Any changes must follow the formal versioning rules, which we will cover in the next subsection.

The importance of a well-constructed PV

A well-constructed PV baseline ensures that:

- Variances between PV and AC reflect the **real performance**, not accounting artifacts.
- Engineering is evaluated, only on the portion of spend that they can control.
- PV aligns with the **same cost type** used for AC, ensuring consistency.
- EVM outputs can be reconciled with Finance, without losing operational meaning.

Obtaining Unit Data

Unit Economics will have its own dedicated chapter later, where we explore how to define units, how to measure them, and how to connect them to value. For now, we will stay focused on the **data and tooling perspective**, because EVM depends on having reliable, consistent unit and usage data before you can calculate Earned Value.

Unit data answers a simple question: "*How much of the thing we produce or deliver did we actually generate?*" Usage data answers the complementary question: "*How much cloud consumption was required to produce it?*"

Both are essential inputs for EV, and both come from systems that sit **outside** the cloud providers.

Unit and Usage Data Common Sources

- **Product analytics platforms:** Tools such as Google Analytics, Mixpanel, Amplitude, or Adobe Analytics track user interactions, transactions, and product events. These systems often provide the **primary unit of value** for digital products, such as:
    - Number of active users
    - Number of transactions
    - Number of API calls
    - Number of sessions
    - Number of processed items

Product analytics is usually the most direct source of unit data.

- **Application telemetry and observability platforms:** Systems, such as Datadog, New Relic, Dynatrace, Prometheus, or OpenTelemetry pipelines, capture operational metrics. These platforms often provide **usage-aligned units**, such as:
    - Requests per second
    - Jobs processed
    - Messages consumed
    - Compute cycles
    - Storage operations

These metrics help connect cloud consumption to workload behavior.

- **Business systems and operational databases:** ERP, CRM, billing systems, or internal operational databases often store business-level units, such as:
    - Orders fulfilled
    - Invoices generated
    - Customers onboarded
    - Shipments processed

These units reflect business value, rather than technical activity.

- **Data warehouses and lakehouses:** Platforms, such as BigQuery, Snowflake, Redshift, or Databricks, often serve as the **integration point** for unit data. They combine product analytics, telemetry, and business data into a single, searchable source that FinOps can use for EV calculations.

- **Custom event pipelines:** Many organizations build their own event streams using Kafka, Kinesis, Pub/Sub, or internal ETL pipelines. These systems provide **high-resolution unit data** tailored to the product's unique value model.
- **ML and data processing platforms:** For data-heavy workloads, unit data may come from processing frameworks, such as Spark, Flink, or Beam. Units often include:
    - Datasets processed
    - Models trained
    - Predictions generated
    - Data volumes transformed

Unit Data and Cloud Billing Systems

Cloud billing systems tell you **how much you spent**, not **what you produced**. Unit data comes from the systems that represent product behavior, customer activity, or operational throughput. This separation is why Unit Economics requires integration across multiple domains—Finance, Engineering, Product, and Data.

What Matters for EVM

For Earned Value, unit data must be:

- **Consistent** (same definition across time.)
- **Traceable** (comes from a reliable system of record.)
- **Aligned with value** (represents something meaningful the workload produces.)
- **Available at the same cadence as AC and PV** (usually monthly.)

Later, in the dedicated Unit Economics chapter, we will explore how to define units, how to validate them, and how to connect them to cost and value. For now, this section gives you the foundation needed to understand how unit data flows into the EVM model.

Designing the EVM Data Pipeline

At this point in the book, all conceptual definitions of AC, PV, and unit data are already established. *Now we are shifting* the focus entirely to **automation**—how to operationalize these inputs, so that the Earned Value can be calculated reliably, repeatedly, and without manual intervention. Designing the EVM data pipeline is about building a flow that ingests these three inputs, normalizes them, aligns them in time, and produces consistent outputs for dashboards, reporting, and governance.

The Role of Automation in the EVM Pipeline

Automation ensures that EVM is not a one-off analysis, but a **continuous operational capability**. The pipeline must be predictable, auditable, and resilient, because AC, PV, and unit data come from different systems, update at different cadences, and follow different governance rules. The design must account for these differences, and unify them into a single, coherent flow.

Core Inputs and Shaping the Pipeline

Even though we are not redefining AC, PV, or unit data here, their **data characteristics** directly influence how the pipeline must be built.

- **AC arrives from cloud billing systems:** AC is typically delivered daily or monthly, depending on the provider, and the chosen data source (Cost Explorer, CUR, Azure EA export, GCP Billing Export, FOCUS, and so on). The pipeline must handle:
    - Ingestion of large billing datasets
    - Late-arriving adjustments
    - Cost-type alignment
    - Allocation metadata
    - Multi-cloud normalization
- **PV arrives from finance systems:** PV is usually updated monthly or quarterly, and follows Finance governance. The pipeline must support:
    - Controlled ingestion of Finance baselines.
    - Versioning and effective-date logic.
    - Separation of controllable versus non-controllable budget components.
    - Alignment with the cost type used for AC.
- **Unit data arrives from product, telemetry, or business systems:** Unit data may update hourly, daily, or monthly depending on the source. The pipeline must handle:
    - Multiple data sources (analytics, telemetry, CRM, ERP, and so on)
    - Different granularities
    - Transformations into monthly unit counts
    - Validation rules to ensure consistency

Designing the Integration Layer

The EVM pipeline needs a **central integration layer**, where all the three inputs converge. This layer typically lives in a data warehouse or lakehouse and must support:

- **Time alignment:** AC, PV, and units must be aggregated to the same time period. Normally, PV comes in a monthly basis, while AC comes in a daily basis (sometimes hourly). Recommendation is to normalize them to a daily basis. It will provide enough grain for a detailed analysis and deviation detection. For this matter, Time Alignment requires careful handling of:

    - Billing periods
    - Invoice months
    - Fiscal calendars
    - Unit timestamps

- **Normalization:** Each input arrives in a different structure. The pipeline must normalize:
    - Currencies
    - Cost types
    - Project or product identifiers
    - Allocation rules
    - Unit definitions
- **Data quality checks:** Automated validation ensures that:
    - AC is complete for the period.
    - PV matches the approved baseline version.
    - Unit data is consistent with expected ranges.
    - No missing or duplicated records exist.

Orchestrating the Pipeline

Automation requires orchestration. The pipeline should run on a predictable schedule, and handle dependencies between inputs.

- **AC ingestion jobs** run daily or monthly depending on the provider.
- **PV ingestion jobs** run only, when Finance publishes a new baseline.
- **Unit ingestion jobs** run at the cadence of the source system (daily or monthly).
- **EVM calculation jobs** run after all three inputs, for the period are available.

This orchestration ensures that EVM outputs are always based on a complete and aligned data.

Output Layer: Making EVM Consumable

Once AC, PV, and unit data are aligned, the pipeline produces the final EVM metrics:

- **EV**

- **CV and SV**
- **CPI and SPI**
- **Forecasting indicators**

These outputs feed dashboards, reports, and governance processes.

Bringing It All Together

Earned Value Management in the cloud is not a theoretical construct. It becomes powerful only when the full workflow runs smoothly, month after month, across Finance, Engineering, and FinOps. This closing section reinforces how the pieces fit together into a single, repeatable operational cycle. The goal is to make EVM a **living capability**, not a one-off analysis.

The End-To-End Workflow

The end-to-end cycle follows a predictable rhythm. Each month, three streams of information converge: **AC from cloud billing**, **PV from Finance**, and **unit data from product or telemetry systems**. Once aligned, these inputs allow you to calculate EV, compare performance, and update forecasts. The cycle then resets and repeats, creating a continuous feedback loop.

This figure illustrates how these monthly inputs flow through a continuous cycle that transforms the raw data into actionable decisions.

***Figure 6.5:** End-to-End FinOps EVM Data Workflow*

- **Ingest AC:** Cloud billing data arrives first. It is ingested from native exports, FinOps platforms or FOCUS datasets, normalized and aligned to the chosen cost type. This establishes the actual cost for the period.
- **Ingest PV:** Finance publishes the approved baseline or updated forecast. FinOps extracts the controllable portion, aligns it with the AC cost type, and loads it into the pipeline. This sets the financial expectations for the period.

- **Ingest unit data:** Product analytics, telemetry, or business systems provide the unit counts for the period. These units represent the value delivered, and are essential for calculating EV.
- **Align the three inputs:** AC, PV, and units are aggregated to the same time period, normalized to the same identifiers, and validated for completeness. This creates a unified dataset ready for EVM calculations.
- **Calculate EV, CV, SV, CPI, and SPI:** With all inputs aligned, the pipeline computes the core EVM metrics. These metrics reveal whether the workload is performing above, below, or on plan.
- **Generate insights and forecasts:** Variances feed into forecasting models, highlighting risks, opportunities, and expected end-of-period outcomes. This is where EVM becomes actionable.
- **Publish dashboards and reports:** The results are delivered to Engineering, Finance, and leadership through dashboards, scorecards, or governance meetings. Transparency drives accountability.
- **Reset and repeat:** The cycle restarts the following month. New AC arrives, PV may be updated, and unit data continues to flow. Over time, the process becomes routine and highly reliable.

Significance of This Cycle

A consistent FinOps EVM cycle creates a shared language between Finance and Engineering. It connects cost, performance, and value in a way that is measurable, predictable, and operationally useful. When automated, the cycle becomes a stable foundation for decision-making, forecasting, and governance.

Conclusion

This chapter brought together all the practical elements required to make FinOps Earned Value Management work as a real, operational capability. We explored how **Actual Cost**, **Planned Value**, and **unit data** each originate from different systems, follow different rhythms, and require different ingestion patterns. We then connected these inputs through automation, showing how data pipelines, orchestration, and tooling patterns transform EVM from a conceptual model into a repeatable workflow.

You saw how AC flows from cloud billing sources, how PV comes from Finance systems, and how unit data emerges from product analytics, telemetry, or business platforms. We examined how these inputs must be aligned, normalized, and processed in a consistent cadence, so that EV, CV, SV, CPI, and SPI can be calculated reliably. The chapter also highlighted how automation—whether through native cloud tools, FinOps platforms, or data warehouses—is the key in making EVM sustainable at scale.

FinOps EVM is still an innovation. At this point, **no commercial tool provides native, end-to-end EVM capabilities.** Market solutions can support parts of the workflow—cost ingestion, allocation, forecasting, dashboards—but none of them deliver a complete EVM engine out of the box. The good news is that most platforms can be **adapted** to accommodate the required inputs and run the custom calculations needed to produce EVM metrics. With the right data model and automation patterns, any organization can build a robust EVM capability on top of its existing FinOps tooling.

In many ways, this chapter serves as a **design blueprint** for building your own EVM data pipeline—a practical guide to assembling the components, connecting the data, and generating the insights that make FinOps EVM so powerful. With these foundations in place, you are well equipped to bring EVM to life in your own environment, and unlock a clearer, more confident understanding of cloud performance.

In the next chapter, we will explore one of the most essential elements of the Earned Value Management technique: the determination of Unit Economics. This is the point where the budgeting process connects cost to value in a measurable way. Understanding how to define Unit Economics correctly will shape the accuracy of percentage complete and the effectiveness of Earned Value calculations. It is the step that enables organizations to track both value creation and cost performance across their cloud investments, with clarity and consistency.

References

- Cloud billing reports. (n.d.). Google Cloud Documentation. Retrieved January 11, 2026, from https://docs.cloud.google.com/billing/docs/reports
- FOCUS - FinOps Open Cost & Usage Specification. (n.d.). Retrieved January 17, 2026, from https://focus.finops.org/
- Open Water Foundation. (n.d.). Cost Explorer - Learn / AWS. https://learn.openwaterfoundation.org/owf-learn-aws/costs/cost-explorer/cost-explorer/
- Structure of Standard data export. (n.d.). Google Cloud Documentation. Retrieved January 11, 2026, from https://docs.cloud.google.com/billing/docs/how-to/export-data-bigquery-tables/standard-usage
- Yujiang. (n.d.). Get started with Cost Management reporting - Azure - Microsoft Cost Management. Azure Docs. Retrieved January 10, 2026, from https://docs.azure.cn/en-us/cost-management-billing/costs/reporting-get-started

CHAPTER 7
Determining Unit Economics

Introduction

Unit Economics provides a practical way to understand, how a workload creates a value relative to the cost required to operate it. In cloud environments, where consumption is dynamic and architectures evolve quickly, traditional financial measures often fail to capture the real relationship between technical activity and business outcomes. Unit Economics fills this gap by focusing on a single meaningful unit that represents progress, output, or value. When this unit is well defined and consistently measured, it becomes the anchor for Earned Value calculations in FinOps EVM, and a reliable indicator of workload performance.

This chapter explores the full lifecycle of determining Unit Economics, from defining what a unit represents to understanding how it behaves, and how costs should be allocated to it. We begin by identifying the Business Units responsible for outcomes, ensuring that accountability is clear and aligned with cloud consumption. We then examine how to collect the data needed to measure both cost and unit in a consistent and actionable way. With this foundation in place, we look at how cost allocation shapes the financial view of a workload, and why consistency across budgeting and reporting is essential.

From there, the chapter introduces the characteristics that make a Unit Economics effective in practice. Behavior and Value Outcome provide the two dimensions needed to interpret how cost and unit relate, whether through elasticity, efficiency, business value, or technical contribution. Finally, we bring these elements together to determine the right Unit Economics for any workload, supported by guiding questions that help teams test assumptions, and select a unit that reflects the reality rather than abstraction.

Structure

In this chapter, the following topics will be covered:

- Defining Unit Economics
- Measuring Unit Economics
- Characteristics of High-Quality Unit Economics
- Determining the Right Unit Economics

Defining Unit Economics

Unit Economics helps us understand the financial performance of a workload, by examining the cost and value of a single meaningful unit. This unit represents the smallest element of work that carries business relevance. It may be a transaction, an API call, a customer session, a processed dataset, or any other unit that reflects how the workload produces value.

When we define Unit Economics, we create a direct connection between the cloud consumption and business outcomes. This connection is essential for FinOps EVM, because Earned Value depends on a reliable measure of percent complete. Percent complete becomes dependable, only when it is tied to a unit that reflects real progress. Without a clear unit, we rely on subjective estimates, or milestones that do not represent the actual state of the workload.

A well-defined unit gives us a stable foundation for measuring cost efficiency, forecasting spend, and evaluating whether the workload is moving toward its intended outcome. It also supports consistent comparisons across teams and time periods, since the unit provides a common lens for analysis.

In practice, Unit Economics becomes the anchor for every calculation that follows in FinOps EVM. It shapes how we measure progress, how we interpret cost signals, and how we make decisions about optimization or investment. When we choose a meaningful unit, and measure it consistently, we gain clarity and control over the financial performance of the workload.

Measuring Unit Economics

Measuring Unit Economics starts with understanding how a workload creates value, and how we can observe that value in a consistent way. To do this, we break the process into clear steps that help us identify the right units, gather the data that represents them, and allocate the costs in a way that reflects the actual consumption. Each step builds on the previous one, giving us a structured path, from raw information to a meaningful insight.

We begin by identifying the business units that matter for the workload. These units define what we want to measure, and set the foundation for all later calculations. Once the units are clear, we focus on collecting the data that describes how often they occur, and how they behave over time. With this data in hand, we move to cost allocation, where we connect cloud spend to the units in a way that is fair, transparent, and repeatable.

Identifying Business Units

Identifying Business Units is the first practical step in measuring Unit Economics. In a cloud context, this step goes beyond organizational charts or formal reporting lines. What matters is establishing a clear hierarchy of accountability that connects cloud consumption to people who can influence decisions and outcomes.

Many organizations already have defined Business Units, and in some cases, these structures are sufficient. However, cloud environments often evolve faster than organizational models. Teams, squads, tribes, and similar constructs are commonly used to describe how work is organized, but they are not always tied to clear financial accountability. For Unit Economics to work, every level in the structure must understand what it owns, and how its decisions affect cost and value.

The goal is to define Business Units in a way that supports transparency, ownership, and decision-making. Each unit should represent a meaningful slice of work, with a clear purpose and a responsible owner. This structure allows accountability to flow from higher-level business objectives down to the workloads that consume cloud resources.

The following steps provide a practical approach for identifying Business Units in a cloud environment:

1. **Start from accountability, not org charts:** Identify who is responsible for outcomes, not just who reports to whom. Business Units should map to decision makers, who can act on cost and performance signals.
2. **Align units with how work is delivered:** Use existing delivery structures, such as teams or squads, when they reflect real ownership. Adjust or refine them, when responsibilities are unclear or shared.
3. **Ensure each unit has a clear scope:** Define what each Business Unit owns, including services, workloads, or platforms. Avoid overlapping responsibilities that dilute accountability.
4. **Create a hierarchy that supports roll up and drill down:** Business Units should fit into a layered structure, where higher levels aggregate results from lower ones. This enables analysis at different levels, without losing consistency.

5. **Validate units against decision-making needs:** Confirm that the defined units support budgeting, optimization, and performance discussions. If a unit cannot influence outcomes, it is likely defined at the wrong level.

By grounding Business Units in accountability and practical ownership, we create a structure that supports meaningful Unit Economics, and prepares the organization for consistent FinOps EVM execution.

Data Collection

Data collection is the step, where Unit Economics moves from concept to execution. The data we collect must support the value outcome that we want to measure, whether that outcome is business-oriented or technical. While the specific metrics will vary depending on the outcome, the underlying principles of data collection remain consistent.

Unit Economics is built on two components: cost and unit. Cost data represents the cloud resources consumed by the workload. Unit data represents the measurable output that reflects progress or value creation. Both sides of the equation must be collected with the same level of care. If either side is incomplete or inconsistent, the resulting Unit Economics will not support reliable analysis or decision making.

In a cloud environment, data is often available, but not always usable in its raw form. Metrics may exist across multiple systems, collected at different frequencies, or defined using different assumptions. The goal of data collection is not to gather everything, but what is necessary, consistent, and actionable.

The following aspects should be considered, when collecting data for Unit Economics:

- **Alignment with the defined unit:** Data must directly represent the unit being measured. If the unit is unclear or loosely defined, the collected data will not reflect real progress.
- **Consistency over time:** Data should be collected using the same definitions and intervals. Changes in measurement logic introduce noise that makes trends difficult to interpret.
- **Traceability between cost and unit data:** It should be possible to explain how cost data relates to unit data. This traceability is essential for transparency and trust.
- **Appropriate level of granularity:** Data should be detailed enough to support analysis, but not so granular that it becomes difficult to manage or explain.
- **Operational availability:** Data must be accessible without excessive manual effort. If data collection cannot be sustained, Unit Economics will not scale.

Data collection sets the boundaries for what Unit Economics can realistically explain. When cost and unit data are collected with clear intent and consistent definitions, they provide a shared reference that teams can rely on. This shared reference reduces ambiguity, and helps align technical signals with business discussions.

In the context of FinOps EVM, **the quality of data directly influences the credibility of percent complete and Earned Value calculations.** Inconsistent or loosely connected data introduces uncertainty that quickly propagates through forecasts, budgets, and performance assessments. Over time, this erodes confidence in the model, and limits its usefulness as a decision support tool.

A disciplined approach to data collection also supports scalability. As workloads evolve and organizations grow, the ability to extend Unit Economics across new services or teams depends on having repeatable data practices. When data collection is treated as an operational capability, rather than a onetime exercise, Unit Economics remains relevant, even as architectures and delivery models change.

At this stage, **the focus is not on selecting the perfect metrics, but on establishing a reliable foundation.** With cost and unit data collected in a structured and transparent way, we are prepared to allocate costs accurately, and evaluate Unit Economics in a manner that supports both financial control and informed decision making.

Cost Allocation

Cost allocation is the step, where cloud spend is connected to the Business Units that consume it. Once Business Units are identified, and the necessary data is collected, allocation provides the financial structure that allows Unit Economics to be calculated and interpreted with confidence.

In a cloud environment, cost allocation is rarely a purely technical exercise. It reflects a set of agreements about how the costs are interpreted, shared, and discussed across the organization. Different cost views can coexist, as long as they are clearly defined and applied consistently. The objective is not to find a single correct allocation model, but to establish one that supports transparency, accountability, and repeatable analysis.

Consistency plays a central role at this stage. Allocated costs must align with how budgets are defined and tracked. If the cost view used for Unit Economics differs from the one used for budgeting or financial reporting, comparisons become difficult, and trust in the numbers erodes. Alignment across these perspectives helps ensure that Unit Economics remains relevant in financial discussions.

It is also important to recognize that cloud costs come in different forms. On-demand usage, committed spend, taxes, credits, and shared services, all influence the final cost picture. Each organization must decide how these elements are treated. What matters is that these decisions are explicit and stable over time, allowing trends and performance to be evaluated without constant reinterpretation.

The following aspects should be considered, when allocating costs for Unit Economics:

- **Alignment with budget structures:** Allocated costs should reflect the same structure used for budgeting and financial tracking.
- **Clear treatment of shared and platform costs:** Shared services and platform components need defined allocation rules to avoid hidden or duplicated costs.
- **Consistent handling of commitments, taxes, and credits:** Decisions on including or excluding these elements should be documented and applied uniformly.
- **Traceability to Business Units:** Each allocated cost should be explainable in terms of ownership and consumption.
- **Stability of allocation logic over time:** Changes to allocation models should be deliberate, and infrequent to preserve comparability.

With a clear and consistent cost allocation approach, Unit Economics becomes a reliable lens for understanding workload performance, and supporting FinOps EVM analysis.

Characteristics of High-Quality Unit Economics

Not every unit is suitable for Unit Economics. While it is often easy to define a unit, it is harder to define one that consistently supports meaningful analysis, decision-making, and financial accountability. A good Unit Economics goes beyond measurement, and becomes a practical tool for understanding how workloads behave and how value is created.

In the context of FinOps EVM, the quality of the unit directly influences the reliability of percent complete and Earned Value calculations. Units that are poorly defined, unstable, or disconnected from outcomes introduce noise into the model and limit its usefulness. Units that are well chosen provide clarity and support conversations that connect the technical execution with financial performance.

This section explores the characteristics that make a Unit Economics effective in practice. It looks at how the units **behave over time**, how they respond to changes in demand, and **how efficiently** they convert cost into output. It also examines how units reflect value, both from a business and a technical perspective.

By understanding these characteristics, we can evaluate whether a unit supports the goals of FinOps EVM and adjust it when necessary. This prepares us to select the units that remain relevant as workloads evolve, and that support consistent measurement across planning, execution, and review cycles.

Pearson Correlation Coefficient

To understand how cost and unit relate to each other, we need a way to observe their relationship beyond a single calculation. The Pearson Correlation Coefficient (PCC) provides a simple and widely used method to describe how two variables move together over time. In this context, it helps us assess whether changes in cost are associated with changes in the unit being measured.

Figure 7.1 illustrates how different values of the Pearson correlation coefficient relate to the patterns seen in real data.

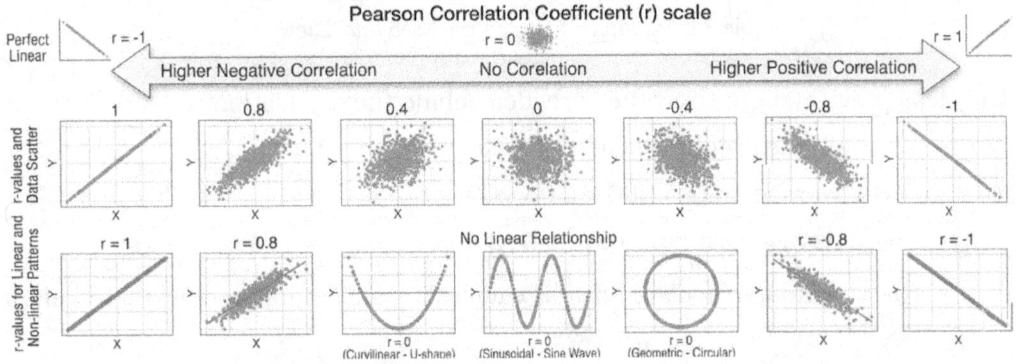

***Figure* 7.1:** *Pearson Correlation Coefficient Scale*

PCC expresses the strength and direction of a linear relationship between two variables. When applied to Unit Economics, it allows us to evaluate whether increases or decreases in cost, tend to align with the increases or decreases in unit volume. A strong positive correlation suggests that cost and unit move in the same direction. A weak or inconsistent correlation indicates that cost changes may be driven by factors unrelated to unit volume.

This distinction matters because Unit Economics is often interpreted as an efficiency signal. Without understanding correlation, it is easy to misread changes in the metric. A rising cost per unit may reflect growing demand, architectural constraints, or operational inefficiencies. Correlation helps separate these patterns by showing whether cost behavior follows unit behavior or diverges from it.

PCC does not explain why costs and units behave in a certain way. It provides a directional signal that helps frame further analysis. This signal becomes the starting point for exploring how Unit Economics responds to changes in volume, and how effectively cost is converted into output. These aspects are examined through elasticity and efficiency in the sections that follow.

Short Worked Example: How PCC is Calculated in Practice

To illustrate how the Pearson Correlation Coefficient is computed, consider a simplified dataset for a batchprocessing workload. The unit is the number of jobs processed per hour, and the cost is the hourly compute charge.

Hour	Units processed	Cost (USD)
1	100	12
2	150	18
3	200	24

Table 7.1: *Example of Units Processed and Their Cost*

The steps provided here show the core idea behind the calculation:

1. Compute the average of each variable.
   - Average units = (100 + 150 + 200) : 3 = 150
   - Average cost = (12 + 18 + 24) : 3 = 18
2. For each hour, calculate how far each value is from its average, then multiply the deviations.
   - Hour 1: (100 – 150) × (12 – 18) = (–50) × (–6) = 300
   - Hour 2: (150 – 150) × (18 – 18) = 0
   - Hour 3: (200 – 150) × (24 – 18) = 50 × 6 = 300
3. Add the products: 300 + 0 + 300 = 600.
4. Compute the standard deviation of each variable (simplified here):
   - Units SD = 50
   - Cost SD = 6
5. Multiply the standard deviations: 50 × 6 = 300.
6. Divide the sum of products by the product of standard deviations: PCC = 600 : 300 = **2.0** Since PCC is bounded between –1 and +1, this simplified example illustrates the mechanics, but with more data points, the value converges toward a realistic number. With a full dataset, this workload would show a PCC close to **1.0**, indicating a strong positive relationship.

The purpose of this example is not the exact numeric result, but the intuition: PCC measures how consistently cost and unit move together. When both increase and decrease in sync, the correlation becomes strongly positive, signaling elastic behavior.

Short Worked Example: Interpreting Correlation in a Cloud Workload

Consider a workload that processes customer orders. The unit is the number of orders processed per day, and the cost comes from compute, storage, and messaging services that scale with activity.

Over a 30-day period, the team observes the following pattern:

- When order volume increases, daily cloud cost also increases.
- When order volume drops, cost drops in the same pattern.
- The Pearson Correlation Coefficient between cost and unit for the period is **0.92**.

A correlation of 0.92 indicates a strong positive relationship. This tells us that the workload behaves elastically: cost closely follows demand. In practice, this means the Unit Economics signal is reliable. If cost per order rises, the team can investigate scaling thresholds, configuration choices, or architectural constraints, knowing that cost and unit are moving together.

Now, consider a second scenario. The same workload shows a PCC of **0.25** over another 30day period. Order volume fluctuates, but the cost remains mostly flat. This weak correlation suggests that cost is being influenced by factors unrelated to demand, such as idle resources, misconfigured autoscaling, or commitments masking real consumption. In this case, the cost per order becomes harder to interpret, because the workload is not responding to the volume changes.

These two examples illustrate how correlation helps determine whether Unit Economics reflects true workload behavior, or whether an additional investigation is needed before drawing conclusions about efficiency.

Behavior

At its simplest, Unit Economics is expressed as cost divided by unit. While this calculation is straightforward, the meaning of the resulting number depends on how cost and unit relate to each other over time. Understanding this relationship is essential before using Unit Economics as an input for analysis or decision-making.

Behavior describes how cost and unit move together, as a workload operates and scales. In some cases, cost increases in line with the unit, suggesting a predictable relationship. In other cases, cost grows faster or slower than the unit, revealing patterns that require a closer attention. These patterns help us understand whether Unit Economics reflects a stable operating model, or the one that changes as demand fluctuates.

In the context of FinOps EVM, behavior matters because Unit Economics is not only a snapshot. It is used to track progress, assess performance, and support percent complete calculations over time. If the relationship between cost and unit is not understood, changes in Unit Economics can be misinterpreted, leading to incorrect conclusions about efficiency or progress.

This subtopic focuses on establishing a baseline understanding of how cost and unit interact. It can be understood in two ways:

- Elasticity
- Efficiency

It sets the foundation for examining how Unit Economics responds to changes in volume, and how effectively it converts cost into output. These aspects are explored in more detail through elasticity and efficiency in the sections that follow.

Elasticity

Elasticity describes a workload, where the cost and unit are strongly correlated. When this behavior is present, changes in one factor tend to produce changes in the other. This means that as unit volume increases, cost increases in a predictable way—and vice versa. This pattern shows a high positive correlation between cost and unit over time.

In elastic workloads, the relationship between cost and unit is not just mathematical—it reflects how the workload responds to demand. If the workload scales linearly, the cost per unit may remain stable. If the workload scales unevenly, the cost per unit may fluctuate, but the overall correlation remains strong. This behavior is useful for forecasting, budgeting, and performance tracking, because it allows teams to anticipate the costs, based on an expected volume.

Elasticity also supports the use of Unit Economics as a planning tool. When the correlation is high, teams can model scenarios with confidence, knowing that cost and unit will move together. This makes it easier to evaluate trade-offs, optimize resource usage, and align financial expectations with operational realities.

To identify elasticity, we look for workloads where:

- Cost and unit data show a strong correlation.
- Volume changes are reflected in cost changes with a minimal lag.
- Cost per unit remains within a predictable range across different volumes.

Elastic workloads are common in cloud environments, where consumption scales with usage. Here are five examples:

- **API Gateway traffic:** Cost scales with the number of API calls processed. As traffic increases, both unit and cost rise in tandem.
- **Data processing pipelines:** Cost correlates with the number of datasets or records processed. More input leads to more compute and storage usage.

- **Serverless functions:** Cost is tied to the number of invocations and execution time. High correlation is typical, when functions are triggered by user activity.
- **Content Delivery Networks (CDNs):** Cost aligns with bandwidth usage and request volume. Elasticity is visible as traffic patterns shift.
- **Batch job execution:** Cost reflects the number of jobs run, or the volume of data handled. When jobs are scheduled based on demand, the correlation remains strong.

Elasticity provides a clear signal that Unit Economics can be used to model and manage workload performance. It sets the stage for evaluating how efficiently cost is converted into output, which is the focus of the next subsection.

Efficiency

Efficiency describes a workload, where cost and unit are not strongly correlated. In this scenario, changes in cost do not reliably track with changes in unit volume. The Pearson Correlation Coefficient (PCC) is low or inconsistent, and the relationship between cost and unit must be interpreted differently. This is the case for most workloads, especially those with higher architectural complexity, or where non-technical factors influence cost directly.

When correlation is weak, Unit Economics shifts from being a predictive signal to being a performance indicator. It becomes a way to express how efficiently a workload converts the cost into an output, rather than how the cost and unit move together. This interpretation is useful for identifying optimization opportunities, comparing workloads, and evaluating whether a workload is delivering a value relative to its spend.

Efficiency behavior is common in environments, where the cost is influenced by shared services, platform dependencies, licensing models, or organizational decisions. In these cases, unit and cost are determined separately, and Unit Economics reflects the outcome of those decisions, rather than a direct operational pattern.

To identify efficiency behavior, we look for workloads where:

- **Cost and unit show low or unstable PCC:** The relationship between cost and unit is weak, inconsistent, or varies across time periods.
- **Unit volume changes without proportional cost impact:** The workload scales in ways that do not produce predictable cost changes, often due to architectural or operational factors.
- **Cost is influenced by external or non-technical factors:** Budget decisions, licensing, or shared infrastructure affect cost independently of workload activity.

Examples of workloads that typically exhibit efficiency behavior include:

- **Data warehouse queries:** Cost depends on compute tier, concurrency, and storage, not just the number of queries or rows processed.
- **Machine learning training jobs:** Cost varies based on model complexity, resource configuration, and training duration, not just the number of models trained.
- **Enterprise SaaS platforms:** Cost is often tied to licensing or subscription tiers, while usage volume may fluctuate independently.
- **Internal developer platforms:** Cost reflects shared infrastructure and tooling, while unit volume depends on team activity, and deployment frequency.
- **Multi-tenant applications:** Cost is influenced by tenant isolation, data segregation, and scaling policies, which may not align with the unit definitions.

Efficiency behavior requires a different approach to interpreting Unit Economics. Instead of expecting cost and unit to move together, we treat the metric as a reflection of how well the workload is performing relative to its financial footprint. This sets the stage for deeper analysis, and supports the conversations about any architectural choices, investment priorities, and operational trade-offs.

The figure, provided here, contrasts correlated and non-correlated perspectives, when evaluating cost and unit behavior.

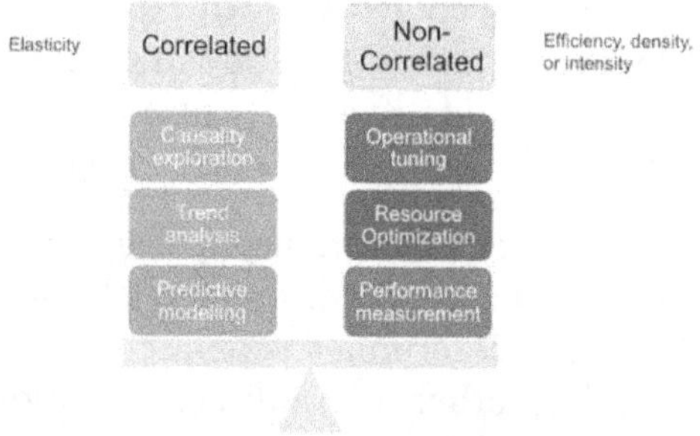

Figure 7.2: *Cost and Unit from a Correlation and Non-Correlation Perspective*

Elasticity versus Efficiency: A Quick Comparison

This quick comparison highlights the practical differences between elastic and efficiency-driven workloads, helping you determine which interpretation of Unit Economics applies to your scenario.

Attribute	Elasticity	Efficiency
PCC (rule of thumb)	**High**; typically **> 0.5**	**Low or unstable**; typically **< 0.3**
When to interpret this way	Cost reliably follows unit volume with consistent slope.	Cost does not track unit volume; other drivers dominate.

Attribute	Elasticity	Efficiency
What Unit Economics signals	Demanddriven scaling and predictable cost per unit.	How well spend is converted to output; potential inefficiencies.
Primary questions to ask	Will cost change if volume changes?	Why does cost change independently of volume?
Typical actions	Use for forecasting, capacity planning, and percentcomplete estimates.	Investigate architecture, reservations, idle resources, licensing.
Operational indicators	Minimal lag between unit and cost; stable cost/unit ratio.	Flat or erratic cost despite volume swings; sudden step costs.
Cloud examples	Serverless APIs; perrequest billing; CDN bandwidth.	Data warehouses with reserved capacity; ML training with variable configs.

Table 7.2: *Quick Comparison of Elasticity versus Efficiency*

Quick guidance: If your workload maps to **Elasticity**, treat Unit Economics as a planning and forecasting input. If it maps to **Efficiency**, treat Unit Economics as a diagnostic metric that prompts architectural and operational investigation.

Value Outcome

Value Outcome defines what the unit is meant to represent. It clarifies whether the workload creates value in a way that is primarily business-oriented, technical, or a combination of both. This distinction matters because Unit Economics is only meaningful, when the unit reflects progress toward an outcome the organization cares about.

In some workloads, value is expressed through business activity, such as transactions, customer interactions, or revenue-related events. In others, value is expressed through technical outputs, such as processed data, delivered compute cycles, or platform capabilities that enable other teams. Both perspectives are valid, and both require a clear understanding of what the unit measures, and why it matters.

Value Outcome also shapes how Unit Economics is interpreted. A business outcome focuses on how cost supports measurable business progress. A technical outcome focuses on how cost supports the operation and performance of the workload itself. The choice influences how teams evaluate efficiency, how they forecast spend, and how they assess whether the workload is delivering the expected return.

This section introduces the concept of Value Outcome and sets the foundation for exploring the two primary categories—Business and Technical—in more detail.

Business Value Outcome

Business Value Outcome focuses on how a workload contributes to the organization's core product or revenuegenerating activities. The closer a workload operates to the revenue generation end of the technology stack, the easier it becomes to define a unit that reflects the business progress. These workloads often have direct, observable interactions with customers, transactions, or product usage, which makes their value outcome more intuitive and measurable.

In many organizations, the technology stack forms a layered structure. At the top, are the workloads that directly support the product or service offered to customers. These workloads often have clear business units, such as orders placed, subscriptions activated, payments processed, or sessions completed. Because these units represent real business events, they naturally align with financial outcomes and strategic goals.

As we move deeper into the stack, workloads become more technical and less directly tied to revenue. Even so, some workloads still support the business value in ways that can be measured. For example, a recommendation engine may not generate revenue on its own, but it influences customer engagement and conversion. In these cases, the Business Value Outcome is still present, but the unit may require more interpretation.

The key idea is that Business Value Outcome becomes easier to define, when the workload is close to the organization's main product. These workloads often share three characteristics:

- **Their output** is visible to customers, or directly tied to customer activity.
- **Their performance** influences revenue, conversion, or product usage.
- **Their units** represent business events, rather than technical operations.

When these conditions are met, Unit Economics can reflect business progress in a straightforward way. The unit becomes a measure of value creation, and the cost associated with it becomes a measure of how efficiently the organization delivers that value.

This perspective sets the stage for exploring Technical Value Outcome, where the value is created through enabling capabilities, rather than direct business events.

Technical Value Outcome

Technical Value Outcome focuses on the value created by workloads that operate deeper in the technology stack, where their contribution is not directly tied to revenue or customer-facing activity. These workloads provide foundational capabilities that enable other systems, teams, or products to function. Their value is real and often essential, but it is not expressed through business events. Instead, it is expressed through technical outputs.

As we move away from the revenue generation end of the stack, workloads tend to become more specialized and more abstract. They support internal processes, platform services, data flows, or operational reliability. Because these workloads do not interact directly with customers or transactions, their units must reflect technical progress, rather than business activity. Examples include processed messages, executed jobs, provisioned environments, or delivered compute cycles.

In these cases, the unit represents the technical work performed, and the value outcome is tied to how effectively the workload enables other parts of the organization. A data ingestion service may not generate revenue, but it ensures that downstream analytics, reporting, and decision-making systems have the information they need. A CI/CD pipeline does not produce business events, but it accelerates delivery, and reduces operational friction.

Technical Value Outcome becomes clearer when workloads share characteristics such as:

- **Their output** enables or supports other workloads, rather than customers directly.
- **Their performance** influences reliability, scalability, or operational efficiency.
- **Their units** represent technical operations, rather than business events.

When these conditions are present, Unit Economics helps quantify how efficiently the workload delivers its technical capabilities. The metric becomes a way to evaluate architectural choices, operational practices, and resource usage. It also supports discussions about investment, capacity planning, and the role the workload plays in the broader ecosystem.

This perspective complements the Business Value Outcome by recognizing that value in an organization is not created only at the top of the stack. Technical workloads form the foundation that allows business-facing systems to operate, and their unit economics provide an insight into how effectively that foundation is maintained.

Figure 7.3 shows how the position of a workload within the service stack, affects the ease of determining its unit economics.

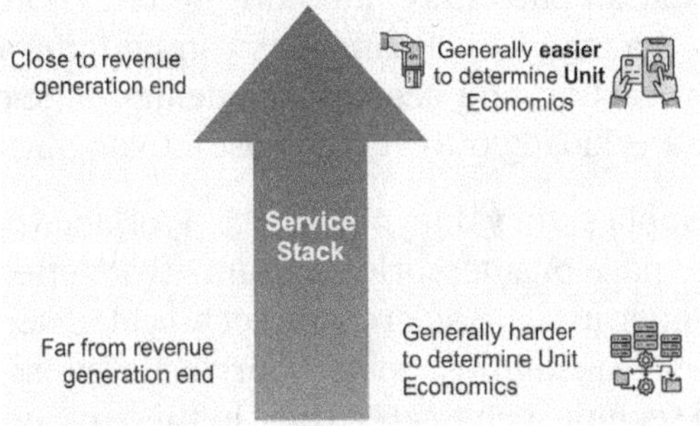

Figure 7.3: *Service Stack and Relation to Unit Economics*

Example: Framing the Same Workload as Business or Technical Value Outcome

A recommendation engine illustrates how the same workload can be interpreted through either a **Business Value Outcome**, or a **Technical Value Outcome**, depending on what the unit is meant to represent.

From a **Business Value Outcome** perspective, the recommendation engine contributes to measurable product performance. Its suggestions influence conversion rates, average order value, and customer engagement. If the unit is defined as *recommendations delivered to customers*, the workload's value is tied to the business events. Cost per recommendation becomes a way to understand how efficiently the system supports revenue-related outcomes.

From a **Technical Value Outcome** perspective, the same engine can be framed around the internal work it performs. If the unit is defined as *models trained*, *feature vectors processed*, or *inference jobs executed*, the value lies in the technical capability, which it provides to the downstream systems. Here, Unit Economics reflects how effectively the workload transforms compute, storage, and data operations into technical output, independent of direct revenue impact.

This dual framing shows why the Value Outcome matters. The workload has one architecture, one cost profile, and one operational footprint—but the meaning of its Unit Economics changes entirely depending on whether the unit represents **business progress** or **technical progress**.

Determining the Right Unit Economics

Determining the right Unit Economics requires an understanding of both how a workload behaves, and what outcome it is meant to represent. Behavior describes the relationship between cost and unit. Value Outcome describes what the unit stands for. When these two dimensions are combined, they form the basis for selecting a unit that is meaningful, stable, and aligned with the purpose of the workload.

Some workloads show clear elasticity, where cost and unit move together with a strong correlation. Others operate under efficiency behavior, where cost and unit are largely independent. Neither pattern is inherently better. What matters is recognizing which one applies, so that the Unit Economics can be interpreted correctly. Elastic workloads support forecasting and scenario modeling. Efficiency-driven workloads highlight how well the workload converts the cost into an output.

The same principle applies to value outcomes. Workloads close to the revenue generation end tend to have businessoriented units that reflect customer or product activity. Workloads deeper in the stack rely on technical units that represent internal operations, or enabling capabilities. Many workloads sit somewhere in between, blending business and technical characteristics. In these cases, the unit must capture the aspect of the value that is the most relevant for decision-making.

The goal is not to force a workload into a single category. It is to understand the combination of behaviors and outcomes that define how the workload operates. When teams recognize whether a workload is elastic or efficiencydriven, and whether its value outcome is business or technical, they can select a unit that reflects reality, rather than an idealized model. This clarity ensures that Unit Economics becomes a reliable tool for analysis, planning, and performance evaluation across the organization.

Questions to Help Determine the Right Unit Economics

Before selecting a unit, it helps to examine how the workload behaves and what outcome it represents. The right Unit Economics becomes clearer, when we look at the workload from different angles, and test our assumptions. The following questions are designed to guide this process. They help identify whether the workload leans toward elasticity or efficiency, and whether its value outcome is business-oriented or technical. Together, they provide a structured way to determine which unit best reflects how the workload creates value and consumes cost.

- What is the reason for service existence?
- What are the main service cost drivers?
- Who are the main customers?
- What business outcome does this service support?
- How does this service contribute to revenue, customer retention, or operational efficiency?
- What are the primary cost components (compute, storage, data transfer, and so on)?
- How does usage scale with demand—linearly, exponentially, or not at all?
- What measurable unit best represents the value delivered (such as per API call, per active user, per GB processed)?
- Can we tie cloud spend directly to this unit (cost per unit)?
- Is the unit meaningful to both engineering and finance teams?
- How does our cost per unit compare to industry benchmarks or internal targets?

Conclusion

Unit Economics brings clarity to how workloads create a value and consume the cost, but its importance becomes even more evident when placed within the FinOps EVM framework. Throughout this chapter, we explored how defining a meaningful unit, collecting consistent data, and allocating cost transparently form the foundation for reliable financial and operational insight. What makes this approach particularly powerful is the connection between Unit Economics and Earned Value. By grounding percent complete in a measurable unit that reflects real progress, FinOps EVM gains a level of precision that traditional project tracking methods often lack. This relationship is both insightful and innovative, as it transforms Unit Economics from a cost-efficiency metric into a core component of performance measurement.

Understanding behavior—whether elastic or efficiency-driven—helps teams interpret how cost and unit interact over time. Recognizing the value outcome—business or technical—ensures that the chosen unit reflects what the workload is truly meant to deliver. When these dimensions are combined, they guide teams toward selecting Unit Economics that are stable, relevant, and aligned with the workload's purpose. The guiding questions at the end of the chapter reinforce this process by helping teams challenge assumptions and validate their choices.

As organizations mature in their FinOps EVM practice, determining the right Unit Economics should not be treated as an isolated exercise. It becomes part of a broader financial planning rhythm. This leads directly into the next chapter, where we will explore the Budgeting Process with FinOps EVM. There, we will propose incorporating the Unit Economics definition and validation into the budgeting cycle itself. Doing so ensures that the financial plans are grounded in measurable outcomes, that percent complete is tied to meaningful progress, and that budgets reflect the real behavior of workloads, rather than abstract estimates.

References

- *Introduction to Cloud Unit Economics.* (n.d.). Retrieved March 6, 2026, from https://www.finops.org/wg/introduction-cloud-unit-economics/
- Oliveira, A. C. (2024, November 7). *A Comprehensive Guide to FINOPs Earned Value Management* - ZEPHYR GLOBE. ZEPHYR GLOBE. Retrieved March 6, 2026, from https://zephyrglobe.com/2024/11/07/a-comprehensive-guide-to-finops-earned-value-management/
- Oliveira, A. C. (2025). *Ultimate FinOps for Azure: Streamline and Optimize Azure Cloud Costs with Proven FinOps Strategies, Native Tools, and Smart Automation (English Edition).* Orange Education Pvt Ltd.

CHAPTER 8

The Budgeting Process with FinOps EVM

Introduction

Up to this point, we have focused on the mechanics of measurement of FinOps Earned Value Management. We explored how to calculate KPIs, how to interpret performance signals, and how to translate cloud activity into meaningful indicators of progress. With these foundations in place, the next step is to understand that where these measurements begin. Every EVM calculation depends on a baseline, and that baseline is created during the budgeting process. This chapter examines how budgets are formed, how they guide financial accountability in the cloud, and why Unit Economics must be incorporated from the very beginning.

Traditional budgeting concentrates on the cost. It defines limits, allocates funds, and establishes expectations for spending. In cloud environments, this is no longer enough. Elastic consumption, distributed ownership, and rapid scaling require a budgeting approach that connects financial planning to business value. Unit Economics provides this connection. By defining the cost of each relevant business unit, such as a customer, transaction, or workload, organizations establish the value baseline that FinOps EVM will later use to determine percentage complete and calculate the Earned Value.

This chapter introduces the structure of enterprise, IT, and cloud budgets, the lifecycle of planning and execution, and the personas involved in shaping financial decisions. More importantly, it shows how budgeting evolves, when value becomes a part of the equation. When Unit Economics is embedded into the planning process, the budget stops being a cost container and becomes a value framework. It sets the targets that EVM will measure against, and ensures that cloud investments are evaluated not only by what they consume, but by what they create.

Structure

In this chapter, the following topics will be covered:

- Foundations of Enterprise Budgeting

- The IT Budget: Planning, Governance, and Accountability
- FinOps versus Traditional IT Financial Management
- Budget Planning in the Cloud Era
- Key FinOps Personas in Cloud Budgeting
- Planning Your First Cloud Budget as a FinOps Lead

Foundations of Enterprise Budgeting

In every successful organization, budgeting serves as a foundational activity. It is not just about setting spending limits — it is about connecting financial plans to business goals. Through budgeting, an enterprise decides how to invest the resources wisely, manage risks, and deliver on strategic objectives.

Think of it as the financial translation of a company's vision. Without a budget, the teams may spend reactively, subsequently losing a sight of the bigger picture. But with a clear budgeting framework in place, departments can align their work with enterprise priorities, making sure that each dollar contributes to the outcomes that matter.

In large enterprises, budgeting is rarely handled in isolation. It involves a collaboration across departments: finance sets the guardrails, business units estimate the needs, and operations track the execution.

The Structure and Hierarchy of Budgets (Enterprise > IT > Cloud)

Budgeting in a modern organization works like a nested system. At the top is the **enterprise budget** — a comprehensive financial roadmap that reflects company-wide priorities, such as revenue targets, investment strategy, and operating expenses.

Beneath that sits the **IT budget**, which is the financial plan for technology operations. It includes the hardware and the software costs, vendor contracts, support services, and—critically—cloud services.

Cloud budgeting is a sub-component of the IT budget. It focuses specifically on cloud infrastructure and services: things like compute resources, storage, networking, and SaaS tools. As enterprises move more workloads to the cloud, this layer is growing rapidly in importance.

Remember:

- Understanding this hierarchy helps clarify how cloud spending is not an isolated concern.
- It rolls up into the broader IT planning, which in turn is a part of a larger business strategy.

Strategic Financial Planning and Business Alignment

Creating a budget is a strategic exercise. Organizations must ensure that each layer of the budget reflects and supports their high-level business goals.

This process is known as **strategic financial planning**. It involves setting long-term financial goals, and aligning each department's plans with those goals. For example, if a company wants to launch a new digital product, IT might need to allocate a budget for cloud infrastructure, licensing, and development environments.

Alignment means that finance and technical leaders speak the same language, and work toward a shared outcome. It also ensures that spending decisions are proactive, not reactive—driven by goals rather than emergencies.

The Role of Technology in Modern Enterprise Cost Structures

Technology is no longer a support function. It is central to how organizations operate, compete, and grow—and it is a major driver of the modern cost structures.

From cloud computing and data analytics to automation and digital security, technology touches nearly every aspect of business operations. This is why IT is often one of the most scrutinized parts of the enterprise budget.

Cloud services in particular have changed the game. Unlike traditional capital investments (like buying servers), cloud spending is **operational**—you pay for what you use, often monthly. This shift from CapEx to OpEx, introduces new flexibility, but also requires new financial management practices.

As cloud spending becomes more dynamic and usage-driven, organizations need financial mechanisms that reveal not only *how much* they spend, but *what value* that spending generates. This is where Unit Economics becomes essential to the budgeting process. By breaking the costs down to meaningful business units—such as cost per customer, per transaction, or per workload—leaders gain visibility into the real efficiency of their technology investments. When integrated with FinOps EVM, these metrics evolve from simple cost indicators into performance signals that connect the cloud consumption to business outcomes. Budgeting then shifts from static allocations to a continuous evaluation of value creation, enabling teams to make informed trade-offs, prioritize highimpact workloads, and align cloud usage with strategic objectives.

A practical example helps illustrate this. Consider a digital subscription platform that processes customer sign-ups through a dedicated onboarding workload. By calculating the Unit Economics for this workload, the team discovers that each new customer requires an average of 0.015 dollars in compute and storage resources. During budget planning, the business forecasts 1.2 million new customers for the year. Instead of estimating the cloud costs, as a broad infrastructure line item, the FinOps team multiplies the expected volume by the cost per unit, and sets a workload budget of 18,000 dollars for onboarding. This approach gives finance and engineering a shared baseline, supports more accurate forecasting, and creates a clear target for optimization. If the cost per customer begins to rise during the year, FinOps EVM will surface this as a performance signal, prompting investigation and corrective action.

The IT Budget: Planning, Governance, and Accountability

A well-run IT budget is more than a financial plan; it is a governance system that brings forecasting, allocation, and tracking together, to ensure that technology spending aligns with business priorities and delivers a measurable value. Understanding the IT Budget as a discipline, its lifecycle, and aligning it with business strategics' priorities is fundamental to the success of Business Units in isolation and for the organization as a whole.

Understanding the IT Budget Disciplines

Effective IT budgeting relies on three core financial disciplines that work together to ensure control, transparency, and alignment with business goals: Forecasting, Allocation, and Tracking.

Forecasting

Forecasting is the process of predicting future IT spending based on historical trends, expected projects, usage patterns, and strategic plans. It is about anticipating what your organization will need — from infrastructure upgrades to software licensing — and estimating the cost.

- A good forecast helps avoid surprises, and supports proactive planning.
- Forecasting in the cloud era often includes elastic usage models (such as scaling services up or down), so it must account for variability and flexibility.
- This is typically done on a monthly, quarterly, or annual basis and adjusted as business conditions evolve.

Allocation

Allocation refers to how budgeted funds are distributed across departments, teams, or initiatives. In an IT context, this could involve dividing the technology budget among infrastructure, security, application development, and now, increasingly, cloud services.

- Allocation ensures that the resources are made available, where they are the most needed.
- It also encourages accountability, as teams are more likely to manage the costs effectively, when they "own" their portion of the budget.
- This can be done through *chargebacks* (billing internal teams for their usage), or *showbacks* (informing them of their usage without a bill).

Tracking

Tracking involves monitoring actual spending in real time or near real time against forecasts, and allocated budgets. It is the heartbeat of financial accountability – helping IT leaders understand:

- Are we staying within budget?
- Are certain areas overspending or underutilized?
- Are optimization efforts (such as cost savings in the cloud) delivering results?

Cloud tools like cost dashboards, alerts, and tagging policies are essential in making this process real-time and actionable.

Introduction to IT Budget Lifecycle

The IT budgeting lifecycle is a continuous, collaborative process that typically includes:

1. **Planning and Forecasting**
2. **Review and Approval**
3. **Allocation and Execution**
4. **Tracking and Adjustment**
5. **Review and Reporting**

Figure 8.1 outlines the continuous cycle of activities that shape how an IT budget is planned, governed, and managed over time. Let us now explore each one of the phases of the lifecycle.

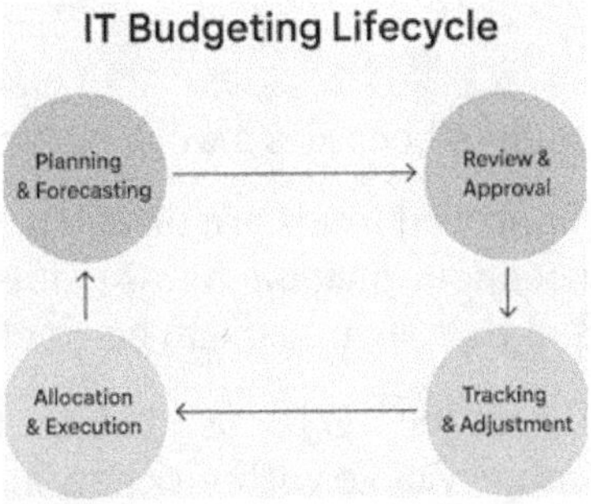

Figure 8.1: *IT Budgeting Lifecycle*

Planning and Forecasting

This stage is where everything begins – before a single dollar is spent, IT leaders, finance partners, and business stakeholders come together to look ahead.

- **Planning** involves gathering an input on technology needs: upcoming projects, infrastructure refreshes, cybersecurity investments, and expected cloud growth. It is not just wish-listing – it is prioritizing, based on the strategic importance, ROI potential, and operational urgency. From the FinOps EVM perspective, it is when expected Unit Economics are determined for the planning period. It takes into account the previous performance to set goals on how the business value will be materialized in the future.
- **Forecasting** uses historical data, vendor roadmaps, usage patterns, and project timelines to estimate future expenses. In cloud environments, forecasting becomes more dynamic, requiring flexible models that account for variability in usage and scaling.
- **The outcome** is a well-informed estimate of what IT will need to spend, and what Unit Economic target to achieve – not only to maintain operations, but to help the business move forward.

Review and Approval

Once forecasts are assembled, they must be validated through financial scrutiny and strategic alignment checks, including Unit Economics.

- This phase includes cross-functional reviews, where finance validates assumptions, business leaders challenge priorities, and IT defends use cases.
- It may involve multiple iterations of the proposed budget, with changes based on risk appetite, enterprise cost constraints, or emerging priorities.
- Approval usually comes from senior leadership, or an executive governance board – ensuring that the IT budget supports top-level objectives while remaining realistic.

This step sets the tone for accountability throughout the year.

Allocation and Execution

With approvals in hand, the budget becomes a working plan, and money starts moving.

- **Allocation** is where approved funds are distributed to teams, departments, or initiatives. It is not just about dividing funds – it is about making sure that the ownership is clear, and that spending can be tracked to outcomes.
- Some organizations use chargebacks (billing teams for their usage) or showbacks (making usage visible without charging) to foster cost ownership.

- **Execution** begins when teams use their allocations to procure services, spin up cloud resources, or contract vendors. This is where the financial plans become operational action.

Tracking and Adjustment

No matter how precise your plan is, things change — and this stage is where real-time agility matters the most.

- Teams monitor actual spending against forecasts and value delivered using dashboards, alerts, and analytics tools, including FinOps EVM.
- Deviations are flagged: maybe, a workload is consuming more than expected, or a cloud service was not shut down on schedule.
- Adjustments may include budget reallocation, initiating cost-optimization efforts (like rightsizing or automation), or delaying discretionary projects to stay within limits.
- Transparency and communication between IT, finance, and business units are essential here, to make smart mid-course corrections.

Review and Reporting

At regular intervals — typically monthly or quarterly — the organization reflects on the performance.

- Teams review budget versus actuals versus earned value, analyze variances, and extract lessons learned. What went according to the plan? Where were the surprises?
- These insights inform not only future forecasting, but also vendor negotiations, cost-saving measures, and internal accountability practices.
- Reporting must be tailored: technical metrics for IT, financial summaries for finance, and strategic overviews for executives.
- As cloud usage continues to grow, reporting practices must evolve to explain dynamic, usage-driven costs in ways, stakeholders understand and trust.

Figure 8.2 outlines the same cycle of activities, but now on a suggested timeline within a year.

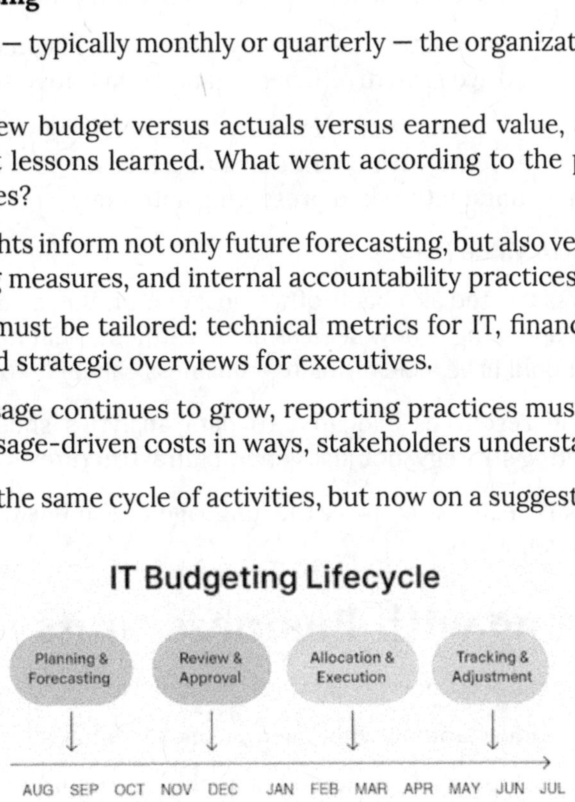

Figure 8.2: *IT Budgeting Lifecycle*

This lifecycle is not a strict sequence – it is a feedback loop. Each phase informs the next, building maturity over time. Well-run IT budgeting processes create not only a financial control, but a greater confidence in how technology drives business value.

Aligning IT Budgets to Strategic Priorities and Business Units

In many enterprises, IT can no longer operate as a siloed department that simply "keeps the lights on." Today, technology is deeply embedded in how business units generate revenue, serve customers, and deliver value. As a result, the IT budget must reflect and support the strategic priorities of the entire organization – and do so in close coordination with individual Business Units (BUs).

The Importance of Alignment with Strategic Priorities

- Strategic initiatives – like launching a new digital product, expanding into new markets, or improving customer experience – often rely on technology.
- If IT budgets are developed without understanding these priorities, the teams may either over-allocate to legacy systems, or underfund an innovation.
- Aligning budgets ensures that money flows to what matters the most: the initiatives that drive growth, efficiency, and competitive advantage.
- Defining Unit Economics and applying FinOps EVM give teams the structure they need to execute with confidence, which is supported by guardrails that maintain accountability, while preserving autonomy.

From Cost Center to Value Driver

Traditionally, IT was treated as a back-office cost center. But, as digital becomes core to the business, IT spending is now seen as an investment. That means every line item in the IT budget should have a clear link to a business capability or outcome.

For example, cloud resources allocated to data analytics should support a sales initiative or marketing strategy, not just general infrastructure.

This shift requires IT leaders to speak the language of the business, and collaborate deeply with BU stakeholders.

Collaborating with Business Units

Effective alignment is not a one-way process. It involves:

1. **Listening:** Understanding what each business unit is trying to achieve.
2. **Translating:** Mapping their needs to technical requirements and associated costs.

3. **Educating:** Helping business leaders understand cost drivers and trade-offs (for instance speed versus resilience).

This collaboration builds trust and accountability – and it helps the BUs feel like co-owners of IT investments.

Budget Structuring for Alignment

To support alignment, IT budgets often include:

- **Initiative-based budgets:** Funding is organized by a strategic program (such as "Customer Experience Initiative"), rather than by system or department.
- **Business unit allocations:** Cloud and service costs are segmented by usage tags or chargebacks to specific teams.
- **Flexible funding pools:** Reserved funds to support agile or experimental projects tied to emerging business opportunities.

Aligning IT budgets with strategic priorities and business units is about shifting the conversation from "How much does IT cost?" to "What value is IT creating – and for whom?" It is one of the clearest signs of IT maturity, and a key principle of FinOps in action.

Impact of Cloud on Traditional IT Financial Models

Cloud has brought a huge impact on traditional IT Financial models. Next, you will find a carousel.

From Capital-Heavy to Operational-Focused

Historically, IT investments were primarily Capital Expenditures (CapEx). Buying servers, networking gear, and data center space required large upfront purchases. These costs were depreciated over time, and treated as long-term assets on the balance sheet.

With the cloud, the model flips: most cloud services operate on a **pay-as-you-go model**, making them Operational Expenditures (OpEx). You pay monthly, based on the actual usage – no massive hardware purchase necessary. This lowers the barrier to entry, but introduces **financial variability** that must be managed continuously.

Greater Financial Flexibility, and Complexity

Cloud services offer remarkable flexibility: you can scale infrastructure up or down instantly, test new environments without procurement delays, and experiment with minimal financial risk.

But, this flexibility comes at a cost – literally:

- Budgets are harder to predict, because usage fluctuates.
- Overprovisioning becomes easy when the resources are a click away.

- Shadow IT (unauthorized spending) can creep in without tight governance.

As a result, IT and finance must adopt new tools and practices to monitor, and control real-time spending.

Need for a Continuous Budget Management

In traditional models, once the hardware was purchased, there was no ongoing infrastructure cost beyond maintenance. In the cloud, every hour of usage has a price tag.

This pushes IT leaders to shift from once-a-year budgeting cycles to **continuous financial oversight.** They need dashboards, alerting mechanisms, and optimization workflows, just to keep the costs within the target – a core pillar of the FinOps discipline.

Changing the Cost-Ownership Culture

In traditional setups, budget responsibility was centralized in IT procurement or finance. In the cloud, spending decisions are made by engineers, DevOps teams, and even business analysts, provisioning resources on demand.

This shift necessitates a decentralized cost culture, where technical teams are not just responsible for building solutions, but also for managing their financial impact. FinOps plays a key role in helping teams adopt this mindset.

Blurring the Lines between Projects and Operations

Previously, IT budgets were cleanly segmented: build something (CapEx) versus run something (OpEx). Cloud blurs this distinction – deploying a product, or launching a new environment may involve both in a single workflow.

This fluidity requires organizations to revisit how they categorize spending, report it to finance, and justify ROI to leadership.

Importance of Unit Economics and Value Measurement

As cloud adoption matures, organizations realize that understanding spending is not enough. They need clarity on the value generated by each unit of consumption. Unit Economics provides this lens by translating cloud usage into business-relevant metrics, such as cost per customer, per transaction, per API call, or per workload.

These measurements help leaders understand whether technology investments are scaling efficiently, or eroding margins as usage grows. When combined with value measurement practices from FinOps EVM, Unit Economics becomes a strategic tool for planning and execution. Teams gain visibility into which services deliver meaningful outcomes, which workloads require optimization, and which initiatives deserve further investment.

This approach strengthens the budgeting process by grounding decisions in measurable value creation, enabling organizations to allocate resources with precision, and maintain financial discipline while supporting innovation.

In summary, the move to cloud has transformed IT financial management from static, centralized, and CapEx-heavy to dynamic, distributed, and OpEx-driven. It demands new tools, policies, cultural norms, and above all, collaboration between finance and technology teams.

FinOps versus Traditional IT Financial Management

FinOps brings finance, engineering, and business teams together to collaborate on cloud spending decisions, using shared data and accountability. It is less about top-down control and more about empowering teams, to make financially responsible decisions within dynamic, cloud-native environments. The following is a side-by-side comparison of the key differences.

Dimension	Traditional IT Financial Management	FinOps (Cloud Financial Operations)
Budgeting Cycle	Annual or quarterly budgeting	Continuous forecasting and frequent recalibration
Spending Model	Capital-intensive (CapEx)	Pay-as-you-go / consumption-based (OpEx)
Ownership of Cost	Centralized with finance and procurement	Decentralized, shared across engineering, product, and finance
Cost Visibility	Delayed, based on monthly or quarterly reports	Near real-time visibility into usage and cost
Governance Approach	Top-down control and policy enforcement	Collaborative, policy-informed but team-empowered
Change Agility	Limited flexibility once budgets are set	High agility — teams can optimize and adjust spending continuously
Tooling and Reporting	Financial systems and spreadsheets	Cost dashboards, tagging, alerts, automated analytics
Accountability	Primarily financial controllers	Shared accountability across cross-functional teams
Performance Metrics	Budget variance and compliance	Business value per dollar spent, utilization rates, cost per customer/event

Table 8.1: *Comparison between FinOps versus Traditional IT Financial Management*

FinOps does not replace financial discipline — it modernizes it.

Instead of relying on outdated assumptions, it helps organizations adapt to the fast-paced, elastic nature of cloud environments, while staying accountable to strategic outcomes.

Budget Planning in the Cloud Era

Cloud computing has redefined the pace, precision, and philosophy behind budgeting in technology. While traditional budgeting was an annual ritual focused on long-term capital planning, the cloud demands a more granular, adaptive, and collaborative approach. In this modern context, budget planning is no longer just a finance exercise – it becomes a powerful mechanism to align strategy, enforce accountability, and empower the engineering teams to act with financial responsibility.

Budget Cycles as a Lever for Accountability

In the FinOps model, the budget cycle is not merely a funding gate – it is a framework for **influencing behavior and reinforcing accountability**, particularly within engineering. Budget planning sets the expectations before any cloud resource is provisioned. When teams participate in budgeting and understand their cost targets, they are more likely to optimize and govern usage continuously. These cost expectations, when transparent and inclusive, drive better habits around architecture choices, automation, and tagging practices.

Defining Clear Accountability Boundaries

To avoid confusion and finger-pointing later on, budget planning must delineate which teams or individuals are responsible for which cost segments. This clarity is especially important in cloud-native environments, where services can sprawl quickly. Whether it is dev teams provisioning compute, analytics teams managing data lakes, or shared platform teams running Kubernetes clusters – every budget line must have a clear owner.

This accountability map should be mirrored in your tagging structure, project codes, or cost center architecture – otherwise, tracking and remediation will become reactive and inefficient.

Granular Budgeting: Cloud versus Finance

Cloud budgets require a much more fine-grained breakdown than traditional financial systems are used to. Engineers think in terms of services, environments, and instance types – while finance may care only about departmental totals, or high-level categories. It is the role of FinOps to bridge these two layers, ensuring that granular budgets (such as "S3 storage for staging data pipeline") roll up cleanly into financial reporting buckets (for example, "Marketing Operations").

This mapping allows both the sides to get the insights they need – without compromising clarity, or introducing redundancy.

Forecasting without Contingency

A common mistake in budget planning is embedding contingency buffers directly into forecasts. This inflates the cost estimates, and distorts usage patterns. Instead, forecasts should reflect realistic expected usage only – clean, lean, and traceable to business assumptions.

Contingency should exist as a separate management reserve, held outside the team's operational budget, and governed by leadership, based on risk or unplanned strategic opportunities.

The figure here illustrates how an IT budget is structured between team-managed funds and the management reserve that supports contingencies.

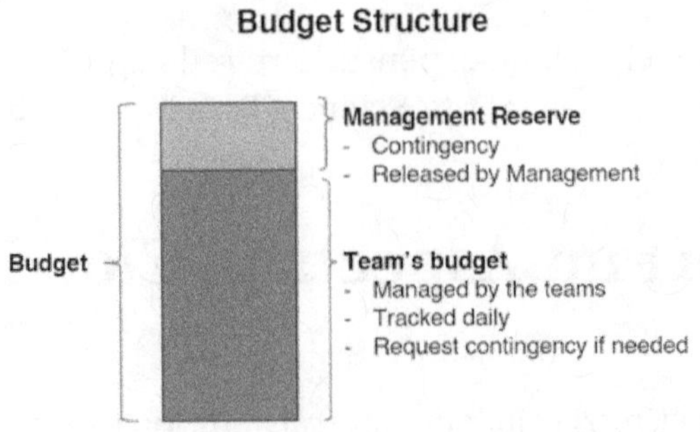

Figure 8.3: *The Budget Structure*

Handling Shared Resources in the Budget

In multi-tenant cloud environments, shared services like networking, logging platforms, or container clusters complicate cost allocation. These are often critical to multiple teams, but owned by none.

To avoid creating budgeting blind spots:

- Define a **fair cost allocation model** (such as usage-based, proportional to business unit headcount, and so on).
- Assign stewardship roles, even for shared infrastructure.
- Clearly communicate how shared costs are recovered (showback/chargeback) or absorbed centrally.

Forecast Monthly, Execute Daily

Cloud budget planning benefits from a **monthly forecasting cadence**, which aligns well with most business rhythms, and helps teams stay close to their commitments. Monthly cycles are short enough to allow course corrections, without overloading the process.

That said, when it comes to **tracking and controlling spending**, FinOps translates these monthly estimates into **daily budget targets**. Why? Because in the cloud, costs can spike within hours. Daily visibility supports real-time alerts, policy enforcement, and workload rebalancing – turning finance from a post-mortem activity into a proactive lever.

Align Breakdown with Accountability

It is critical that the **structure of the budget aligns with how teams are organized and measured**. If a single budget line includes spending from multiple teams or cloud projects, it becomes impossible to drive responsibility or action. Every budget entry must correlate directly with a team, product, or initiative that can respond and optimize.

Budget entries like "general cloud expenses" are red flags. Replace them with precise units, like "ML Training Nodes - Data Science Team" or "Customer Portal Front-End - Retail BU."

Other Important Aspects in Cloud Budget Planning

Beyond the core budgeting disciplines, several additional factors play a crucial role in shaping effective cloud budget planning.

- **Scenario Planning:** Cloud enables rapid scale-up/down, so that budgeting should accommodate best-case and worst-case business demand models, not just a single forecast.
- **Tagging Hygiene:** Budget planning should reinforce the importance of tagging standards. Forecasting accuracy collapses without clear resource attribution.
- **Budget-to-Actual Feedback Loop:** Embed periodic variance reviews to adjust assumptions, improve team performance, and increase forecast accuracy.
- **Tool Enablement:** Empower teams with dashboards that show their portion of the budget, and how their actions influence it in real-time.
- **Cultural Change:** Train both engineers and business managers on the why behind the budget structure – not just the what.

A Practical Example

A practical example helps illustrate how cloud budgets are structured in real organizations. Consider a company with three engineering teams that share a common cloud platform. During budget planning, each team builds its forecast based on expected usage, planned initiatives, and Unit Economics targets.

The Data Engineering team estimates that its data pipeline will process 18 billion events during the year. Based on a cost of 0.000004 dollars per event, the team sets a workload budget of 72,000 dollars for its streaming and storage services. The Application Services team plans to expand its customer portal and expects a 40 percent increase in traffic. It forecasts 110,000 dollars for compute and content delivery based on historical usage patterns and the cost per request. The Machine Learning team anticipates several training cycles for new models, and allocates 95,000 dollars for GPU workloads, calculated from the cost per training hour and the number of expected iterations.

These forecasts are created without contingency padding. Each team presents only the expected cost of its workloads, based on realistic assumptions and Unit Economics. Contingency is managed at a higher level as part of a central management reserve. Leadership holds this reserve to support unplanned strategic opportunities, or to absorb risks that cannot be assigned to a specific team. This separation keeps the team forecasts clean, and prevents inflated budgets that distort performance signals.

Shared platform services, such as networking, logging, and Kubernetes clusters are budgeted separately. These costs are allocated proportionally to each team based on usage metrics from the previous year. This structure gives every team a clear ownership boundary and a predictable budget target. It also allows finance to consolidate the numbers into a single IT budget, without losing the granularity needed for daily FinOps operations.

The company uses a monthly forecasting cadence to keep the plan aligned with business conditions. Each team reviews its consumption trends, adjusts its forecast for the remaining months, and updates leadership on expected variances. While forecasting happens monthly, execution happens daily. Teams monitor their workloads through dashboards and alerts that translate the monthly budgets into daily spending targets. This helps them detect anomalies early, correct misconfigurations, and maintain accountability throughout the month.

FinOps **transforms** budget planning from a static requirement into a **dynamic, collaborative, and measurable process.**

It unites cost awareness with cloud agility, empowering teams to deliver innovation **without sacrificing accountability**.

Key FinOps Personas in Cloud Budgeting

Understanding the different FinOps personas involved in the cloud budgeting process is critical to building alignment, and driving financial accountability across the organization. FinOps is not one person's job — it is a cross-functional collaboration between finance, technology, and business teams, each bringing unique insights and responsibilities to the table.

The figure here illustrates the FinOps Personas and Allies, according to FinOps Foundation framework.

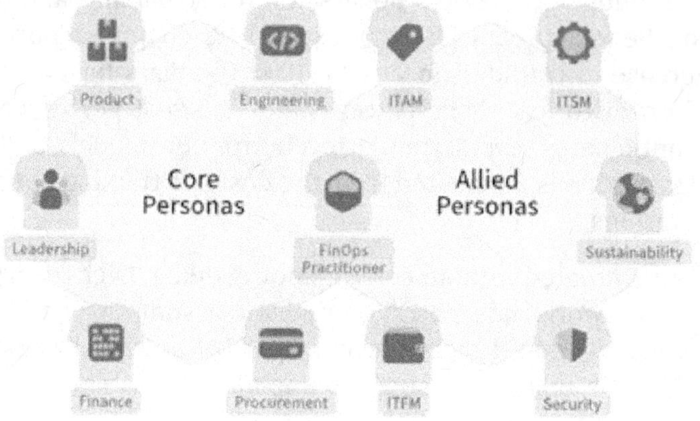

Figure 8.4: *FinOps Personas by FinOps Foundation*

Here is an expanded look at the primary personas, what they care about, and how they contribute during the budgeting process:

Finance Lead (like Cloud Financial Analyst, CFO Controller)

Primary Focus: Governance, forecasting accuracy, and financial health.

Responsibilities in Budgeting:

- Sets the overall financial targets and fiscal constraints.
- Works with technical teams to understand forecast assumptions.
- Defines how cloud expenses roll up into enterprise-level financial planning.
- Tracks budget variance, and manages reforecast cycles.
- Builds models to separate operational budget from management reserves.

What they need: Clean, structured data; monthly forecasts; clarity on cloud cost drivers.

Engineering/Product Owner (like DevOps Manager, Engineering Lead, Application Owner)

Primary Focus: Service performance, reliability, and delivery speed

Responsibilities in Budgeting:

- Provides technical estimates for workload resource needs.
- Plans anticipated usage levels and growth scenarios.
- Implements tagging policies for accountability.

- Takes action on budget versus actual deviations.
- Participates in rightsizing, cost-optimization, and reserved instance planning.

What they need: Forecast targets, cost dashboards, alerting mechanisms, and visibility into spend tied to the workloads they manage.

FinOps Practitioner / Cloud Cost Manager

Primary Focus: Bridging finance and engineering with shared data and accountability

Responsibilities in Budgeting:

- Facilitates the budgeting process, and educates the stakeholders.
- Builds forecast models using historical usage, business growth inputs, and cost trends.
- Ensures that cost allocation models reflect shared versus dedicated resources.
- Aligns forecast granularity with team-level accountability.
- Maintains alignment between monthly forecasts and daily spend tracking.

What they need: Cost tools, cloud billing data, strong collaboration with all other personas, and authority to nudge improvements.

Executive Stakeholder (like CIO, CTO, Business Unit Leader)

Primary Focus: Strategic investments, risk management, and value creation

Responsibilities in Budgeting:

- Approves major budget allocations aligned to business goals.
- Communicates high-level priorities to technical and financial teams.
- Helps arbitrate trade-offs across departments.
- Holds leaders accountable for financial and operational performance.

What they need: High-level budget summaries, KPI rollups, risk exposure reporting, and scenario comparisons.

Business Unit Manager / Project Sponsor

Primary Focus: Delivery of business outcomes within budget

Responsibilities in Budgeting:

- Reviews team-level forecasts, and validates against project roadmaps.

- Influences the allocation of funding across features or teams.
- Collaborates with Engineering and Finance to align timelines and cost estimates.
- Interprets cloud costs through a value lens (cost per sale, transaction, customer).

What they need: Budget breakdown aligned to their scope, visibility into burn rate, and ongoing support from FinOps.

Procurement Lead (like Sourcing Manager, Cloud Contracts Specialist)

Primary Focus: Vendor engagement, contract optimization, and purchase governance

Responsibilities in Budgeting:

- Negotiates pricing, discount tiers, and usage commitments with cloud providers and third-party vendors.
- Reviews forecast data to guide committed use purchases (for instance, Reserved Instances, Savings Plans, Volume Licensing).
- Validates that cloud purchases comply with enterprise procurement policies.
- Collaborates with Finance to manage the timing of purchases to avoid budget overages.
- Coordinates with Engineering and FinOps teams to ensure that the contracts support actual usage patterns and growth forecasts.

What they need: Visibility into upcoming project needs, forecast models, provider usage data, and timely engagement from technical teams.

Bringing It All Together

Each persona owns a piece of the puzzle – and success comes from balancing their perspectives:

- Finance enforces fiscal boundaries.
- Engineering brings workload-specific knowledge.
- FinOps connects the dots and enables real-time collaboration.
- Executives ensure a strategic alignment.
- Business Owners focus on outcomes and ROI.

Here is a matrix that summarizes the responsibilities of each role, during the Budgeting Lifecycle.

Persona	Forecast and Planning	Review and Approval	Allocation and Execution	Tracking and Adjustment
Finance Lead	• Sets budget ceilings. • Validates assumptions. • Aligns budget to corporate targets.	• Approves forecasts. • Reviews business justification. • Challenges overalloca-tions.	• Distributes funds. • Monitors financial risk. • Coordinates reserve access.	• Analyzes variances. • Triggers reforecast cycles. • Reports KPIs to executives.
Engineer-ing Owner	• Estimates cloud usage. • Assesses workload architecture. • Validates feasibility.	• Defends resource needs. • Collaborates on ROI discussion.	• Tags and launches resources. • Implements usage guardrails. • Monitors active spend.	• Optimizes workloads. • Responds to alerts. • Adjusts deployment behavior.
FinOps Practi-tioner	• Builds forecast models. • Facilitates team inputs. • Ensures tagging/ ownership.	• Consolidates inputs. • Validates structure versus accountability. • Advises finance.	• Supports usage attribution. • Enables dashboards. • Reinforces policy compliance.	• Drives cost reviews. • Facilitates optimization. • Leads communication loops.
Executive Stakehold-er	• Sets business priorities. • Advocates strategic funding.	• Approves high-level plans. • Resolves con-flicts. • Aligns cross-BU invest-ments.	• Monitors goal align-ment. • Sponsors transforma-tion projects.	• Reviews impact versus strategy. • Adjusts direc-tion, if needed. • Champions accountability.
Business Unit Manager	• Shares road-map insight. • Projects re-source needs. • Aligns with product goals.	• Validates pro-posed alloca-tions. • Ensures busi-ness readi-ness.	• Engages in charge-backs/ showbacks. • Oversees execution alignment.	• Tracks ROI metrics. • Participates in QBRs. • Reassesses priorities.

Persona	Forecast and Planning	Review and Approval	Allocation and Execution	Tracking and Adjustment
Procurement Lead	• Advises on vendor constraints. • Plans reservation strategies. • Reviews pricing trends.	• Supports negotiation strategy. • Confirms contract terms.	• Executes purchases. • Validates entitlements. • Ensures contract compliance.	• Rebalances contracts. • Tracks consumption versus commitment. • Flags renewal windows.

Table 8.2: *FinOps' Roles and Responsibilities during Budgeting Lifecycle*

The real power of FinOps lies in **orchestrating these voices** into a shared budgeting rhythm. One where transparency, speed, and accountability replace friction and surprise.

Planning Your First Cloud Budget as a FinOps Lead

Planning your first cloud budget as a FinOps Lead is less about filling in numbers, and more about establishing the practices, assumptions, and guardrails that will shape how your organization manages cloud spend going forward. It is the moment, where financial discipline meets technical reality, where you translate business goals into actionable forecasts, and where you define the level of accountability and visibility teams will operate with throughout the year.

Forecasting and Planning

The success of a cloud budget hinges not just on the numbers, but on the **readiness of the organization** to plan, forecast, and act in a FinOps-aligned way. Before launching into the Forecasting and Planning phase, a FinOps Lead must first ensure that the key structures, inputs, and stakeholders are well-prepared. Here is what needs to be in place:

Pre-Budget Readiness Checklist for FinOps Leads:

- **Defined Ownership and Accountability Structures**
    - Identify and document who is responsible for which workloads, projects, environments, and shared services.
    - Ensure that every anticipated cost category (such as compute, storage, data transfer, third-party services) maps clearly to a team or business owner.
    - Reinforce the principle: "*You cannot forecast what no one owns.*"

  - Define what Unit Economics will be used to measure performance on value delivery.

- **Historical Usage and Cost Data Availability**
  - Compile at least 3–6 months of cloud usage and billing reports for key services.
  - Ensure granularity via tagging, cost allocation keys, or linked accounts to enable team-level forecasting.
  - Clean up anomalies or missing data that might distort historical trends.
- **Tagging Standards and Coverage**
  - Validate that tagging and metadata policies are applied to at least 80–90% of deployed resources.
  - If shared services are not tagged, plan for proportional chargeback/showback strategies.
  - Define the source of Unit metrics for Unit Economics and FinOps EVM metric calculations.
- **Visibility Tools and Dashboards**
  - Ensure that budgeting stakeholders (engineering, product, finance) have access to spend dashboards, breakdown views, and forecasting tools.
  - If tools are new, prepare short onboarding or training sessions.
  - Ensure that the dashboards incorporate FinOps EVM metrics.
- **Awareness of Key Business Drivers**
  - Meet with product managers, business unit leaders, or strategic planners to understand **upcoming launches, growth targets, or planned shifts** that may impact cloud needs.
  - Identify **seasonality, business cycles, or expected experiments** (such as machine learning training spikes).
- **Financial Rules of Engagement**
  - Clarify with Finance which costs are:
    - Operational versus capital
    - Pre-approved versus discretionary
    - Fixed versus variable
  - Understand the thresholds for review/approval, and the process for requesting budget increases.

- **Reserved Capacity and Discount Commitments**
    - Document any existing committed-use discounts (Reserved Instances, Savings Plans, and so on).
    - Ensure that these are reflected in cost modeling to avoid inflated forecast estimates.
- **Forecasting Calendar and Cadence**
    - Set a timeline and expectations: When are forecasts due? Who reviews them? How often are they updated?
    - Recommend monthly granularity, but clarify the need for **daily tracking, once execution begins**.
- **Define Forecasting Methodology**
    - Establish that whether teams should forecast based on:
        - Unit cost × usage volume
        - Fixed allocation from historical data
        - Target capacity per environment

This **standardizes assumptions** and makes rolling up totals consistent.

- **Educate Participants on Purpose**
    - Brief stakeholders on why their forecasts matter:
        - Drives accountability.
        - Enables proactive optimization.
        - Secures headroom for innovation.
        - Builds trust with Finance.

Treat the budgeting exercise as a **collaborative strategy ritual**, not a bureaucratic box-check.

Once these pieces are in place, you are not just forecasting cloud costs – you are laying the foundation for **real-time financial intelligence, technical accountability, and business-aligned decision-making.**

Review and Approval

Before stepping into the **Review and Approval** phase of the cloud budgeting lifecycle, a FinOps Lead must ensure that all the groundwork, laid during the forecasting and planning has been validated, communicated, and structured in a way that enables smooth collaboration and decision-making. This stage is not just about getting rubber-stamped approval – it is about building confidence across the stakeholders that the budget is **aligned, justified, and strategically sound**.

Here is a checklist of what should be ready before launching Review and Approval:

Pre-Review Readiness for FinOps Leads

- **Consolidated and Validated Forecasts**
  - All team-level forecasts have been collected, documented, and double-checked for accuracy.
  - Forecasts reflect a realistic usage (no embedded contingency), with clear assumptions.
  - Shared service costs have been appropriately distributed across consumers.
- **Visibility of Forecast Drivers**
  - Key assumptions (such as traffic growth, workload scaling, launch dates) are clearly documented.
  - Supporting evidence, such as historical trends, diagrams, or usage scenarios are available.
  - Strategic initiatives tied to budget entries are mapped and labeled.
- **Cross-Team Budget Alignment**
  - There is consistency between engineering estimates and business goals.
  - Finance, Procurement, and Business Units have reviewed their portions and raised early flags.
  - No orphaned budget areas – every cost is linked to a known team or initiative.
- **Clear Rollups for Finance and Executives**
  - Line items have been grouped into summary views for executive decision-makers.
  - CapEx and OpEx distinctions are clearly flagged.
  - Budget entries map cleanly to enterprise cost categories (for instance cost centers, GL codes).
- **Variance and Sensitivity Modeling**
  - Forecasts include low, expected, and high scenarios (where appropriate).
  - Key risk areas are annotated – for example, “subject to traffic spike” or “dependent on vendor rollout”.
  - Adjustments for pending reservations or renewals are transparently captured.

- **Communication and Presentation Materials**
    - Slide decks, summary tables, or dashboards are prepared for budget reviewers.
    - Notes and Q&A briefs are available to help team leads defend their assumptions.
    - Any forecast conflict or overlap between the teams is flagged for discussion.
- **Budget Approval Workflow Prepared**
    - Meeting schedule or async approval timeline is confirmed.
    - Defined approvers per business unit or cost category are documented.
    - Contingency reserve governance and escalation path are clearly understood.

Going into Review and Approval, without this level of structure risks delays, confusion, and misalignment.

With everything in place, the FinOps Lead ensures that reviews are **fast, focused, and credible** – enabling stakeholders to say "yes" with confidence, or raise meaningful improvements without derailing the entire plan.

Allocation and Execution

The **Allocation and Execution** phase is where your planning finally translates into action. It is the moment where numbers become real infrastructure, and accountability shifts from intent to behavior. To enable this phase to succeed, a FinOps Lead must ensure not just that budgets and unit metrics are approved, but that **teams are prepared, systems are aligned, and governance is activated**.

Here is a detailed checklist of what needs to be in place:

Pre-Allocation and Execution Readiness for FinOps Leads

- **Finalized and Authorized Budget Map**
    - Budget is locked in and aligned to clearly defined teams, workloads, or business units.
    - Allocations match forecast ownership – no surprises or unassigned costs.
    - Shared service costs are distributed fairly and consistently.
- **Budget Visibility at the Right Level**
    - Engineering and business owners have **access to their budget segments** via dashboards or cost portals.

  - Budgets and Unit Economics are broken down by **service, environment, project, or cost center** – no vague rollups.
  - Daily or weekly burn projections are available to compare usage versus budget.
- **Cost and Value Allocation Mechanisms Activated**
  - **Chargeback or showback models** are finalized and understood.
  - **Unit Economics models** are finalized and connected to reports.
  - Tagging enforcement or account hierarchies are live to **track spend per team/product.**
  - A process exists for **attributing untagged or misaligned spending.**
- **Cloud Tooling Ready for Execution**
  - Budgets and thresholds are **set up in cloud cost management tools**.
  - Alerts are configured to notify the stakeholders when usage exceeds target levels.
  - **Guardrails or automated policies** (for instance size caps, auto-shutdown scripts) are deployed.
- **Governance and Communication Paths Defined**
  - Teams know **who to contact** when nearing or breaching budgets.
  - Approval processes are documented for **overage justification or contingency reserve requests.**
  - Stakeholders are briefed on **budget expectations and financial behaviors** (such as no overprovisioning "just in case").
- **Reserved Commitment Strategy Reflected**
  - Active Reserved Instances, Savings Plans, or negotiated rates are applied to forecasts.
  - Engineering is aware of which workloads must use reserved capacity to realize savings.
  - Plans are in place to evaluate reservation coverage monthly.
- **Performance Metrics and Accountability Tracked**
  - Each budget line is linked to an accountable owner with decision rights and optimization levers.
  - Unit Economics like *cost per feature*, *utilization rate*, or *cost per customer*, are introduced where applicable.

  - A cadence is in place for budget-to-actual reviews (such as biweekly syncs or monthly reports).

- **Education and Enablement Completed**
  - Teams understand their budget targets, and what behaviors support them.
  - FinOps office hours or FAQ channels are available for real-time support.
  - Stakeholders know how to interpret spend reports, and adjust architecture decisions accordingly.

With these elements in place, you are not just releasing money – you are equipping the teams to **spend with intent, monitor with insight, and adapt with agility**.

Tracking and Adjustment

The Tracking and Adjustment phase is where all the upstream discipline pays off. This is the point in the budget lifecycle where forecasts meet reality, and where the FinOps Lead enables a continuous feedback loop that prevents waste, surfaces insights, and drives optimization. But to achieve that, several foundational elements need to be established ahead of time.

Pre-Tracking and Adjustment Readiness for FinOps Leads

Daily Budget Baseline Defined

- Monthly budget and unit economics targets have been broken down into **daily thresholds.**
- Daily burn expectations are mapped per team, service, or environment.
- Shared service components (such as platform, logging, data pipeline) are assigned proportionally.

Why it matters: *Daily thresholds enable proactive alerts and mid-month corrections – not just month-end surprises.*

Real-Time Spend Visibility Tools are Live

- Dashboards are configured and accessible to **each budget owner.**
- Drill-down views are enabled by account, tag, service, and region.
- Cloud provider budgets and alerts are active, and aligned with the internal thresholds.
- The source of unit metrics is established to allow automatic unit economics calculation.

- Any discrepancies between the finance tools and cloud provider tools are understood.

Alerting and Escalation Framework in Place

- Budgets have **alerts for threshold breaches** (like 80%, 90%, 100%).
- CPI from FinOps EVM **alerts for threshold breaches** (such as 0.8, 1.20).
- Owners are clearly defined for triage (for example, who gets the Slack, email, or ticket).
- Escalation policies are documented, including access to management reserve triggers.

Optional: *Integrate cost alerts with incident tools, like PagerDuty or Jira, for formalized responses.*

Example: Action Plan When Budget or CPI Thresholds are Reached

A simple escalation ladder helps teams know exactly when to act, and what to do. The following example shows how a team should respond as budget consumption approaches key thresholds, and as CPI signals move outside expected ranges.

Budget Consumption Thresholds

- **80 percent threshold:** The team reviews recent usage, and validates that the trend is accurate. No escalation is required at this stage. The team checks for configuration drift, unused resources, or upcoming deployments that may influence the forecast. This step confirms that the remaining budget is still aligned with the monthly plan.
- **90 percent threshold:** The team performs a short analysis to understand the drivers of the increase. If the overrun is caused by a known event, the team updates the monthly forecast and informs the FinOps lead. If the cause is unclear, the team investigates usage patterns, and prepares a brief summary of findings. Corrective actions may be initiated, if the trend suggests the budget will be exceeded.
- **100 percent threshold:** The team escalates to the Tactical Forecast Review. A formal summary is required, including root cause, expected impact, and proposed actions. Leadership decides whether to use the management reserve, adjust scope, or authorize temporary overspend. The team implements corrective actions immediately.

CPI Thresholds (Lower and Higher)

- **CPI slightly below target (0.90 to 0.85):** The team validates the signal and checks for anomalies. No escalation is required yet. The team reviews efficiency metrics, and identifies early opportunities to improve performance.

- **CPI below 0.85 for the first period:** The team investigates the cause, and prepares a short internal summary. Corrective actions may begin, if the issue is operational. No formal escalation is required until the second consecutive period.
- **CPI below 0.85 for two consecutive periods:** This triggers mandatory escalation. The team submits a formal report to the FinOps lead and product owner. Leadership reviews whether the workload requires optimization, scope adjustment, or additional funding.
- **CPI above target (such as above 1.10)** The team validates the signal and confirms that the workload is delivering more value than planned. No escalation is required. The team documents the improvement, and updates the forecast if the trend is expected to continue.

Accountability Routines and Cadence

- Weekly or biweekly **FinOps EVM health check-ins** are scheduled with budget owners.
- Roles are clarified for those, who adjusts infrastructure versus who requests budget reallocation.
- Ownership maps are updated, so that no costs go unreviewed.

Optimization Playbooks and Levers Prepared

- Engineering teams have access to **rightsizing recommendations,** or underutilized asset reports.
- Reserved instance coverage is monitored and adjusted.
- Scripting/tooling exists to automate non-critical shutdowns or cleanups.
- Cloud-native savings tools (such as Spot, Savings Plans) are actively used.

Tracking Format Consistency

- Team-facing cost reports and Finance tracking rollups are **aligned in granularity and language.**
- Reports show **forecast versus actual versus variance**, not just raw spend.
- Forecasting models allow for inline annotations and rationale tracking.

Mid-Cycle Reforecasting Readiness

- Workflow exists for teams to update projections mid-quarter or month.
- Finance has thresholds for when reforecasting is required.
- Stakeholders are trained on how and why to adjust projections (not just react to spending).

Executive and BU Reporting Expectations Aligned

- Strategic stakeholders understand what metrics they will see, and how to interpret them.
- Variance narratives are prepared, so that the leaders can contextualize spend shifts.
- Unit Economics, such as cost-to-deliver, cost-per-user, or ROI per product, are accessible.

  By ensuring that all of this is in place, before entering Tracking and Adjustment, FinOps Lead transforms budgeting from a passive compliance exercise into **an active, intelligent control system** – one that empowers teams to react, correct, and optimize *in real time.*

Orchestrating Value: The FinOps Lead as a Budget Architect

The FinOps Lead acts as the architect of a budget, designed to orchestrate value, rather than simply control spending. By applying FinOps EVM and grounding decisions in Unit Economics, this role ensures that the budget becomes a strategic instrument that guides the teams toward measurable outcomes.

Instead of treating the budget as a constraint, the FinOps Lead shapes it as a framework that clarifies priorities, aligns investments with expected value, and enables the teams to execute with autonomy, supported by a clear accountability. This approach strengthens the organization's ability to pursue value deliberately, using financial signals to steer delivery, validate assumptions, and continuously refine, where the resources should flow to generate the greatest impact.

Conclusion

The budgeting process is where FinOps Earned Value Management begins to take shape. Earlier chapters established how EVM metrics are calculated, and how they reveal the performance, but those calculations only gain a meaning, when they are anchored in a well-constructed budget. This chapter showed how enterprise, IT, and cloud budgets form a connected structure that guides financial decisions and operational behavior. It also demonstrated how cloud environments require a more granular, collaborative, and adaptive approach than traditional financial models can support.

The most important evolution introduced here, is the integration of Unit Economics into the budgeting process. Cloud spending is inherently dynamic, and cost alone cannot describe whether a workload is progressing in a healthy direction. By defining

Unit Economics during planning, organizations establish a measurable link between consumption and value. These units become the reference point for determining percentage complete in FinOps EVM and for calculating Earned Value in a way that reflects business outcomes. Budgeting then becomes more than a financial exercise. It becomes the foundation for value measurement, accountability, and strategic alignment.

The chapter also highlighted the roles of finance leaders, engineers, product owners, executives, and business managers. Each persona contributes to the accuracy of the budget and the clarity of the value targets that EVM will later evaluate. Their collaboration ensures that cloud investments are planned with intention and monitored with shared responsibility.

With the budgeting structure defined and Unit Economics embedded into the planning baseline, the next step is to understand how forecasts evolve throughout the execution cycle. The following chapter explores how to build, refine, and manage forecasts using FinOps EVM, turning planned value into a living model that adapts to real usage and real business conditions.

References

- Oliveira, A. (n.d.). *FinOps Budgeting Course*. Retrieved February 10, 2026, from https://www.learningfinops.com/finops-budgeting
- Oliveira, A. (2024, November 7). *A Comprehensive Guide to FinOps Earned Value Management*. ZEPHYR GLOBE. Retrieved December 8, 2025, from https://zephyrglobe.com/2024/11/07/a-comprehensive-guide-to-finops-earned-value-management/
- PMI (2020). *The standard for earned value management. Project Management Institute.*
- FinOps Foundation. (2024). *Budget Management*. Retrieved February 10, 2026. https://www.finops.org/framework/previous-capabilities/budget-management/
- U.S. Government Accountability Office. (2020). GAO *Cost Estimating and Assessment Guide: Best Practices for Developing and Managing Program Costs* (GAO20195G). Retrieved February 10, 2026. https://www.gao.gov/products/gao-20-195g
- KPMG. (2024). *Taking control of cloud costs: The FinOps imperative*. Retrieved February 10, 2026. https://kpmg.com/us/en/articles/2023/financial-operations-cloud-cost.html

Chapter 9
Forecasting with FinOps EVM

Introduction

Forecasting with FinOps EVM brings together every concept introduced so far, and turns them into a practical, decision-ready model. Earlier chapters established the foundations: how Earned Value is represented graphically, how AC, EV, and PV are calculated, and how to obtain the data that feeds each indicator. With these building blocks in place, this chapter focuses on the step that gives FinOps EVM its real power: projecting the future based on current performance in value terms.

Traditional cloud forecasting, often relies on simple spend trends or static budget curves. Scenario 2 from the earlier discussion in *Chapter 4, The FinOps EVM Framework*, showed why this approach can be misleading. A workload may appear under budget when comparing Actual Cost to the plan, yet still be underperforming, when measured against the business value. FinOps EVM corrects this by incorporating Percent Complete, Earned Value, and CPI into the forecasting process, ensuring that the projections reflect both financial and operational efficiency.

In this chapter, we will construct the full forecasting model step by step. We begin with the plan, open it into daily granularity, calculate Percent Complete, derive CPI, and finally apply CPI to Planned Value to generate a forecast curve. We then extend the model to teams and business units, showing how the same mechanics scale across the organization. By the end, you will see how FinOps EVM transforms forecasting from a budget exercise into a value-aware management tool.

For the purpose of this discussion, **'Forecasting'** refers to projecting future cloud spend, based on current performance efficiency, using CPI-adjusted Planned Value to estimate how the budgeting period will evolve, if the present trends continue.

Structure

In this chapter, the following topics will be covered:

- Recap of Scenario 2: Over Budget
- Putting Together the Plan
- Determining the Percent Complete
- Calculating the CPI
- Calculating the Forecast
- Forecasting by Teams and Business Units

Recap of Scenario 2: Over Budget

In *Chapter* 4, we discussed the Scenario 2, that will be the basis of our explanation. It highlights a situation, where surface level budget tracking leads to the wrong conclusion. When Actual Cost is compared directly to Planned Value, the numbers suggest a favorable outcome. Spending appears to be under control, and the initiative seems to be performing within financial limits. This is precisely the type of situation, where many organizations would feel comfortable, and move on.

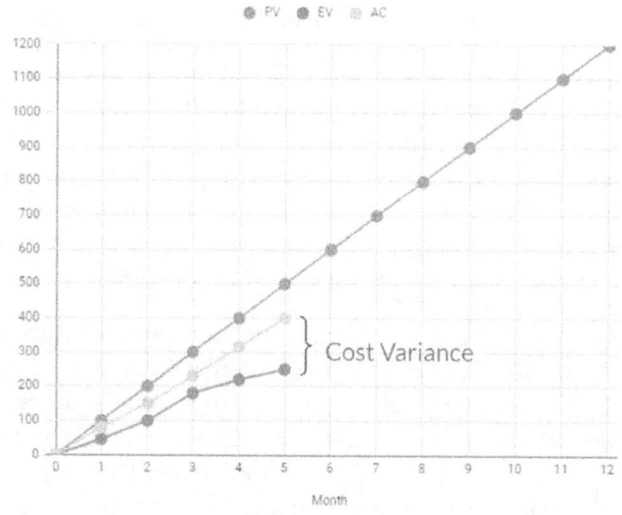

Figure 9.1: *FinOps Earned Value Cumulative Values*

Once Earned Value is introduced, the picture changes. In this scenario, unit economics drifted away from the target. Even though total spend remained below the plan, the cost per unit increased, reducing the percent complete. As a result, Earned Value fell below the Actual Cost, revealing that the organization was converting cloud spend into business outcomes, less efficiently than expected.

The negative cost variance makes this explicit. While the plan versus actual comparison shows a small apparent saving, the Earned Value comparison exposes a real shortfall in delivered value. The Cost Performance Indicator reinforces this conclusion. A CPI below 1 confirms that the initiative is over budget, when measured against the business value, not just financial limits.

This scenario is foundational for *Chapter* 9, because it explains why forecasting cannot rely on spend alone. Forecasts built only on Planned Value and Actual Cost, assume that efficiency remains constant. Scenario 2 shows that this assumption breaks down quickly, when unit economics deteriorate. Without Earned Value and CPI, future projections would be based on misleading signals, masking inefficiencies that compound over time.

Scenario 2 establishes the need for value aware forecasting. It demonstrates that being under budget does not guarantee success, and that effective forecasting must account for how well spending is translated into outcomes. This insight becomes critical, as we move into planning, percent complete calculation, and CPI driven forecasts in the sections that follow.

Putting Together the Plan

Forecasting in FinOps EVM does not start with formulas or projections. It starts with the plan. Before any CPI can be calculated or any forecast line drawn, there must be a clear, structured baseline that represents what the organization intended to achieve. This section reconnects the mechanics of the planning table with the budgeting principles established earlier, setting the foundation for everything that follows.

Reintroducing the Planning Table

The planning table represents the operational expression of the budget. Each row corresponds to a time slice, typically a month, and each column captures a specific dimension of the plan and its execution.

At its core, the table establishes three essential elements:

- **Budget** defines the expected spend for each period.
- **Planned Value (PV)** accumulates that budget over time, forming the baseline curve.
- **Time** provides the structure that allows he performance to be assessed cumulatively, rather than in isolation.

This cumulative view is critical. Planned Value is not a monthly target. It is the total value that should have been earned up to that point in time. Without this accumulation, Earned Value and CPI lose their meaning.

Month	Budget	PV	% Complete	EV	Actual	AC	CPI	Forecast
0	0	0						
1	100	100						
2	100	200						
3	100	300						
4	100	400						
5	100	500						
6	100	600						
7	100	700						
8	100	800						
9	100	900						
10	100	1000						
11	100	1100						
12	100	1200						

Table 9.1: *Planned Value (PV) as a Cumulative Sum of the Budget by Month*

At this stage, the table is intentionally incomplete. Columns such as percent complete, Earned Value, Actual Cost, CPI, and Forecast remain empty. That is by design. The plan must exist before the performance can be measured against it.

Budgeting Considerations

Chapter 8, The Budgeting Process with FinOps EVM, established that budgeting in a FinOps context is not a static financial exercise. It is a value driven planning process that connects the expected spend to expected outcomes through Unit Economics.

Several principles from that chapter directly shape how this plan is constructed:

- **Budgets must reflect accountability.** Each budget line should map to a team, product, or business unit that can act on deviations.
- **Forecasting should be clean.** The plan should represent expected usage, without embedded contingency. Risk buffers belong to outside the operational baseline.
- **Monthly planning, daily execution.** While the table is structured monthly, it supports daily tracking and adjustment once execution begins.
- **Unit Economics are defined upfront.** The target unit economics established during budgeting will later determine percent complete and Earned Value.

The planning table is where these principles become concrete. It translates strategic budgeting decisions into an operational baseline that FinOps EVM can work with.

The Importance of a Well Established Plan

Forecasting depends on performance signals. Performance signals depend on Earned Value. Earned Value depends on percent complete. Percent complete depends on Unit Economics. And all of these depend on a well-defined plan.

This is why putting the plan together is the first step in forecasting. Without a clear Planned Value curve, CPI has nothing to act on. Without CPI, forecasts are reduced to linear extrapolations of spend, repeating the same mistakes, as highlighted in Scenario 2.

By establishing the plan first, you create a stable reference point. From here, execution data can be layered in, percent complete can be calculated, CPI can be derived, and forecasts can begin to reflect reality rather than assumptions.

This table is not just a spreadsheet. It is the bridge between budgeting and forecasting, between intention and outcome. Everything that follows builds on this foundation.

Opening up the Plan: From Monthly Budget to Daily Baseline

Once the monthly budget is defined, and the Planned Value curve is established, the next step is to open that plan into a daily structure. This is essential, because cloud spending behaves daily, not monthly. Costs fluctuate with usage patterns, deployments, scaling events, and operational changes. A monthly number alone cannot support the level of control and visibility required for FinOps EVM forecasting.

Daily granularity gives teams the ability to monitor performance in near real time, detect deviations early, and understand how actual consumption is tracking against the plan. It also prepares the structure needed for real time forecasting, later in the chapter.

Importance of Daily Granularity

A monthly budget is a strategic view. A daily budget is an operational one. FinOps EVM needs both.

Daily granularity supports:

- **Real time variance detection:** A spike on the 12th of the month is invisible in a monthly-only view, until it is too late.
- **Accurate Earned Value tracking:** Percent complete and Earned Value can be calculated at any point in the month.
- **Consistent communication with engineering teams:** Engineers operate daily. A daily target aligns financial expectations with operational rhythms.
- **A stable foundation for forecasting:** Forecasting requires a baseline that matches the cadence of actual consumption.

To achieve this, the monthly budget must be translated into daily values.

Approaches for Converting the Monthly Budget to Daily Budget

There are two common approaches. Both are valid, but each has some implications that must be understood and agreed upon with Finance.

Approach 1: Monthly Budget Divided by Days in the Month

This is the most intuitive method. Each month has its own daily rate.

For example, if the monthly budget is 100:

Month	Days	Monthly Budget	Daily Budget
January	31	100	3.23
February	28	100	3.57
March	31	100	3.23

Table 9.2: *Monthly Budget Divided by Days in the Month*

This produces a daily number that varies month to month.

Implications:

- Daily targets reflect the actual length of each month.
- The cumulative PV curve remains perfectly aligned with the monthly plan.
- Daily monitoring is accurate, but slightly uneven across months.

This method is simple and mathematically consistent with the original budget.

Approach 2: A Single Daily Budget Applied across the Entire Year

In this method, the annual budget is divided by 365 (or 366), and the same daily value is used every day.

If the annual budget is 1200:

- Daily budget = 1200 : 365 = 3.29 per day
- Monthly totals will vary depending on the number of days in each month.

Example:

Month	Days	Daily Budget	Monthly Total
January	31	3.29	102.00
February	28	3.29	92.10
March	31	3.29	102.00

Table 9.3: *A Single Daily Budget Applied across the Entire Year*

Implications:

- Daily targets are consistent and easy to communicate.
- Monthly totals no longer match the original monthly budget.
- Finance must explicitly approve this shift, since it changes the shape of the PV curve.

This method is useful, when teams want a stable daily target, but it requires an alignment with Finance, because it alters the monthly distribution of the plan.

Stakeholder alignment

Alignment with Finance is essential here. Regardless of the method chosen, the daily plan becomes the baseline for performance measurement. That means that:

- Percent complete will be calculated against it.
- Earned Value will be derived from it.
- CPI will be interpreted relative to it.
- Forecasts will project forward from it.

If the daily baseline is not aligned with Finance, the organization will end up with conflicting interpretations of performance.

Finance may believe that the team is under budget, while the FinOps EVM model shows an over budget condition, or vice versa. To avoid this, the conversion method must be:

- Explicitly chosen
- Documented
- Approved by Finance
- Communicated to all stakeholders

This ensures that everyone understands how the plan was constructed, and how the performance will be evaluated.

Bringing It Back to the Forecasting Process

Opening the plan into daily granularity is not a side exercise. It is the first operational step in forecasting. Once the daily PV curve is established:

- Actual Cost can be compared daily.
- Percent complete can be updated as soon as new unit economics data is available.
- CPI becomes a living indicator.
- Forecasts can be recalculated continuously.

This daily baseline is the foundation for the forecasting engine that will be built in the next sections ahead.

Determining the Percent Complete

Percent Complete is the point where the plan you built and the performance you observe finally meet. It is the first moment in the FinOps EVM cycle where real data interacts with the baseline. Everything that follows – Earned Value, CPI, and ultimately the forecast – depends on getting this step right. To make this clear, we revisit the table used in the overbudget scenario and connect it with the principles introduced earlier about data, unit economics, and the budgeting process.

Revisiting the Planning Table

The table used in the overbudget scenario contains the essential structure for calculating Percent Complete. It includes:

- **Budget** for each month.
- **Planned Value (PV)** as the cumulative baseline.
- **Percent Complete**, which reflects performance.
- **Earned Value (EV)**, derived from PV and Percent Complete.
- **Actual Cost (AC).**
- **CPI** and **Forecast**, which depend on EV and AC.

Month	Budget	PV	% Complete	EV	Actual	AC	CPI	Forecast
0	0	0	0%					
1	100	100	45%					
2	100	200	50%					
3	100	300	60%					
4	100	400	55%					
5	100	500	50%					
6	100	600						
7	100	700						
8	100	800						
9	100	900						
10	100	1000						
11	100	1100						
12	100	1200						

Table 9.4: *Recap of Scenario 2 - Adding Percent Complete*

In the scenario, the Percent Complete column already shows values, such as 45 percent, 50 percent, 60 percent, and so on. These values are not estimates or opinions. They are the direct result of comparing actual unit economics with the target unit economics defined during the planning period.

This is the key idea: Percent Complete is a measure of value delivered, not time elapsed.

Calculation of Percent Complete

Percent Complete is determined by comparing the **target unit economics** defined during budgeting with the **actual unit economic**, observed during execution. The formula is straightforward:

$$Percent\ Complete = \frac{Target\ Unit\ Economic}{Actual\ Unit\ Economic}$$

This expresses how efficiently the workload is performing relative to the plan.

If actual unit economics match the target, Percent Complete equals 100 percent. If actual unit economics are worse than the target, Percent Complete drops below 100 percent. If actual unit economics outperform the target, Percent Complete rises above 100 percent.

It is important to emphasize that, in FinOps EVM, Percent Complete does not represent the traditional project progress. Instead, it acts as an **efficiency factor**, derived from Unit Economics. Rather than measuring how much of the work has been delivered, it measures how effectively the workload is performing relative to its target Unit Economics.

This is why the Percent Complete values in the table vary month to month. They reflect how the workload behaved in each period, not how much time has passed.

Budgeting and Planning Process Shaping Percent Complete

During the budgeting cycle, Finance and FinOps define:

- The target cost per unit
- The expected unit volume
- The value outcome the unit represents

This becomes the Unit Plan. It is the reference point for all Percent Complete calculations.

The Unit Plan is a part of the budget baseline. When the plan is approved, the target unit economics become the performance expectation for the entire period. Percent Complete measures how well the workload is meeting that expectation.

Data and Tooling Influencing Percent Complete

Percent Complete depends on two data sources:

- **Actual Cost**, obtained from cloud billing systems.

- **Unit data**, obtained from product or workload telemetry.

Chapter 6, Data, Tooling, and Automation, emphasized that these data sources must be:

- Accurate
- Timely
- Consistent
- Traceable

If cost allocation is inconsistent, or the unit data is incomplete, Percent Complete becomes unreliable. This is why the data pipeline matters. Percent Complete is only as strong as the data behind it.

Connecting Percent Complete to the Scenario Table

In the over budget scenario, the Percent Complete values reflect a deterioration in unit economics. Even though Actual Cost stayed below the planned amount, the workload delivered less value per dollar than expected. This is why Percent Complete fell, and why the Earned Value ended up lower than Actual Cost.

The table makes this visible:

Month	PV	% Complete	EV	AC	CPI
1	100	45%	45	–	–
2	200	50%	100	–	–
3	300	60%	180	–	–
4	400	55%	220	–	–
5	500	50%	250	–	–

Table 9.5: *Earned Value Ending up Lower Than the Actual Cost*

Percent Complete is the first signal that something is off. It shows that the workload is not converting spend into value at the expected rate. This is the foundation for the CPI calculation that follows.

Importance of Percent Complete

Percent Complete is the anchor of the entire FinOps EVM model. It connects:

- The budget baseline
- The unit economics
- The actual performance
- The Earned Value

- The CPI
- The forecast

Without Percent Complete, the model collapses into a simple spend-versus-plan comparison. With it, you gain a value-aware view of the performance that reveals efficiency, not just cost.

Calculating the CPI

With Percent Complete established and Actual Cost collected, you now have the two ingredients required to calculate the Cost Performance Index. CPI is the moment, where the FinOps EVM model reveals its core insight: how efficiently the workload is converting cloud spend into the value defined during planning. It is a simple calculation, but it carries a significant meaning, because it reflects the combined effect of budgeting, unit economics, and real execution.

To make this concrete, we return to the table used in the overbudget scenario. At this stage in the process, the table already contains:

- **Planned Value (PV)** as a cumulative baseline.
- **Percent Complete**, derived from unit economics.
- **Earned Value (EV)**, calculated as PV multiplied by Percent Complete.
- **Actual Cost (AC)**, now collected and ready to be used.

CPI is calculated only after AC is available, because it compares the value delivered (EV) with the cost incurred (AC).

Calculation of CPI

The formula is direct:

$$CPI = \frac{Earned\ Value}{Actual\ Cost}$$

Let us remember how CPI should be interpreted:

- A CPI **greater than 1** indicates that the workload is delivering more value than the cost incurred.
- A CPI **lower than 1** indicates that the workload is delivering less value than the cost incurred.
- A CPI **equal to 1** indicates that value delivery is aligned with cost.

This is why CPI is such a powerful indicator. It compresses the entire performance picture into a single number.

Revisiting the Scenario Table

In the overbudget scenario, the table shows Percent Complete values that reflect deteriorating unit economics. Once AC is added, the EV column can be calculated, and CPI becomes visible.

A simplified view of the table at this stage looks like this:

Month	PV	% Complete	EV	AC	CPI
1	100	45%	45	100	0.45
2	200	50%	100	200	0.5
3	300	60%	180	300	0.6
4	400	55%	220	400	0.55
5	500	50%	250	500	0.5

Table 9.6: *Calculating the CPI per Month*

These numbers illustrate the core issue: even though the Actual Cost is aligned with the plan, the workload is not delivering the expected value. CPI exposes this immediately.

Actual Cost Role in Forecasting

Actual Cost in FinOps EVM is cumulative. This means that AC for May includes all spending from January through May. This cumulative structure is essential because:

- PV and EV are cumulative.
- CPI must compare cumulative value with cumulative cost.
- Variance analysis depends on cumulative alignment.

If AC were monthly instead of cumulative, CPI would lose its meaning, and could not be compared across periods.

As stated on *Chapter 6, Data, Tooling, and Automation*, Actual Cost comes from cloud billing systems. As described earlier, AC must be:

- **Accurate**, reflecting real consumption.
- **Consistent**, using the same cost type across all periods.
- **Timely**, aligned with the cadence of EVM reporting.
- **Traceable**, with clear allocation to workloads or business units.

Cloud billing includes usage charges, commitment-related charges, credits, adjustments, and sometimes taxes. Before extracting AC, teams must decide:

- Whether to use invoiced or amortized values.
- Whether to include or exclude credits.

- Whether taxes should be a part of the AC.
- How shared or platform costs will be allocated.

Once these decisions are made, they must remain stable throughout the budgeting period. CPI depends on consistency.

CPI Importance

CPI is the first indicator that tells you whether the workload is delivering value at the expected efficiency. It is not a judgment. It is a signal. A CPI below 1 does not mean failure. It means that the workload is not converting spend into value at the planned rate. A CPI above 1 indicates efficiency gains that may justify a further investment.

CPI is also the foundation for forecasting. Once CPI is calculated, it becomes the multiplier, applied to future Planned Value to project the expected cost trajectory. This is where the forecasting process begins.

Calculating the Forecast

As stated in the Introduction of this chapter, and for the purpose of this discussion, **'Forecasting'** means estimating the expected total cloud spend for the budgeting period by applying the latest CPI to the remaining Planned Value. This allows us to project future outcomes based on how efficiently the value is being delivered today.

The Forecast uses the most recent CPI as the performance multiplier. The logic is:

$$\textit{Forecast for a future month} = \textit{PV for that month} \times \textit{Latest CPI}$$

You do not recalculate CPI for future months. You carry forward the last known CPI, as the best estimate of how the workload will continue to perform unless something changes.

In the scenario table, the last calculated CPI is 0.63. This becomes the divider for every future PV point.

Month	Budget	PV	% Complete	EV	Actual	AC	CPI	Forecast
0	0	0	0%	0	0	0		
1	100	100	45%	45	80	80	0.56	
2	100	200	50%	100	70	150	0.67	
3	100	300	60%	180	80	230	0.78	
4	100	400	55%	220	85	315	0.70	
5	100	500	50%	250	85	400	0.63	
6	100	600						960
7	100	700						1120
8	100	800						1280
9	100	900						1440
10	100	1000						1600
11	100	1100						1760
12	100	1200						1920

Table 9.7: *Calculating the Forecast Based on the Last CPI*

For example:

- PV at month 6 is 600.
- Forecast = 600 / 0.63 = 960.

Using CPI on Forecasting

CPI is a cumulative indicator. It reflects everything that has happened up to the current point:

- All unit economics variations
- All cost allocation decisions
- All architectural inefficiencies
- All optimization gains

Because it is cumulative, the latest CPI is the most stable and representative measure of performance. Using it to project the future is consistent with how EVM is forecasting.

How This Differs from the Earlier Explanation

Earlier in the book, the focus was on the mechanics: PV, EV, AC, and CPI. The forecasting step was described conceptually, but without the visual impact.

Here, the graph makes the story impossible to ignore.

- PV continues to rise steadily.
- EV and AC flatten, because the workload is underperforming.
- The Forecast line shoots upward, far above PV.

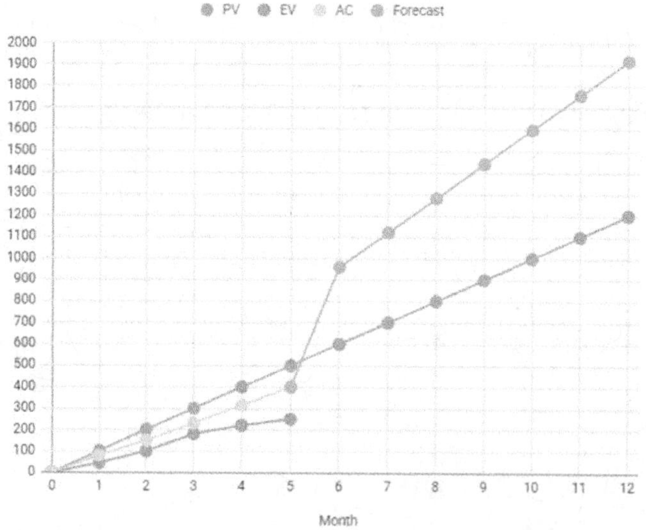

Figure 9.2: *Graph with Cumulative View of Forecast*

This visual gap is the heart of the insight. It shows that **if nothing changes, the workload will finish the period significantly over budget**, even though the early months looked harmless, when viewed only through Actual Cost.

This is why visualization matters. It turns a numeric signal into a narrative.

Interpreting the Forecast Graph

When you look at the graph, interpret it in three layers:

1. **PV: What you planned to spend**

   This is the baseline. It rises smoothly, because it reflects the approved budget.

2. **EV and AC: What actually happened**

   These lines flatten early in the scenario, showing that value delivery and cost accumulation slowed down. On their own, they might not look alarming.

   EV and AC stops at month 5 because the actual data is only available up to that month, when the measurement is taken.

3. **Forecast: What will happen, if the performance continues**

   This is the critical line. It projects the cumulative cost trajectory based on the latest CPI. If CPI is below 1, the forecast line rises faster than PV. If CPI is above 1, the forecast line rises slower than PV.

   In the scenario, CPI is 0.63, which means that the workload is delivering only 63 percent of the expected value per dollar. When you apply this to the remaining PV, the forecast curve climbs sharply, revealing a significant overbudget outcome.

The total cost expend represented on the Forecast line represent how much the organization need to spend, if they were to deliver the same Units, as previously anticipated during the Budgeting period.

This is the moment when stakeholders understand the risk. The graph makes the inefficiency visible in a way that tables alone cannot.

The Importance of Forecast Graphical Representation

This is the step that transforms FinOps EVM from a reporting tool into a decision tool. Once the forecast is visible:

- Engineering teams can investigate the root causes of inefficiency.
- Product teams can reassess priorities.
- Finance can anticipate budget pressure.

- Leadership can make informed trade-offs.

The forecast is not a prediction. **It is a warning**. It tells you what will happen **if nothing changes**.

And that is exactly the kind of insight FinOps exists to provide.

Forecasting by Teams and Business Units

Once you understand how to build a forecast at the aggregate level, the natural next step is to break it down by teams and business units. The mechanics do not change. You still calculate Percent Complete from unit economics, derive Earned Value, compute CPI, and apply the latest CPI to Planned Value to generate the forecast. What changes is the richness of the analysis, and the volume of data you must handle.

When you introduce teams and business units into the model, you move from a single forecast line to a layered view of performance. Each team has its own PV, EV, AC, CPI, and forecast curve. Each business unit aggregates the teams beneath it. This creates a more precise understanding of where value is being created, where inefficiencies are emerging, and where corrective action is needed.

Example Containing Business Unit and Teams

Let us use this table to illustrate.

Month	Business Unit	Team	Budget	PV	% Complete	EV	Actual	AC	CPI	Forecast
1	Marketing	Alpha	100	100	45%					
2	Marketing	Alpha	100	200	50%					
3	Marketing	Alpha	100	300	60%					
1	Sales	Beta	80	80	100%					
2	Sales	Beta	80	160	100%					
3	Sales	Beta	80	240	95%					
1	Sales	Gama	50	50	110%					
2	Sales	Gama	50	100	110%					
3	Sales	Gama	50	150	110%					

Table 9.8: *Example Containing Business Unit and Teams*

1. **Multiple Organizational Layers**

   Each row represents a specific combination of:

   - **Month**
   - **Business Unit**
   - **Team**

   This means that the dataset is no longer a single sequence of months. It is a *matrix* of months × business units × teams.

2. **Budget and Planned Value (PV) per Team**

   Each team has its own:

   - **Budget** for the month
   - **Cumulative PV** up to that month

   For example:

   - Marketing → Team Alpha has 100 per month.
   - Sales → Team Beta has 80 per month.
   - Sales → Team Gama has 50 per month.

   PV accumulates independently for each team.

3. **Percent Complete per Team**

   The **% Complete** column reflects each team's performance, based on its own unit economics.

   Examples:

   - Team Alpha ranges from 45% to 60%.
   - Team Beta is consistently near 100%.
   - Team Gama exceeds expectations at 110%.

   This already tells you that different teams are performing at very different efficiency levels.

4. **Placeholders for EV, AC, CPI, and Forecast**

   These columns are empty, because this table is meant to illustrate the *structure* before the calculations are applied.

   Once filled, each team will have its own:

   - Earned Value
   - Actual Cost
   - CPI
   - Forecast

   This is where the forecasting becomes richer and more actionable.

   Example of FinOps EVM Breakdown by Business Unit and Teams

   Now, let us explore the benefits of the breakdown approach based on this example. Let us consider the following numbers for this example.

Month	Business Unit	Team	Budget	PV	% Complete	EV	Actual	AC	CPI	Forecast
1	Marketing	Alpha	100	100	45%	45	95	95	0.47	
2	Marketing	Alpha	100	200	50%	100	90	185	0.54	
3	Marketing	Alpha	100	300	60%	180	90	275	0.65	
1	Sales	Beta	80	80	100%	80	75	75	1.07	
2	Sales	Beta	80	160	100%	160	75	150	1.07	
3	Sales	Beta	80	240	95%	228	78	228	1.00	
1	Sales	Gama	50	50	110%	55	52	52	1.06	
2	Sales	Gama	50	100	110%	110	55	107	1.03	
3	Sales	Gama	50	150	110%	165	51	158	1.04	

***Table 9.9**: Example Containing Business Unit and Teams with Actuals and CPI*

Considering that the Actuals occurred, as shown in the table, at the end of Month 3:

- Alpha team spent $275 (AC), below Plan (PV), but above the Earned Value of $180 (EV).
    - EV = PV × % Complete = 300 × 60% = 180
    - AC = Accumulated Actual Cost
    - CPI = EV / AC = 180 / 275 = 0.65

1. **Forecasting by Team**

    Each team will have its own CPI, and therefore its own forecast curve. This allows you to see:

    - Which teams are driving efficiency
    - Which teams are creating budget pressure
    - How each team contributes to the business unit's overall performance

    Let us use the Gama team as an example.

Month	Business Unit	Team	Budget	PV	% Complete	EV	Actual	AC	CPI	Forecast
1	Sales	Gama	50	50	110%	55	52	52	1.06	
2	Sales	Gama	50	100	110%	110	55	107	1.03	
3	Sales	Gama	50	150	110%	165	51	158	1.04	158.0
4	Sales	Gama	50	200						208.9
5	Sales	Gama	50	250						261.1
6	Sales	Gama	50	300						313.3
7	Sales	Gama	50	350						365.5
8	Sales	Gama	50	400						417.7
9	Sales	Gama	50	450						469.9
10	Sales	Gama	50	500						522.2
11	Sales	Gama	50	550						574.4
12	Sales	Gama	50	600		654.3				626.6

***Table 9.10**: Forecasting by Business Unit and Teams*

Considering that the Actuals occurred, as shown in the table, at the end of Month 3:

- Gama team spent $158 (AC), above Plan (PV), but earned more than plan and actual on $165 (EV).
    - EV = PV × % Complete = 150 × 110% = 165

  - AC = Accumulated Actual Cost
  - CPI = EV / AC = 165 / 158 = 1.04
- Taking the CPI and multiplying the PV by month, you can build the progression of Forecasting.
- Remember that we are still on Month 3. From there, you can calculate what will occur in each month.
  - Forecast = PV of the month × CPI (month 3)
- At the end of Month 12:
  - Forecast = PV (month 12) × CPI (month 3)
  - Forecast = 600 × 1.04 = 626.6
- Also, in Month 12, considering that performance remains stable, we can use the CPI formula to obtain the EV of month 12. The Forecast cost will be the new AC forecasted for month 12.
  - CPI = EV / AC or
  - EV = CPI × AC
  - EV = 1.04 × 626.6 = 654.3

The conclusion is that, although Forecast shows that Gama Team will spend more than Planned ($626.6 versus $600 Planned), the expected value is much higher ($654.3).

2. **Forecasting by Business Unit**

By aggregating the teams under each business unit, you can build:

- A Marketing forecast
- A Sales forecast
- A company-wide forecast

This mirrors how organizations make decisions.

Let us use the Sales Business Unit as example. Starting from the same initial scenario:

Month	Business Unit	Team	Budget	PV	% Complete	EV	Actual	AC	CPI	Forecast
1	Marketing	Alpha	100	100	45%	45	95	95	0.47	
2	Marketing	Alpha	100	200	50%	100	90	185	0.54	
3	Marketing	Alpha	100	300	60%	180	90	275	0.65	
1	Sales	Beta	80	80	100%	80	75	75	1.07	
2	Sales	Beta	80	160	100%	160	75	150	1.07	
3	Sales	Beta	80	240	95%	228	78	228	1.00	
1	Sales	Gama	50	50	110%	55	52	52	1.06	
2	Sales	Gama	50	100	110%	110	55	107	1.03	
3	Sales	Gama	50	150	110%	165	51	158	1.04	

Table 9.11: *Sales Business Unit and Teams*

As Sales has two teams, now let us consolidate it into just the Business Unit level.

Month	Business Unit	Team	Budget	PV	% Complete	EV	Actual	AC	CPI	Forecast
1	Sales		130	130		135	127	127	1.06	
2	Sales		130	260		270	130	257	1.05	
3	Sales		130	390		393	129	386	1.02	

***Table 9.12:** Consolidated Data by Sales Business Unit*

Here is how to calculate each column:

- **Budget, PV, EV, Actual and AC:** Sum of each value of Beta and Gama teams by month.
- **% Complete:** No need to be calculated, as the Unit Economics of each team are not comparable.
- CPI is calculated considering the resulting PV and AC. In Month 3:
    - CPI = EV / AC = 393 / 386 = 1.02

  Now that we have the CPI, we can forecast the Sales Business Unit:

Month	Business Unit	Team	Budget	PV	% Complete	EV	Actual	AC	CPI	Forecast
1	Sales		130	130		135	127	127	1.06	
2	Sales		130	260		270	130	257	1.05	
3	Sales		130	390		393	129	386	1.02	386.0
4	Sales		130	520						543.0
5	Sales		130	650						678.8
6	Sales		130	780						814.6
7	Sales		130	910						950.3
8	Sales		130	1040						1086.1
9	Sales		130	1170						1221.8
10	Sales		130	1300						1357.6
11	Sales		130	1430						1493.4
12	Sales		130	1560		1658.7				1629.1

***Table 9.13:** Forecasting by Business Unit*

  Remember that we are still in Month 3. From there, you can calculate what will occur in each month.

- At the end of Month 12:
    - Forecast = PV (month 12) × CPI (month 3)
    - Forecast = 1560 × 1.02 = 1629.1
- Also in Month 12, considering that performance remains stable, we can use the CPI formula to obtain the EV for Month 12. The Forecast cost will be the new AC forecasted for Month 12.
    - CPI = EV / AC or
    - EV = CPI × AC
    - EV = 1.02 × 1629.1 = 654.3

The conclusion is that, although Forecast shows that Sales will spend more than Planned ($1629 versus $1560 Planned), the expected value is much higher ($1659).

3. **A Much Richer Performance View**

   Instead of a single CPI for the entire organization, you now have:

   - CPI per team
   - CPI per business unit
   - CPI for the whole portfolio

   This reveals patterns that are invisible at the aggregate level.

In Summary

This table demonstrates the **scalability** of FinOps EVM. The same formulas apply, but the insights become far more precise.

It also highlights the **data challenge**:

- More teams = more rows.
- More months = more rows.
- Daily granularity = exponential growth.

This is why Business Intelligence tools become essential. Spreadsheets cannot handle this volume effectively.

The Key Principle behind the Table

As emphasized earlier in the budgeting discussion:

The budget breakdown must match the structure used for Actual Cost and Unit Economics.

If:

- Budgets are defined by business unit.
- Actuals are tagged by team.
- Unit economics are measured by product.

Then, the model will not reconcile.

Advantages of Forecast Breakdown

Breaking the forecast down by teams and business units gives you several advantages:

- **You see where performance diverges.** One team may be highly efficient while another struggles. The aggregate CPI hides this.

- **You can target interventions.** Instead of broad cost-cutting, you can focus on the specific teams or workloads driving the variance.
- **You align financial accountability.** Teams see the direct impact of their decisions on the forecast.
- **You support business-aligned reporting.** Leaders can view forecasts in the structure they recognize: business units, products, or functional areas.

This is where FinOps EVM becomes a management tool rather than a reporting exercise.

The Trade-Off: Higher Cardinality

The downside is that the dataset grows quickly. Each team adds a new set of PV, EV, AC, CPI, and forecast values. If you add daily granularity on top of that, the cardinality increases dramatically.

For example:

- 10 business units
- 40 teams
- 365 daily entries per team

You now have more than 14,000 rows per year before adding any additional dimensions such as environment, service, or region.

This is why some level of Business Intelligence becomes essential. Spreadsheets alone will not scale, especially when you need to compute Actual Cost into it. You need dashboards, drill-downs, filters, and automated refreshes to make the data usable.

The Importance of Budget Alignment

As emphasized earlier in the budgeting discussion, **the budget breakdown must match the structure used for actuals and unit economics**. If Finance allocates budget by business unit but actuals are tagged by team without a clear mapping to Business Unit, the model will not reconcile. If unit economics are measured at the product level but budgets are set at the cost-center level, Percent Complete becomes meaningless.

The structure must be consistent across:

- Budget
- Actual Cost
- Unit data
- Forecast

Without this alignment, the forecast will be technically correct but operationally unusable.

Additional Insights to Consider

1. **Forecasting at lower levels increases volatility:** Smaller teams have smaller volumes. A small shift in unit economics can swing the CPI sharply. This is normal. It requires an interpretation, rather than alarm.
2. **Aggregation smooths the signal:** Business unit forecasts are more stable, because they average the performance of multiple teams. Use both views: the team level for diagnosis, and the business unit level for strategic decisions.
3. **Teams need visibility into their own CPI:** Forecasting becomes a coaching tool. Teams can see how their architectural choices, scaling patterns, and operational habits influence long-term cost outcomes.
4. **Forecasting supports capacity and hiring decisions:** If a team's CPI is consistently strong, it may justify additional investment. If it is consistently weak, it may indicate an architectural debt, or operational inefficiency.
5. **Daily granularity enables real-time course correction:** A daily PV baseline allows teams to detect deviations early. This is especially valuable for the workloads with variable demand or rapid scaling.
6. **Forecasting by team strengthens accountability:** When teams see their own forecast line diverging from PV, the conversation shifts from abstract cost control to concrete performance improvement.

The Importance of Forecasting Breakdown

Forecasting by teams and business units uses the same EVM mechanics, but it delivers a richer and more actionable view of performance. It reveals where value is being created, where inefficiencies are emerging, and where leadership should focus attention. It also requires more sophisticated data handling, because the volume and complexity of the dataset grow quickly.

When done correctly, this breakdown transforms FinOps EVM from a single forecast curve into a multi-layered performance system that mirrors how the organization actually operates. It gives every team a clear view of its financial trajectory, and gives leadership the insight needed to steer the business with confidence.

Conclusion

Forecasting with FinOps EVM brings together every concept introduced throughout the earlier chapters and transforms them into a practical, value-driven decision framework. By combining Planned Value, Actual Cost, Unit Economics, Percent Complete, Earned Value, and CPI, we move beyond traditional cost tracking and into a model that reveals how efficiently cloud spend is being converted into business outcomes. This chapter demonstrated how each of these components builds on the previous one, culminating in a forecast that reflects real performance rather than assumptions.

The over-budget scenario served as a powerful reminder that surface-level comparisons between Actual Cost and budget can be misleading. Only when Earned Value and CPI are introduced does the true picture emerge. The forecasting graph makes this visible in a way that numbers alone cannot: a widening gap between PV and the projected cost trajectory signals inefficiency that, if left unaddressed, will compound over time. This visualization is not merely informative — it is actionable. It gives leaders the clarity needed to intervene early, adjust priorities, and prevent budget overruns before they materialize.

We also expanded the forecasting model to teams and business units, showing how the same mechanics scale across organizational layers. This breakdown increases insight but also increases data complexity, reinforcing the need for strong data governance, consistent budget structures, and appropriate analytical tooling. When aligned correctly, this multi-layered view becomes a strategic asset, enabling targeted optimization and more accurate financial planning.

Ultimately, FinOps EVM forecasting is not about predicting the future — it is about revealing the trajectory created by current performance. It empowers organizations to act with foresight rather than hindsight.

In the next chapter, we will shift from methodology to adoption. We will explore how to drive organizational alignment, embed these practices into daily operations, and ensure that FinOps EVM becomes a sustainable capability rather than a one-time exercise.

References

- Oliveira, A. C. (2024, November 7). A *Comprehensive Guide to FinOps Earned Value Management* - ZEPHYR GLOBE. ZEPHYR GLOBE. Retrieved March 29, 2026, from https://zephyrglobe.com/2024/11/07/a-comprehensive-guide-to-finops-earned-value-management/
- PMI (2020). *The standard for earned value management. Project Management Institute.*
- FinOps Foundation. (2024). *Forecasting*. Retrieved March 29, 2026. https://www.finops.org/framework/capabilities/forecasting/
- FinOps Foundation. (2024). *Exploring Cloud Cost Forecasting*. Retrieved March 29, 2026. https://www.finops.org/wg/cloud-cost-forecasting/

CHAPTER 10

Driving Organizational Adoption

Introduction

We have been on a practical journey through FinOps Earned Value Management, learning the mechanics, and the data that makes it meaningful. Now, it is time to implement the model across your organization. This chapter focuses on the work required to move from understanding to doing. It shows how to organize people, processes, and tools, so that Planned Value, Earned Value, Actual Cost, and the Cost Performance Index become routine signals that can drive decisions.

Implementation is an operational program. It requires a clear vision, executive sponsorship, a governance model that produces fast decisions, and a data pipeline that teams trust. It also requires training, playbooks, and a cadence of reviews that turn anomalies into corrective action. The goal is to change how teams plan, prioritize, and act, so that the organization pursues value rather than chasing cost alone.

This chapter is structured to be immediately useful. The first section lays out a phased adoption roadmap with milestones, success criteria, and a resource plan. The second section defines the organizational design and the RACI assignments, which you need to avoid ambiguity. The governance section prescribes decision forums, escalation thresholds, and the artifacts that make decisions auditable. The data and tooling section explains the pipelines, dashboards, and validation steps required to scale daily EVM. The change management section provides training curricula, communication templates, and remediation playbooks to embed the practice.

Read this chapter as a field manual. Use the examples, follow the cadence, and adapt the thresholds to your context. The work is practical and iterative. Start small, prove value, and expand with discipline. When FinOps EVM is adopted, forecasts become warnings you can act on, and CPI becomes the language leaders use to allocate resources to value. Begin the work with urgency and discipline.

Structure

In this chapter, the following topics will be covered:

- Adoption Strategy and Roadmap
- Organizational Design, Roles, and Accountability
- Governance Model
- Using FinOps EVM KPIs for Decision Making and Governance

Adoption Strategy and Roadmap

This section organizes the adoption work into three practical categories, so that you can move from plan to action, without getting lost in detail. The first category, **Strategy and Governance**, covers vision, sponsorship, decision forums, cadence, PV/BAC controls, and the phased rollout plan; it defines who decides what and when. The second category, **Data, Tooling, and Operations**, covers AC and unit data pipelines, PV time phasing, BI and automation, dashboards, and the operational playbooks that make daily EVM possible. The third category, **Change Management and Enablement**, covers stakeholder engagement, training, communication cadences, remediation playbooks, incentives, and the measures that sustain adoption over time. We will treat each category as a self-contained workstream with clear milestones, owners, and artifacts, so that you can pilot quickly, validate results, and scale with confidence.

Figure 10.1 shows how combining governance, operational capability, and organizational enablement creates the conditions needed for successful adoption.

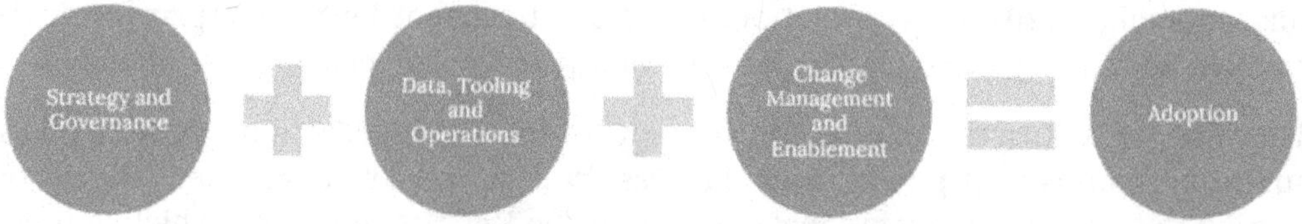

Figure 10.1: *Adoption Strategy and Roadmap Components*

Strategy and Governance

Here are the components that makes a good Strategy and Governance, in the context of FinOps EVM.

Vision and objectives

Define a clear, measurable vision for FinOps EVM adoption and the objectives that will guide execution. This statement anchors every decision, and keeps the teams aligned on the value you expect to realize. Make the objectives specific, time-bound, and tied to business outcomes, such as improved cost per unit, earlier detection of inefficiency, or predictable budget variance reduction.

- **Example objectives**: Reduce cost variance by X within 12 months; achieve consistent CPI reporting across top 10 workloads; and, enable daily PV versus AC monitoring for critical teams.
- **Why this matters**: A concise vision prevents scope creep, and gives leadership a single metric set to evaluate progress.

Stakeholder alignment and sponsorship

Secure executive sponsorship, and identify the core stakeholders who will own the outcomes. Adoption succeeds when finance, engineering, product, and operations share accountability and a common language.

- **Sponsor role**: Remove blockers, approve budget, and enforce governance.
- **Stakeholder map**: List owners for Budgeting, Data, Engineering, Product, FinOps practice, and BI.
- **Engagement plan**: Regular steering committee cadence; monthly operational reviews; escalation path for disputes.

Governance model and decision rights

Design a governance model that defines, who approves PV changes, who validates unit economics, and who signs off on forecasts. Governance must be lightweight, but enforceable.

- **Policies to define**: PV versioning rules; AC data source and cost type; allocation rules for shared services.
- **Decision rights**: Designate owners for budget adjustments, CPI interpretation, and forecast exceptions.
- **Auditability**: Require documented approvals, and a single source of truth for PV and BAC.

Organizational structure and roles

Map the roles required to operate FinOps EVM, and how they integrate with existing teams. Clarify responsibilities to avoid duplication and to enable a rapid action on signals.

- **Core roles**: FinOps lead, Data engineer, Cost analyst, Unit economics owner, Engineering steward, Finance liaison.
- **Team model**: Central FinOps practice for standards and tooling; embedded FinOps practitioners within business units for day-to-day support.
- **RACI**: Produce a RACI matrix for PV updates, AC reconciliation, percent complete calculation, and forecast publication.

Phased rollout plan

Adopt a phased approach: pilot, validate, scale, and institutionalize. Each phase has clear entry and exit criteria.

Figure 10.2: *Implementation Phases*

- **Phase 1: Pilot**: Select 2 to 4 representative workloads; validate unit economics, AC pipeline, and CPI calculation. Exit, when forecasts match manual expectations, and stakeholders accept the methodology.
- **Phase 2: Validate**: Expand to a business unit; introduce daily PV and automated CPI refresh; run weekly forecast reviews. Exit when BI dashboards and alerts are stable.
- **Phase 3: Scale**: Onboard remaining teams, add daily granularity, and integrate with budgeting systems.
- **Phase 4: Institutionalize**: Embed FinOps EVM into monthly financial reviews and performance incentives.

Timeline, milestones, and resource plan

Produce a realistic timeline with milestones, resource allocation, and budget. Keep the plan modular, so that it can adapt to discoveries.

- **Milestones**:
  - Pilot launch
  - First CPI-driven forecast
  - Business unit rollout
  - BI automation complete
  - Governance sign off
- **Resources**: Headcount for FinOps practice, data engineering hours, BI development, training budget.
- **Contingency**: Reserve time and budget for unexpected data cleanup or rework.

Data, Tooling, and Operations

Successful FinOps EVM adoption begins with a solid strategic foundation, and that foundation is built through clear governance, aligned stakeholders, defined roles, and a structured rollout plan. Before any dashboards, forecasts, or unit economics models come to life, the organization needs shared intent, decision-making clarity, and a roadmap that guides how the practice will scale. The elements that follow establish this groundwork, ensuring that FinOps EVM is not just implemented as a set of tools or reports, but embedded as an operating model that the teams trust, and can execute consistently.

KPIs, success criteria, and measurement

Define the metrics that will prove adoption and business impact. Use a small set of leading and lagging indicators.

- **Leading indicators**: Percent of workloads with daily PV; time to reconcile AC; number of CPI-driven interventions.
- **Lagging indicators**: Change in average CPI; variance at completion; reduction in emergency budget reallocations.
- **Targets and thresholds**: Set thresholds that trigger remediation playbooks.

Data and tooling readiness

Ensure that the data pipeline, cost model, and tooling are production-ready before broad rollout. Data quality is the foundation of trust.

- **Data checklist**: AC source selected and consistent; PV time-phased and versioned; unit data available and traceable; allocation rules documented.
- **Tooling**: BI dashboards for PV/EV/AC/CPI; automated ETL for daily ingestion; alerting for CPI drift.
- **Validation**: Reconciliation tests between billing, FOCUS or provider exports, and finance systems.

Processes, playbooks, and runbooks

Create repeatable processes for percent complete calculation, CPI updates, forecast generation, and exception handling. Document step-by-step playbooks for operational teams.

- **Playbook elements**: Data validation steps; CPI calculation method; forecast publication schedule; remediation playbook when CPI < threshold.
- **Runbooks**: Automated scripts for data refresh; manual reconciliation steps; contact list for rapid incident response.

Communication and stakeholder cadence

Establish a communication plan that keeps the stakeholders informed and focused on outcomes. Frequency and content must match audience needs.

- **Cadences**: Daily operational alerts for teams; weekly forecast reviews for managers; monthly executive summaries for leadership.

- **Content**: CPI trends, forecast delta versus BAC, root cause summaries, and recommended actions.
- **Transparency**: Publish PV versions and data lineage, so that stakeholders can trace the numbers.

Reporting, dashboards, and decision support

Design the reporting suite that supports daily operations and strategic decisions. Reports must be actionable and tailored.

- **Operational dashboards**: Per-team PV/EV/AC/CPI with alerts for CPI drift.
- **Manager dashboards**: Rollups by business unit, forecast delta versus BAC, and remediation status.
- **Executive reports**: Concise narrative, top risks, and recommended tradeoffs.

Budget alignment and incentives: Align budgeting cycles and incentives to reinforce the desired behavior. Ensure that the budget structure supports the unit economics used for EVM.

- **Budget rules**: Require budgets to be broken down to the level used for AC and unit data.
- **Incentives**: Recognize teams that improve CPI sustainably; tie a part of the performance reviews to forecast accuracy and remediation effectiveness.

Change Management and Enablement

Driving lasting adoption requires more than processes and tooling; it depends on how well people understand the practice, embrace new behaviors, and feel supported, as they transition into a FinOps EVM operating model. The elements that follow outline the training, risk mitigation, and continuous-improvement mechanisms that help teams internalize the change, and sustain it over time.

Training, enablement, and change management

Design a training program that teaches the why, the how, and the actions to take when signals appear. Training must be role-specific and practical.

- **Curriculum**: Executive briefings, practitioner workshops, engineering clinics, and finance alignment sessions.
- **Formats**: Hands-on labs with real datasets; short reference cards; recorded sessions for on-demand access.
- **Adoption tactics**: Coaching during the first forecast cycles; office hours; success stories to build momentum.

Risk management and mitigation

Identify risks to adoption and prepare mitigations. Treat data, culture, and tooling risks explicitly.

- **Common risks**: Inconsistent tagging; misaligned budget breakdowns; resistance from engineering.
- **Mitigations**: Tagging enforcement, alignment workshops with finance, pilot success stories, and incremental rollout to reduce shock.

Continuous improvement and sustainment

Adoption is ongoing. Define how the practice will evolve, how feedback will be collected, and how improvements will be prioritized.

- **Feedback loops**: Postmortems after forecast cycles; quarterly stakeholder surveys; KPI reviews.
- **Improvement backlog**: Prioritize data quality, automation, and new unit economics as business needs evolve.
- **Governance review**: Schedule periodic reviews to update PV rules, allocation logic, and escalation paths.

Final checklist before scale

Before the broad rollout, validate a short checklist to confirm readiness.

- **Checklist items:**
    - Pilot success criteria met.
    - Data pipeline automated and reconciled.
    - Governance approved.
    - Training completed for initial cohort.
    - BI dashboards validated.

This adoption strategy and roadmap give you a practical, phased path to embed FinOps EVM into your organization. Each element is actionable and designed to reduce friction, while increasing the clarity and speed of decision-making. Follow the phases, keep the governance light but firm, and treat data quality as the non-negotiable foundation of trust.

Organizational Design, Roles, and Accountability

This section defines who must own what for FinOps EVM to work. Clear roles and crisp accountability reduce debate and accelerate action. You will find practical responsibilities, and the behavioral expectations that make the practice operational rather than theoretical.

Core Personas and Responsibilities

The following personas are the minimum set required to run FinOps EVM at scale. Each persona has a distinct sphere of influence and a set of deliverables that must align with the budgeting, data, and unit economics work, which is already described in the earlier chapters. Treat these descriptions as operational job cards: assign a named owner, set measurable outcomes, and review them in every FinOps cadence.

Figure 10.3 presents the core personas that form the foundation of a FinOps EVM operating model.

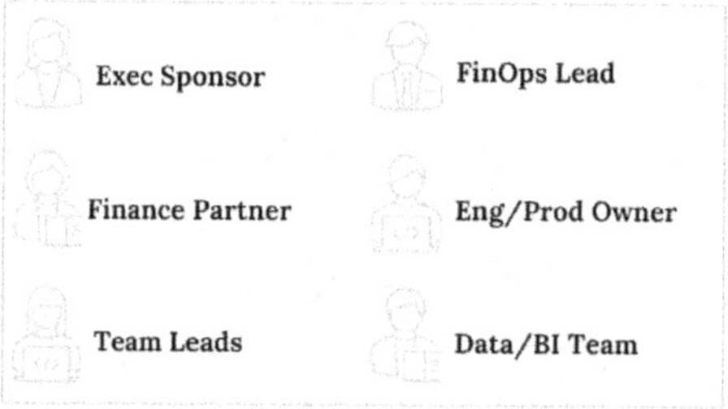

***Figure* 10.3:** *Core Personas for FinOps EVM Adoption*

Executive Sponsor

Mandate and resource allocation

The Executive Sponsor secures the mandate and the resources that make FinOps EVM possible. This person signs off on the budget structure, enforces cross-functional cooperation, and removes organizational blockers that prevent teams from acting on CPI signals. Their role is to convert the strategic intent into operational permission, so that the teams can change behavior without political friction.

The Sponsor also holds leadership accountable for outcomes. They expect regular, concise reporting that links CPI-driven forecasts to business decisions. When forecasts show material risk, the Sponsor convenes the right leaders to decide on tradeoffs, reallocation, or escalation.

FinOps Lead

Practice owner and cross-functional coordinator

The FinOps Lead runs the day-to-day practice, and translates EVM mechanics into repeatable workflows. This person owns the data pipeline definitions, the cadence for percent complete updates, and the templates used to calculate EV, CPI, and forecasts. They act as the translator between engineering, finance, and product, so that the unit economics become operational signals, rather than academic metrics.

The FinOps Lead also drives continuous improvement. They run retrospectives on forecast accuracy, maintain the playbook for remediation actions, and coach teams on interpreting CPI. Their success metric is adoption: how often teams use EVM outputs to change behavior and reduce forecast variance.

Finance Partner

PV, BAC, governance

The Finance Partner provides the authoritative Planned Value and Budget at Completion figures and enforces governance around baseline changes. They own the formal budget lifecycle, approve the daily-to-monthly PV conversion method, and ensure that the forecasts reconcile with corporate reporting requirements. Their involvement guarantees that FinOps EVM outputs remain auditable and aligned with financial controls.

Finance also defines the rules for Actual Cost treatment, such as whether to use amortized or billed values, and how to handle credits and taxes. They participate in scenario reviews, and validate EAC and VAC calculations, so that the operational forecasts can be trusted by executives and auditors.

Engineering/Product Owners

Unit data, tagging, and remediation

Engineering and Product Owners supply the unit data that drives Percent Complete and Earned Value. They are responsible for defining the unit, instrumenting telemetry, and maintaining tagging discipline, so that the costs map to the right units. Without their consistent data, CPI becomes unreliable, so that their role is fundamentally operational and continuous.

These owners also lead remediation when forecasts indicate risk. They translate CPI signals into technical actions, such as rightsizing, architectural changes, or feature prioritization. Their accountability is to deliver measurable improvements in unit economics and to report progress in the FinOps cadence.

Data/BI Team

Pipelines, dashboards, automation

The Data and BI team builds and maintains the pipelines that join billing, unit telemetry, and budget baselines into a single source of truth. They automate EV and CPI calculations, create dashboards for different personas, and ensure data lineage and traceability. Their work turns manual spreadsheets into reliable, repeatable outputs.

They also own alerting and data quality processes. When data gaps or anomalies appear, the BI team triages root causes and implements fixes so that the percent complete and forecasts remain trustworthy. Their performance is measured by data freshness, pipeline uptime, and the reduction of manual reconciliations.

Team Leads

Local CPI owners and action takers

Team Leads are the frontline owners of CPI for their scope. They receive the team-level forecast, interpret what it means for delivery, and execute the remediation playbook. Their responsibilities include short feedback loops with engineers, implementing cost controls, and reporting the impact of actions on unit economics.

They also act as the bridge between tactical fixes and strategic decisions. When local actions cannot close the gap, Team Leads escalate with clear options and estimated impact. Their accountability is practical: reduce forecast variance through targeted, measurable interventions.

RACI Chart: FinOps EVM Core Activities

Use the RACI chart as a practical starting point to get your FinOps EVM program moving. It captures the typical assignments for core activities, and clarifies who should be responsible, accountable, consulted, and informed. Every organization is different, so review these assignments with your stakeholders, replace generic roles with named people, and adjust the chart to reflect local reporting lines, capacity, and governance needs, before you lock it into policy.

Legend: R = Responsible; A = Accountable; C = Consulted; I = Informed

Activity / Decision	Exec Sponsor	FinOps Lead	Finance Partner	Eng / Product Owners	Data / BI Team	Team Leads
Set adoption vision and objectives	A	C	C	I	I	I
Approve budget and allocate resources (BAC, funding)	A	C	R	I	I	I
Define Planned Value (PV) time phasing method	I	C	A	C	I	I
Define Unit Economics (unit definition, target)	I	C	C	A	I	C
Tagging and instrumentation standards	I	C	I	A	C	R
AC source selection and cost treatment rules (amortized versus billed)	I	C	A	C	I	I
Build and maintain data pipelines (billing + unit data)	I	C	I	C	R	I

Activity / Decision	Exec Sponsor	FinOps Lead	Finance Partner	Eng / Product Owners	Data / BI Team	Team Leads
Implement EV / CPI calculation logic	I	R	C	C	R	I
Generate CPIadjusted forecasts (EAC)	I	R	C	C	R	I
Publish dashboards and reports (operational / manager / exec)	I	R	C	C	R	I
Daily/weekly data validation and reconciliation	I	R	C	C	R	I
Run weekly forecast review cadence	I	R	C	C	I	R
Execute remediation actions (technical fixes)	I	C	I	R	I	A
Approve PV / BAC changes (formal baseline changes)	A	C	R	C	I	I
Governance, policy, and audit controls	A	C	R	I	C	I
Training, enablement, and coaching	I	R	C	C	C	I
Escalation for material forecast risk	A	R	C	C	I	I
Continuous improvement backlog prioritization	I	R	C	C	C	I

Table 10.1: *RACI Chart – FinOps EVM Core Activities*

Notes and guidance:

- **Single accountable owner:** Each activity has one Accountable (A) column to ensure that the decisions are clear. Executive Sponsor holds strategic approvals and escalations; Finance Partner is accountable for formal budget controls; FinOps Lead is accountable, for operational delivery of the practice.
- **Separation of duties:** Finance owns authoritative budget figures and cost treatment rules; Data/BI owns pipelines and automation; Engineering/Product owns unit definitions and remediation execution.
- **Team Leads as action owners:** Team Leads are accountable for local remediation, and are responsible for executing fixes that change CPI at the team level.

- **Consulted versus informed:** Consulted roles must be engaged early (C) to avoid rework; Informed roles receive outputs and summaries (I) to maintain transparency.
- **Practical use:** Use this chart as the baseline RACI. For each pilot or business unit, convert these generic assignments into named people, and update the RACI to reflect local structure and capacity.

Governance Model

A governance model turns FinOps EVM from a set of calculations into a repeatable decision system. It defines the forums where decisions are made, the cadence for reviews, the thresholds that trigger escalation, and the artifacts that prove a decision was made and executed. Good governance keeps the practice lightweight, predictable, and action-oriented.

The figure here, outlines the core components that work together to form an effective governance model.

Figure 10.4: *Governance Model*

Decision Forums and Their Purpose

These forums define where decisions are made, and how different levels of the organization engage.

- **Operational Review:** A weekly forum for teams, FinOps, and data owners to validate data, review teamlevel CPI and forecasts, and agree on immediate remediation actions. This meeting focuses on facts, root cause hypotheses, and short-term fixes that teams can implement within one to two sprints. Typical attendees: FinOps Lead, Team Leads, Data/BI representative, and Engineering steward. Typical outputs: validated CPI numbers, assigned remediation tasks, and data quality tickets.

- **Tactical Forecast Review:** A biweekly or monthly forum for managers and product owners to review aggregated forecasts by business unit, evaluate tradeoffs, and approve reallocation of discretionary budget. This meeting balances operational fixes with product priorities, and short-term funding decisions. Typical attendees: FinOps Lead, Finance Partner, Product Owners, Engineering Leads, Team Leads as required. Typical outputs: approved reforecast scenarios, prioritized remediation backlog, and decision log entry.
- **Steering Committee:** A monthly or quarterly forum for executives to review portfolio-level forecasts, approve material baseline changes, and decide strategic tradeoffs. This is where the Executive Sponsor and senior finance leaders sign off on actions that affect BAC or crossBU allocations. Typical attendees: Executive Sponsor, Finance Lead, FinOps Lead, selected Business Unit leaders. Typical outputs: executive decisions, PV/BAC version approvals, escalation resolutions.
- **Emergency War Room:** An ad hoc forum triggered, when forecast variance exceeds a predefined threshold. The goal is rapid containment and a clear remediation plan with owners and timelines. Trigger conditions: forecast EAC exceeds BAC by a defined percentage, or CPI drops below a critical threshold for multiple critical workloads. Typical attendees: Executive Sponsor or delegate, FinOps Lead, Finance Partner, affected Engineering and Product Owners. Typical outputs: immediate containment actions, communication plan, follow-up schedule.

Cadence and Meeting Structure

These rhythms establish how often each forum meets, and what each session is designed to accomplish.

- **Daily**: Automated alerts and short standups for teams with active remediation tasks. Keep these under 15 minutes and focused on blockers.
- **Weekly**: Operational Review, 45 to 60 minutes. Agenda: data health check, team CPI review, action assignment, verification of previous actions.
- **Biweekly or Monthly**: Tactical Forecast Review, 60 to 90 minutes. Agenda: consolidated forecasts, scenario analysis, budget tradeoffs, and approval of reforecast proposals.
- **Monthly or Quarterly**: Steering Committee, 60 minutes. Agenda: portfolio health, strategic decisions, PV/BAC approvals, policy updates.
- **Ad hoc**: Emergency War Room, duration as needed until containment and plan are in place.

Decision Rights and Change Control

These guidelines clarify who can authorize changes, and how those changes are governed.

- Define who can approve PV and BAC changes, and under what conditions. Require a documented request, impact analysis, and sign off from the Finance Partner and Executive Sponsor for material changes.
- Use versioned PV baselines. Every change creates a new baseline with a clear rationale and an audit trail. Keep prior baselines accessible for retrospective analysis.
- Set thresholds for automatic escalation. Example thresholds: CPI below 0.85 for two consecutive reporting periods, EAC exceeding BAC by 10 percent, or a single workload forecast exceeding a materiality threshold. When thresholds are met, the escalation path is automatic and time-boxed.

Artifacts and Decision Records

These artifacts ensure that the decisions are documented, traceable, and supported by consistent reporting.

- Maintain a decision log that records the request, analysis, decision, approvers, and follow-up actions. Link each decision to the PV version, and to the forecast that prompted it.
- Publish a monthly forecast pack that includes PV, EV, AC, CPI, EAC, and a short narrative of root causes and recommended actions. Tailor the pack for managers, and for the executives as well.
- Keep the runbooks and playbooks for common remediation actions. Each playbook should include an expected impact on CPI, estimated effort, and rollback criteria.

Data Governance and Auditability

These practices maintain data integrity and enforce the standards required for a reliable forecasting.

- Require a single source of truth for AC, PV, and unit data. The Data/BI team enforces lineage, freshness, and reconciliation rules.
- Define acceptable data latency and completeness thresholds. If data falls below these thresholds, pause automated forecasts, and surface the issue in the Operational Review.

- Schedule periodic audits of allocation rules, tagging coverage, and amortization logic. Use audit findings to update policies, and to prioritize data cleanup work.

KPIs for Governance Effectiveness

These metrics help evaluate whether the governance model is working as intended.

- **Time to detect variance:** Average time from data arrival to CPI anomaly detection.
- **Time to remediate:** Average time from assignment to verified remediation.
- **Forecast accuracy:** Variance between EAC and actuals at key milestones.
- **Adoption metrics:** Percent of workloads with daily PV, percent of teams using the remediation playbook, and percent of forecasts reviewed on cadence.

Practical Tips for Running Governance

These recommendations help keep governance lightweight, effective, and trusted by teams.

- Keep meetings short and outcome-focused. Use dashboards to drive the conversation, rather than slides.
- Start with a small set of thresholds, and expand as the organization matures. Avoid over-escalation early on.
- Make decisions reversible when possible. Use short-term containment, while you validate longer-term fixes.
- Publish decisions and rationale promptly, to build trust and reduce repeated debates.

This governance model provides a clear, repeatable structure for turning FinOps EVM signals into decisions and actions. Adapt the forums, cadence, and thresholds to your organization, but keep the principles: fast detection, clear ownership, documented decisions, and measurable follow-up.

Using FinOps EVM KPIs for Decision Making and Governance

FinOps EVM KPIs must be the language leaders use to assess health and make decisions quickly. These KPIs translate unit economics and cost signals into a small set of actionable indicators that executives, finance, and engineering can read at a glance. The following guidance explains which KPIs to track, how to interpret them, how to set escalation thresholds, and how to use CPI as an input to investment and prioritization decisions.

Core KPIs to Surface in Governance

These KPIs provide the essential signals leaders need to assess financial health and efficiency.

- **Cost Performance Index (CPI)**: EV divided by AC, cumulative. This is the primary efficiency signal.
- **Estimate at Completion (EAC) versus Budget at Completion (BAC)**: It indicates the forecasted total cost compared to approved budget.
- **Forecast Delta**: EAC minus BAC, shown as an absolute value and percent.
- **Data health metrics**: Tag coverage, unit data completeness, AC reconciliation rate, data latency.

Display these KPIs at three levels: team, business unit, and portfolio. Executives need the portfolio view with a short narrative. Managers need rollups and drilldowns. Teams need the raw signals and remediation tasks.

Decision Thresholds and Automatic Escalation

Define clear, time-boxed thresholds that trigger the governance workflow. Use cumulative CPI and forecast deltas to avoid reacting to noise.

- **CPI threshold**: CPI below 0.85 for two consecutive reporting periods triggers a tactical review and an immediate remediation plan.
- **EAC threshold**: EAC exceeding BAC by 10 percent triggers escalation to the Steering Committee, and a required reforecast with options.
- **Materiality threshold**: A single workload forecast exceeding a materiality threshold (for example, 5 percent of BAC or a fixed monetary value) triggers an emergency war room.
- **Data health threshold**: Unit data completeness below 90 percent pauses the automated forecasts for affected workloads until the data is restored.

When a threshold is met, the escalation path is automatic and time-boxed. For example, a CPI breach moves from Operational Review within 48 hours to Tactical Forecast Review within 5 business days, with a remediation plan due at the Tactical Review and executive notification, if the plan cannot close the gap within the agreed timeframe.

Using CPI in Investment and Prioritization Decisions

CPI is a normalized measure of how efficiently the spend converts into a value. Use it to guide these three types of decisions.

- **Continue, adjust, or stop**: For ongoing investments, a sustained CPI below the threshold requires either targeted remediation, or a pause in further investment until unit economics improve. Document the expected improvement and the decision rationale.
- **Reallocate funding**: When CPI indicates persistent underperformance in one area and strong CPI in another, reallocate discretionary funds toward higher CPI workloads that deliver more value per dollar. Use EAC and business impact to quantify tradeoffs.
- **Invest to improve**: A workload with strategic importance, but low CPI may justify targeted investment in optimization. Approve investment, only when the expected improvement in CPI, and the payback period are documented and accepted, by Finance and Product.

Decision rules should require a short business case for any investment to improve CPI, including estimated CPI uplift, cost of remediation, and timeline to impact.

Operationalizing KPI-Driven Governance

These dashboards translate KPIs into actionable views tailored to executives, managers, and teams.

- **Executive dashboard**: One page with portfolio CPI, top 5 forecast deltas, and a short narrative of risks and recommended actions.
- **Manager dashboard**: Business unit rollups, CPI by team, EAC versus BAC, and remediation status.
- **Team dashboard**: Daily PV/EV/AC, percent complete, CPI trend, and active remediation tasks.

Use automated alerts for threshold breaches, and prepare a documented remediation plan with the owner, actions, expected impact on CPI, and verification criteria.

Example table: CPI by team to spot troubled projects

Team	Business Unit	PV Cumulative	AC Cumulative	EV Cumulative	CPI	Status
Alpha	Marketing	300,000	320,000	210,000	0.66	Escalate
Beta	Sales	240,000	230,000	232,000	1.01	Healthy
Gamma	Data Platform	180,000	175,000	160,000	0.91	Monitor
Delta	Product	120,000	110,000	132,000	1.20	Opportunity
Epsilon	Analytics	90,000	95,000	70,000	0.74	Remediate

Table 10.2: *CPI by Team to Spot Troubled Projects*

The status column in this table is illustrative only, and is not specific to FinOps EVM. Use terms and qualitative labels that reflect the CPI thresholds in your organization's context.

Use this table in weekly Operational Reviews. Highlight the teams in red when CPI is below the escalation threshold, and in green when CPI is above 1.0. For each red or amber team, you will require a oneline remediation summary and an owner.

Triage and Remediation Playbook

When CPI indicates trouble, follow a short, repeatable playbook.

- **Validate data**: Confirm AC, unit data, and PV baseline integrity within 24 hours.
- **Root cause**: Identify whether the issue is unit economics drift, tagging misallocation, architectural inefficiency, or oneoff cost events.
- **Quick wins**: List the actions that can reduce AC, or improve unit economics within 1–2 sprints. Estimate CPI impact.
- **Medium-term fixes**: Plan architectural or product changes with estimated cost and CPI improvement.
- **Decision**: Manager approves quick wins immediately; Steering Committee approves medium-term investments if required.
- **Verify**: Measure the CPI change after actions and close the loop in the next Operational Review.

Final Guidance

Remember these final tips:

- Keep the KPI set small and stable.

- CPI is the primary signal, EAC versus BAC is the financial consequence, and data health metrics protect trust.
- Use thresholds to automate escalation, but keep the decisions time boxed and reversible.

When leaders see CPI and EAC clearly presented, they can act decisively, and keep the organization focused on value, rather than raw spend.

Conclusion

This chapter closes the book by turning the concepts you have learned into a practical program for change. Over the preceding pages, we moved from the mechanics of FinOps EVM to the operational work required to make it part of how your organization plans, builds, and runs cloud services. Here you found a phased adoption roadmap, a clear set of roles and accountabilities, a governance model with decision forums and escalation thresholds, and the data and tooling patterns that make daily EVM reliable. You also received concrete guidance on training, communication, and remediation playbooks, so that the teams can act on CPI signals with speed and confidence. The material is organized to be used as a field manual: pick the phase that matches your current maturity, assign named owners, and follow the cadence until the practice becomes routine.

The governance guidance in this chapter gives you a repeatable decision system. Operational Reviews, Tactical Forecast Reviews, and a Steering Committee provide the right level of scrutiny at the right cadence. Thresholds such as CPI below 0.85 for consecutive periods or EAC exceeding BAC by a material percentage create automatic, time-boxed escalation paths that force decisions rather than delay them. The data and BI patterns show how to build a single source of truth for AC, PV, and unit telemetry so forecasts are trusted and actionable. The reporting templates, and the CPI by team example give you the tools to spot trouble quickly and to prioritize remediation where it will deliver the most value.

On a personal note, this book represents my effort to change how organizations think about cloud finance. I have worked to move the conversation from raw spend to delivered value, and to make unit economics the anchor of financial accountability. The FinOps EVM approach I present is the result of practical experiments, pilot programs, and repeated refinements in real environments. My contribution is not only the formulas and dashboards, but the operational patterns that make those signals useful in daily decision-making. I wrote this book to shorten your learning curve, to give you templates that work, and to show how leaders can use CPI and EAC as a common language across finance, product, and engineering.

Adopting FinOps EVM is a change in practice and in mindset. Start with a focused pilot, prove the model with measurable outcomes, and expand deliberately. Use the governance and playbooks in this chapter to keep your decisions fast and accountable. If you apply these steps with discipline, you will not only control cloud spend, but you will also steer investment toward the outcomes that matter. That is the real promise of FinOps EVM: a repeatable way to measure, forecast, and manage cloud spending in terms of business value.

References

- Oliveira, A. C. (2024, November 7). A *Comprehensive Guide to FinOps Earned Value Management* - ZEPHYR GLOBE. ZEPHYR GLOBE. Retrieved April 11, 2026, from https://zephyrglobe.com/2024/11/07/a-comprehensive-guide-to-finops-earned-value-management/
- *FinOps Domains.* (n.d.). Retrieved April 11, 2026, from https://www.finops.org/framework/domains/
- *Project Management Institute – The Standard for Earned Value Management.* (n.d.). Retrieved April 11, 2026, from https://www.pmi.org/standards/earned-value-management

Appendix

Introduction

This appendix is designed to provide a quick access to references that can be highly beneficial for FinOps practices. It encompasses examples of Unit Economics, the codes utilized in various chapters, and a comprehensive glossary of the terms.

- Appendix 1: Article - The Pursuit of Value in the AI Era
- Appendix 2: Unit Economics Examples
- Appendix 3: RACI Chart
- Appendix 4: FinOps EVM Formulas
- Appendix 5: Glossary of Terms

Appendix 1: Article - The Pursuit of Value in the AI Era

We are living through the first wave of an AI revolution that feels both inevitable and experimental. Companies are pouring operational budgets into models, agents, and data platforms with the urgency of discovery; the conversation is dominated by what we can build, not yet by what we should keep. This spending looks a lot like R&D: opexheavy, iterative, and tolerant of failures. The risk is not that we spend too much, but that we spend without a shared language, for what "value" actually means when the work is partly done by code and partly by people.

Value has always been easier to see in some roles than others. Sales and direct revenue streams have clear metrics; marketing and product can point to adoption and retention. But most organizations are full of people, whose daily contributions are less visible: administrators who keep the processes moving, finance teams reconciling accounts, procurement negotiating terms, HR managing talent flows, and IT keeping systems alive. AI agents are beginning to do work in those similar domains—drafting contracts, reconciling ledgers, summarizing candidate pools, automating ticket triage. If we are serious about pursuing value, we must learn to see the outputs of the agents the same way, in which we see the outputs of people: as measurable contributions to outcomes that matter.

Start by asking different questions. Instead of "How much does this model cost?" ask "What work does this capability replace, accelerate, or improve?" Can we reduce the time spent on projects by eliminating repetitive coordination? Can we produce reports faster, and with fewer errors? Can we reconcile accounts correctly and earlier in the month, so that the decisions are based on a fresher data? Can complex spreadsheet work—consolidations, scenario runs, formula audits—be turned into minutes instead of days? These are the kinds of value statements that translates the AI activity into business outcomes for nonrevenue functions.

Value in the AI era, is often a compound of speed, quality, and risk reduction. For an HR screening agent, value might be measured in hours saved per hire, and a reduction in timetooffer, combined with a quality gate that tracks candidate fit. For procurement, value could be a faster contract turnaround and fewer missed renewal opportunities, plus measurable savings from better negotiation support. For finance, value is earlier close cycles, fewer reconciliation exceptions, and higher confidence in forecasts. For IT and operations, value shows up as reduced mean time to resolution, fewer escalations, and more predictable capacity planning. These are not exotic metrics; they are operational levers that leaders already care about—made visible and measurable by the AI.

This is also a cultural challenge. Organizations must move from treating AI as a magic box to treating it as a portfolio of capabilities that require stewardship. That means defining the unit of value for each capability, instrumenting outcomes, and accepting that many experiments will fail or underperform. It also means rethinking incentives: reward teams for improving throughput and accuracy, not just for launching models. Celebrate reductions in cycle time and error rates as much as you celebrate new features.

There is a moral and managerial dimension too. As agents take on routine tasks, the human role shifts from doing to stewarding: people become the ones who set boundaries, judge outputs, and handle exceptions. That shift creates new responsibilities—designing prompts and workflows, defining quality gates, monitoring performance, and deciding when to intervene. These are not purely technical chores; they require domain knowledge, ethical judgment, and an ability to translate ambiguous outputs into business decisions.

Practical stewardship means building clear acceptance criteria and confidence thresholds, so that automation can run at a speed without creating any hidden risks. It means training people to read model behavior, spot drift, and trace errors back to data or prompt design. It also means creating escalation paths and psychological safety, so that the teams can pause an agent, report failures, and iterate without blame.

The skills that matter change: data literacy to understand what the agent consumes and produces; prompt and workflow design to shape useful outputs; and process design to map where humans must review, and where the agents can act autonomously. Measure the human contribution by outcomes—hours saved, error rates reduced, cycle times shortened, and exceptions resolved—and reward improvements in those metrics.

Finally, the pursuit of value in the AI era is an invitation to be deliberate. Experiment quickly, yes, but measure deliberately. Translate outcomes into time saved, errors avoided, decisions accelerated, and risk reduced. When you can point to a concrete improvement—faster reconciliations, reports produced overnight, projects delivered with fewer coordination hours—you stop arguing about hype and start arguing about priorities. That is how AI stops being a cost center, and becomes a multiplier of human work: not by replacing people, but by making their contributions clearer, faster, and more impactful.

Appendix 2: Unit Economics Examples

The importance of Unit Economics was explained in *Chapter 10, Driving Organizational Adoption*. This Appendix contains some ideas of Unit Economics that can be applied in any business. Of course, not all of them are needed. It is important to evaluate the ones that are relevant to the business, and that can be mapped directly to the cloud cost invested.

Unit Economics in this Appendix will be divided into Business and Technical Examples.

Business Examples:

- **Cost Per User**: Calculate the cost of supporting each user on your platform. This metric helps in understanding the efficiency of your user acquisition strategies, and the overall cost of maintaining your user base. By comparing this cost with the revenue generated per user, you can assess the profitability of your user base.
- **Cost Per Transaction**: Determine the cost associated with processing each transaction. This metric is crucial for businesses like e-commerce platforms, where understanding the cost per transaction can help in optimizing the pricing strategies and improving the overall operational efficiency.
- **Customer Lifetime Value (CLV)**: Calculate the total revenue expected from a customer over their entire relationship with your business. By comparing CLV with the cost of acquiring and retaining customers, you can make informed decisions about marketing spend and customer retention strategies.
- **Revenue Per Employee**: Measure the revenue generated per employee. This metric helps in assessing the productivity and efficiency of your workforce. By correlating this with employee costs, you can identify the areas for improvement, and optimize resource allocation.

- **Profit Margin Per Unit**: Calculate the profit margin for each unit of product or service sold. This metric helps in understanding the profitability of different products or services and can guide pricing and product development decisions.
- **Cost Per Customer**: Calculate the total expenses associated with acquiring and serving each customer. This metric includes marketing, sales, and customer support costs, providing insights into the efficiency of customer acquisition strategies and the overall value of each customer.
- **Cost Per Sale**: Measure the total cost involved in making a sale, including marketing, sales team expenses, and promotional costs. This metric helps in optimizing sales processes, and improving the return on investment for sales activities.
- **Cost Per Lead**: Determine the cost of acquiring each potential customer or lead. This includes advertising, marketing campaigns, and lead generation activities. Understanding this metric helps in assessing the effectiveness of marketing efforts, and optimizing lead acquisition strategies.
- **Cost Per Click**: Calculate the cost associated with each click in online advertising campaigns, such as Pay-Per-Click (PPC) advertising. This metric helps in optimizing the online ad spend and evaluating the performance of digital marketing campaigns.
- **Cost Per Conversion**: Measure the total expenses required to convert a lead into a paying customer. This includes marketing, sales, and onboarding costs. Understanding this metric helps in optimizing conversion strategies and improving overall profitability.
- **Cost Per Feature**: Calculate the cost of developing and maintaining each feature within a product or service. This metric helps in prioritizing feature development, based on its cost-effectiveness and impact on the overall product.
- **Cost Per Acquisition (CPA)**: Determine the total cost of acquiring a new customer, including all marketing and sales expenses. This metric helps in evaluating the efficiency of acquisition channels and optimizing marketing budgets.
- **Cost Per Engagement**: Measure the cost of engaging with customers through various channels, such as social media, email marketing, or customer support. This metric helps in assessing the effectiveness of engagement strategies and optimizing resource allocation.
- **Cost Per Subscriber**: Calculate the total expenses associated with acquiring and maintaining each subscriber, including marketing, sales, and subscription management costs. This metric is particularly important for subscription-based businesses, to optimize their revenue model.

- **Cost Per Retention**: Determine the cost of retaining an existing customer, including loyalty programs, customer support, and retention marketing efforts. This metric helps in assessing the effectiveness of retention strategies and improving customer loyalty.
- **Cost Per Unit Sold**: Measure the total cost associated with producing and selling each unit of a product. This includes production, distribution, and marketing expenses. Understanding this metric helps in optimizing pricing strategies and improving profit margins.
- **Cost Per Support Ticket**: Calculate the cost of resolving each customer support ticket, including personnel, tools, and resources involved in the support process. This metric helps in optimizing support operations and reducing customer service costs.
- **Cost Per Training Session**: Determine the total expenses associated with conducting each training session for employees or customers, including trainer fees, materials, and facility costs. This metric helps in assessing the effectiveness of training programs and optimizing training budgets.
- **Cost Per Project**: Measure the total cost involved in executing a project, including personnel, materials, and overhead expenses. This metric helps in evaluating project efficiency and optimizing project management processes.
- **Cost Per Marketing Campaign**: Calculate the total expenses associated with running a marketing campaign, including advertising, creative development, and distribution costs. This metric helps in assessing the effectiveness of marketing efforts and optimizing marketing budgets.

Technical Examples:

- **Cost Per API Call**: Calculate the cost associated with each API call made by your application. This metric is important for applications that rely heavily on APIs, as it helps in optimizing API usage and reducing costs.
- **Cost Per Compute Hour**: Determine the cost of running a Virtual Machine (VM) or container for one hour. This metric helps in optimizing resource utilization and identifying opportunities for cost savings, such as resizing VMs or using spot instances.
- **Cost Per GB of Storage**: Measure the cost of storing one gigabyte of data. This metric is crucial for businesses that handle large amounts of data, as it helps in optimizing storage solutions and reducing costs.
- **Cost Per Data Transfer**: Calculate the cost of transferring data between different services or regions. This metric helps in optimizing data transfer strategies and minimizing costs associated with data movement.

- **Cost Per Batch Job**: Calculate the cost associated with running a batch job. This metric is essential for organizations that rely on batch processing for data analysis, large-scale computations, or automated tasks. By understanding the cost per batch job, you can optimize job scheduling, resource allocation, and identify the opportunities for using spot instances or reserved capacity to reduce costs.
- **Cost Per Query**: Measure the cost of executing a query in data analytics services like Azure Synapse Analytics or Azure Data Explorer. This metric helps in optimizing query performance, managing resource allocation, and reducing the costs associated with data processing. By analyzing the cost per query, you can identify inefficient queries and optimize them for better performance and lower costs.
- **Cost Per Event**: Calculate the cost associated with processing each event in event-driven architectures using Azure Event Grid or Azure Event Hubs. This metric helps in understanding the cost implications of real-time data processing, and optimizing event handling strategies to reduce costs.
- **Cost Per Build/Deployment**: Determine the cost of building and deploying applications using Azure DevOps or GitHub Actions. This metric helps in optimizing CI/CD pipelines, managing build resources, and reducing costs associated with application development and deployment.
- **Cost Per Backup**: Measure the cost of backing up data using Azure Backup or other backup solutions. This metric helps in optimizing backup schedules, managing storage costs, and ensuring data protection while minimizing expenses.
- **Cost Per Stream**: Calculate the cost associated with streaming data using services like Azure Stream Analytics or Azure Media Services. This metric is crucial for organizations that rely on real-time data streaming or media streaming. By understanding the cost per stream, you can optimize streaming configurations, manage resource allocation, and reduce costs.
- **Cost Per ML Model Training**: Determine the cost of training machine learning models using Azure Machine Learning. This metric helps in managing the costs associated with model training, optimizing training configurations, and identifying opportunities for using cost-efficient compute resources.
- **Cost Per Container Instance**: Measure the cost of running container instances using Azure Kubernetes Service (AKS) or Azure Container Instances (ACI). This metric helps in optimizing container deployments, managing resource utilization, and reducing costs associated with containerized applications.
- **Cost Per API Gateway Request**: Calculate the cost of handling requests through API Gateway services like Azure API Management. This metric helps in

managing the costs associated with API traffic, optimizing API configurations, and identifying opportunities for reducing expenses.

- **Cost Per Message**: Measure the cost of sending messages using messaging services like Azure Service Bus or Azure Queue Storage. This metric helps in optimizing message handling strategies, managing resource allocation, and reducing costs associated with messaging and communication between services.

Appendix 3: RACI Chart

Use the RACI chart as a practical starting point to get your FinOps EVM program moving. It captures the typical assignments for core activities and clarifies who should be responsible, accountable, consulted, and informed. Every organization is different, so review these assignments with your stakeholders, replace generic roles with named people, and adjust the chart to reflect local reporting lines, capacity, and governance needs before you lock it into policy.

Legend: R = Responsible; A = Accountable; C = Consulted; I = Informed

Activity / Decision	Exec Sponsor	FinOps Lead	Finance Partner	Eng / Product Owners	Data / BI Team	Team Leads
Set adoption vision and objectives	A	C	C	I	I	I
Approve budget and allocate resources (BAC, funding)	A	C	R	I	I	I
Define Planned Value (PV) timephasing method	I	C	A	C	I	I
Define Unit Economics (unit definition, target)	I	C	C	A	I	C
Tagging and instrumentation standards	I	C	I	A	C	R
AC source selection and cost treatment rules (amortized versus billed)	I	C	A	C	I	I
Build and maintain data pipelines (billing + unit data)	I	C	I	C	R	I
Implement EV / CPI calculation logic	I	R	C	C	R	I
Generate CPIadjusted forecasts (EAC)	I	R	C	C	R	I

Activity / Decision	Exec Sponsor	FinOps Lead	Finance Partner	Eng / Product Owners	Data / BI Team	Team Leads
Publish dashboards and reports (operational / manager / exec)	I	R	C	C	R	I
Daily/weekly data validation and reconciliation	I	R	C	C	R	I
Run weekly forecast review cadence	I	R	C	C	I	R
Execute remediation actions (technical fixes)	I	C	I	R	I	A
Approve PV / BAC changes (formal baseline changes)	A	C	R	C	I	I
Governance, policy, and audit controls	A	C	R	I	C	I
Training, enablement, and coaching	I	R	C	C	C	I
Escalation for material forecast risk	A	R	C	C	I	I
Continuous improvement backlog prioritization	I	R	C	C	C	I

Table A.1: *RACI Chart – FinOps EVM Core Activities*

Notes and guidance:

- **Single accountable owner:** Each activity has one Accountable (A) column to ensure that the decisions are clear. Executive Sponsor holds strategic approvals and escalations; Finance Partner is accountable for formal budget controls; FinOps Lead is accountable for operational delivery of the practice.
- **Separation of duties:** Finance owns authoritative budget figures and cost treatment rules; Data/BI owns pipelines and automation; Engineering/ Product owns unit definitions and remediation execution.
- **Team Leads as action owners:** Team Leads are accountable for local remediation and are responsible for executing fixes that change CPI at the team level.
- **Consulted versus informed:** Consulted roles must be engaged early (C) to avoid rework. Informed roles receive outputs and summaries (I) to maintain transparency.
- **Practical use:** Use this chart as the baseline RACI. For each pilot or business unit, convert these generic assignments into named people, and update the RACI to reflect local structure and capacity.

Appendix 4: FinOps EVM Formulas

Input Metrics

Planned Value (PV)

PV = Planned percentage of work completed × BAC

Planned Value represents the authorized budget for the work planned to be completed by a given date. In FinOps, PV represents the expected cloud spend for the amount of progress that should have been achieved according to the plan. PV is cumulative, meaning that it represents the total value accumulated up to the point of analysis.

Example: A workload has a total annual budget (BAC) of $1,200,000. By the end of Q1, the plan expects 25% of value to be delivered. PV = 0.25 × $1,200,000 = $300,000.

Earned Value (EV)

EV = PV × Percent Complete

Earned Value is the budgeted value of the work actually completed to date. In FinOps, EV reflects the value of cloud-enabled progress delivered so far, based on Unit Economics, comparing the actual Unit Economics against what was expected according to the what was budgeted. Like PV, EV is cumulative for the assessment period.

Example: Cumulative PV through March is $300,000, and Percent Complete is 92.6%. EV = $300,000 × 0.926 = $277,800. The workload has earned $277,800 of its planned value.

Actual Cost (AC)

AC = Sum of actual cloud costs incurred to date

Actual Cost is the total cost incurred for the work performed and resources used up to a specific point in time. In FinOps, AC represents the real cloud spend captured in billing data. AC must be traceable, reproducible, and aligned with the same period used for PV and EV.

Example: Cloud billing data shows $310,000 of actual spending through the end of Q1. AC = $310,000.

Budget at Completion (BAC)

BAC = Total planned cloud budget for the initiative

Budget at Completion is the total authorized budget for the entire initiative or budgeting period. In FinOps, BAC represents the expected total cloud spend allocated for delivering the full scope of work within a budget cycle, which is normally defined on a yearly basis. BAC serves as the reference point for all planning and forecasting.

Example: The approved annual cloud budget for a product is $1,200,000. BAC = $1,200,000.

Percent Complete and Unit Economics

Percent Complete

Percent Complete = Target Unit Economic : Actual Unit Economic

In FinOps EVM, Percent Complete is not measured by traditional task-based progress. It is derived from Unit Economics by comparing the target cost per unit defined during budgeting with the actual cost per unit observed during execution. If actual unit economics match the target, Percent Complete equals 100%. If actual unit economics are worse (higher cost per unit), Percent Complete drops below 100%. If actual unit economics outperform the target (lower cost per unit), Percent Complete rises above 100%.

Example: The target cost per order is $0.50, and the actual cost per order in March is $0.54. Percent Complete = $0.50 : $0.54 = 92.6%. The workload is delivering value at 92.6% of the planned efficiency.

Current-Status Output Metrics

Cost Variance (CV)

CV = EV – AC

Cost Variance measures the difference between the value earned and the actual cost incurred. A positive CV indicates that the initiative is delivering value at a lower cost than planned. A negative CV signals that cloud spending is exceeding the value delivered. CV is often used in executive reviews to highlight financial performance.

Example: EV = $277,800 and AC = $310,000. CV = $277,800 – $310,000 = –$32,200. The workload is over budget by $32,200 relative to the value it has delivered.

Cost Performance Index (CPI)

CPI = EV : AC

The Cost Performance Index expresses cost efficiency as a ratio. It shows how much value is being earned for each dollar or euro spent. CPI is one of the most influential metrics in FinOps EVM because it provides a clear, normalized indicator that can be compared across teams, workloads, or time periods. CPI is also the primary input for forecasting metrics, such as EAC.

Example: EV = $277,800 and AC = $310,000. CPI = $277,800 : $310,000 = 0.90. For every dollar spent, only $0.90 of value has been earned. CPI > 1 means cost efficiency; CPI = 1 means on plan; CPI < 1 means overspending relative to value.

Schedule Variance (SV)

SV = EV – PV

Schedule Variance measures the difference between the value earned and the value planned. It indicates whether the initiative is ahead of, or behind the planned pace of progress. In cloud operations, a negative SV means the business unit will achieve the expected value later than planned.

Example: EV = $277,800 and PV = $300,000. SV = $277,800 – $300,000 = –$22,200. Value delivery is behind schedule by $22,200.

Schedule Performance Index (SPI)

SPI = EV : PV

The Schedule Performance Index expresses schedule efficiency as a ratio. It shows the rate at which value is being delivered compared to the planned rate. SPI is useful for identifying delivery bottlenecks and assessing the impact of delays. Schedule delays often translate into extended cloud consumption.

Example: EV = $277,800 and PV = $300,000. SPI = $277,800 : $300,000 = 0.93. The workload is delivering the value at 93% of the planned pace. SPI > 1 means ahead of schedule; SPI = 1 means on plan; SPI < 1 means behind schedule.

Forecast Output Metrics

Estimate at Completion — Based on Current CPI (EAC)

EAC = BAC : CPI

This is the default EAC formula for cloud environments. It assumes that the current cost efficiency (CPI) will continue for the rest of the initiative. It is the most commonly used EAC variation in FinOps.

Example: BAC = $1,200,000 and CPI = 0.90.

EAC = $1,200,000 : 0.90 = $1,333,333.

The workload is projected to cost $1,333,333, exceeding the budget by $133,333.

Estimate at Completion — Remaining Work at Planned Efficiency (EAC)

EAC = AC + (BAC – EV)

Use this formula when past performance is not representative of future performance. This often happens after a major optimization effort, architectural redesign, or cost-saving initiative. It assumes future work will be completed at the original planned efficiency, not the current CPI.

Example: AC = $310,000, BAC = $1,200,000, EV = $277,800.

EAC = \$310,000 + (\$1,200,000 – \$277,800) = \$1,232,200.

After optimizations are applied, the remaining work is expected to follow the original plan.

Estimate at Completion — Remaining Work at Current CPI (EAC)

EAC = AC + (BAC – EV) : CPI

Use this when past inefficiencies are expected to continue. It anchors the calculation in actual cost already spent, while projecting the remaining work at the current efficiency. It is more conservative than the BAC : CPI version, because it separates the past and future performances.

The assumption is that the remaining work will continue at the current CPI, but AC is already sunk and should not be recalculated.

Example: AC = \$310,000, BAC = \$1,200,000, EV = \$277,800, CPI = 0.90.

EAC = \$310,000 + (\$1,200,000 – \$277,800) : 0.90 = \$310,000 + \$1,024,667 = \$1,334,667.

Estimate at Completion — Combined CPI and SPI (EAC)

EAC = AC + (BAC – EV) : (CPI × SPI)

Use this when both cost and schedule performance are influencing future spend. This is common in cloud initiatives, where delays increase consumption, such as extended use of temporary environments, prolonged migration windows, or delayed decommissioning of legacy systems. This formula is the most pessimistic one, and often produces the highest EAC.

Example: AC = \$310,000, BAC = \$1,200,000, EV = \$277,800, CPI = 0.90, SPI = 0.93.

EAC = \$310,000 + (\$1,200,000 – \$277,800) : (0.90 × 0.93) = \$310,000 + \$922,200 : 0.837 = \$1,411,792.

Estimate at Completion — Manual Forecast (EAC)

EAC = AC + New Forecast for Remaining Work

Use this when neither CPI nor SPI reflects the reality, often due to major changes in scope, architecture, or business priorities. This version relies on engineering and FinOps collaboration to produce a realistic forecast. Common in situations, such as sudden traffic surges, new compliance requirements, major architectural redesign, or unexpected vendor price changes.

Example: AC = \$310,000, and the engineering team estimates \$850,000 to complete.

EAC = \$310,000 + \$850,000 = \$1,160,000.

Estimate at Completion — Re-baselined Budget (EAC)

EAC = Revised BAC

Use this when the budget itself has changed due to new scope or strategic decisions. The original BAC is no longer valid. This is not a calculation, but a formal reset of expectations. Common in large enterprises where new features are added, business units expand usage, or regulatory requirements increase workload.

Example: The original BAC was $1,200,000, but new compliance requirements added $200,000 of expected spend. EAC = Revised BAC = $1,400,000.

Estimate to Complete (ETC)

ETC = EAC – AC

Estimate to Complete represents the expected cost required to finish the remaining work. It isolates the future portion of the spending forecast. ETC helps FinOps teams plan future budgets, evaluate the financial impact of delays, and determine whether the upcoming work requires optimization.

Example: EAC = $1,333,333 and AC = $310,000. ETC = $1,333,333 – $310,000 = $1,023,333.

The workload is expected to spend an additional $1,023,333 to complete the budgeting period.

Variance at Completion (VAC)

VAC = BAC – EAC

Variance at Completion measures the difference between the original budget and the forecasted total cost. It shows whether the initiative is expected to finish under or over the approved cloud budget. A positive VAC means under budget; zero means on budget; a negative VAC means expected overspend.

Example: BAC = $1,200,000 and EAC = $1,333,333.

VAC = $1,200,000 – $1,333,333 = –$133,333.

The workload is forecasted to exceed its budget by $133,333.

To-Complete Performance Index — Against BAC (TCPI)

TCPI = (BAC – EV) : (BAC – AC)

TCPI against BAC measures the required cost efficiency for the remaining work to meet the original budget. If CPI shows what happened, TCPI shows what must happen next. A TCPI greater than 1 means the team must operate more efficiently than it has so far. A TCPI equal to 1 means the current efficiency is enough. A TCPI less than 1 means the target can be met even with lower efficiency.

Example: BAC = $1,200,000, EV = $277,800, AC = $310,000.

TCPI = ($1,200,000 – $277,800) : ($1,200,000 – $310,000) = $922,200 : $890,000 = 1.04.

The team must operate at 104% efficiency relative to the plan to stay within the original budget.

To-Complete Performance Index — Against EAC (TCPI)

TCPI = (BAC – EV) : (EAC – AC)

TCPI against EAC measures the required cost efficiency for the remaining work to meet the revised forecast. Use this when the original budget is no longer achievable, and the team is working toward the revised estimate.

Example: BAC = $1,200,000, EV = $277,800, EAC = $1,333,333, AC = $310,000.

TCPI = ($1,200,000 – $277,800) : ($1,333,333 – $310,000) = $922,200 : $1,023,333 = 0.90.

The team can meet the revised forecast even at 90% efficiency.

Forecasting Application

CPI-Based Forecast for Future Periods

Forecast for a future month = PV for that month : Latest CPI

When projecting future cloud spend, the most recent CPI is used as the performance multiplier applied to the remaining Planned Value. You do not recalculate CPI for future months. You carry forward the last known CPI as the best estimate of how the workload will continue to perform unless something changes.

Example: The latest CPI is 0.90, and PV for June is $100,000.

Forecast for June = $100,000 : 0.90 = $111,111.

At the current efficiency, the workload is expected to cost $111,111 in June, instead of the planned $100,000.

Appendix 5: Glossary of Terms

This Appendix offers a glossary of terms that acts as a helpful guide for the readers, explaining important concepts and definitions found in the book. This resource is designed to make the terms easier to understand, and ensure a consistent interpretation, promoting clearer communication and comprehension among the readers.

A

Actual Cost (AC)

The total cloud spend actually incurred for work performed during a given period. In FinOps EVM, AC is derived from cloud billing data, and represents the real expenditure against the planned and earned value.

Amortized Cost

A cost representation that distributes upfront payments, such as Reserved Instance or Savings Plan fees, evenly across the commitment period, rather than recording them as a lump sum at purchase.

Anomaly Detection

The practice of identifying unusual or unexpected changes in cloud spending patterns that may indicate waste, misconfiguration, or opportunities for optimization.

At-Completion Variance (VAC)

The projected budget surplus or deficit, at the end of a project or planning period, calculated as BAC minus EAC. A negative VAC signals expected overspend.

B

Baseline

A fixed reference point representing the approved budget, schedule, or scope against which the actual performance is measured. In FinOps EVM, the cost baseline aligns planned cloud spend with expected value delivery.

Billed Cost

The amount invoiced by the cloud provider for a billing period, reflecting charges after discounts, credits, and negotiated rates have been applied.

Blended Cost

An averaged cost rate that combines on-demand and discounted pricing across an organization, smoothing rate differences to simplify internal cost allocation.

Budget at Completion (BAC)

The total authorized budget for the cloud workload or project over its full lifecycle. BAC serves as the ceiling against which all EVM metrics are measured.

Business Value

The measurable benefit an organization derives from its cloud investments encompasses revenue generation, cost avoidance, customer satisfaction, and strategic enablement beyond simple cost reduction.

C

Capability

A functional area within the FinOps Framework that describes a specific practice an organization must develop, such as cost allocation, forecasting, or rate optimization.

Capital Expenditure (CapEx)

Spending on long-term assets that are capitalized on the balance sheet and depreciated over time. Cloud commitments, such as Reserved Instances, may receive CapEx treatment depending on accounting standards.

Chargeback

A cost allocation model in which actual cloud costs are billed directly to the consuming business unit or team, creating direct financial accountability for usage.

Cloud Cost Management

The discipline of monitoring, analyzing, and optimizing cloud expenditures to ensure spending aligns with business objectives and delivers maximum value.

Cloud Provider

A vendor that delivers computing resources, storage, networking, and services on demand over the internet, such as AWS, Microsoft Azure, or Google Cloud Platform.

Commitment-Based Discount

A pricing model in which the customer agrees to a minimum usage level or spend over a defined term in exchange for reduced rates, as compared to on-demand pricing.

Contracted Cost

The cost derived from negotiated agreements, such as Enterprise Discount Programs or Private Pricing Agreements, reflecting organization-specific rates rather than public list prices.

Cost Allocation

The process of assigning cloud costs to specific teams, projects, products, or business units so that spending can be traced to the organizational entity responsible.

Cost Performance Index (CPI)

The ratio of Earned Value to Actual Cost (EV divided by AC) indicates cost efficiency. A CPI below 1.0 means that the project is spending more than planned per unit of value delivered.

Cost Variance (CV)

The difference between Earned Value and Actual Cost (EV minus AC). A negative CV indicates a cost overrun relative to the value delivered.

Crawl-Walk-Run

The FinOps maturity progression model describing three stages of practice adoption: Crawl establishes foundational visibility, Walk introduces optimization and governance, and Run achieves continuous, data-driven cost and value management.

D

Data Pipeline

The automated flow of cloud billing, usage, and metadata through ingestion, transformation, enrichment, and storage stages to produce the cost and value metrics required for FinOps EVM analysis.

Discount Coverage

The percentage of eligible cloud usage that is covered by commitment-based discounts, such as Reserved Instances, Savings Plans, or Committed Use Discounts.

Domain

A high-level organizational area within the FinOps Framework that groups related capabilities, such as Understanding Cloud Usage and Cost, Performance Tracking and Benchmarking, or Cloud Rate Optimization.

E

Earned Value (EV)

The budgeted cost of work actually completed, expressed in monetary terms. In FinOps EVM, EV quantifies how much planned value has been realized based on delivered outputs or outcomes.

Earned Value Management (EVM)

A project management methodology that integrates scope, schedule, and cost data to provide objective measures of project performance and progress, enabling early detection of variances.

Effective Cost

The net cost after all discounts, credits, refunds, and amortization adjustments have been applied, representing the true economic cost of cloud resource consumption.

Estimate at Completion (EAC)

The projected total cost of the project or workload when finished, typically calculated using current performance trends, such as BAC divided by CPI.

Estimate to Complete (ETC)

The expected cost required to finish the remaining work, calculated as EAC minus AC. ETC informs budget replanning and resource allocation decisions.

Executive Sponsor

A senior leader who champions the FinOps EVM initiative, secures funding and organizational support, removes cross-functional barriers, and ensures a strategic alignment.

F

FinOps

A cloud financial management discipline that brings together technology, business, and finance teams to collaborate on data-driven spending decisions, enabling organizations to get maximum business value from their cloud investments.

FinOps EVM (FinOps Earned Value Management)

FinOps EVM is a framework that adapts classic Earned Value Management to cloud financial operations by translating Planned Value, Actual Cost, and Earned Value into cloud-native terms, such as unit economics and continuous spend. It measures how efficiently cloud spending converts into business outcomes by using Percent Complete, based on real versus target unit economics, enabling leaders to assess performance through indicators like CPI and Cost Variance. In essence, it provides a disciplined, value-oriented way to evaluate whether cloud investments are delivering the expected results, going beyond simple budget comparisons to reveal the true relationship between cost, efficiency, and business value.

FinOps Framework

The operating model defined by the FinOps Foundation that provides principles, personas, domains, capabilities, and a maturity model for managing cloud costs and driving business value.

FinOps Foundation

The industry body, part of The Linux Foundation, that advances the FinOps discipline through community collaboration, training, certification, and the development of standards and best practices.

FinOps Lifecycle

The iterative cycle of Inform, Optimize, and Operate that organizations follow to continuously improve cloud financial management practices.

FinOps Open Cost and Usage Specification (FOCUS)

An open standard that defines a consistent schema for cloud billing data across providers, enabling unified cost analysis, tooling interoperability, and cross-cloud comparisons.

Forecast

A projection of future cloud costs or value delivery based on the historical trends, current performance indices, and known upcoming changes, used to guide budgeting and planning decisions.

G

Governance

The framework of policies, decision forums, escalation paths, and review cadences that ensure FinOps EVM practices are followed consistently, and that variances trigger appropriate corrective action.

I

Idle Resource

A provisioned cloud resource that is running and incurring cost, but is not being used or is significantly underutilized, representing waste that can be eliminated or reduced.

Inform Phase

The first phase of the FinOps Lifecycle focused on providing visibility into cloud costs and usage, establishing baselines, building shared understanding, and enabling data-driven conversations.

K

Key Performance Indicator (KPI)

A measurable value that demonstrates how effectively an organization is achieving its objectives. In FinOps EVM, KPIs include CPI, SPI, unit cost metrics, and discount coverage rates.

Kubernetes Cost Allocation

The practice of attributing shared Kubernetes cluster costs to individual namespaces, workloads, or teams based on resource requests, limits, or actual utilization.

L

Lifecycle

See FinOps Lifecycle.

List Cost

The published on-demand price for a cloud service before any discounts, negotiations, or credits are applied serving as the baseline against which the savings are measured.

M

Maturity Model

A structured framework for assessing an organization's current level of FinOps practice adoption, and defining a roadmap for progressive improvement through the Crawl, Walk, and Run stages.

Metric

A quantifiable measure used to track and assess the status of a specific process or activity. FinOps EVM relies on metrics such as CPI, SPI, EAC, and unit economics to evaluate performance.

N

Negotiate Phase

An aspect of FinOps practice focused on securing favorable pricing through commitment-based discounts, enterprise agreements, and strategic negotiations with cloud providers.

O

On-Demand Pricing

The standard pay-as-you-go pricing model offered by cloud providers, with no upfront commitment, typically representing the highest per-unit cost.

Operational Expenditure (OpEx)

Ongoing spending that is expensed in the period incurred rather than capitalized. Most cloud consumption follows an OpEx model, enabling flexibility but requiring active cost governance.

Operate Phase

The third phase of the FinOps Lifecycle focused on executing optimization actions, enforcing policies, automating governance, and continuously aligning cloud operations with business objectives.

Optimize Phase

The second phase of the FinOps Lifecycle, focused on identifying and implementing specific actions to improve cloud cost efficiency, such as rightsizing, commitment purchases, and waste elimination.

Organizational Alignment

The coordination of people, processes, and incentives across finance, engineering, product, and executive teams to ensure shared accountability for cloud cost and value outcomes.

P

Percent Complete

Percent Complete in FinOps EVM is the **efficiency ratio** that compares the *actual unit economics* achieved in the period with the *target unit economics* defined during budgeting. Instead of measuring physical progress like traditional EVM, it measures how effectively the workload is converting cloud spend into business outcomes. Formally, it is calculated as **Target Unit Economic : Actual Unit Economic**, producing a value above 100 percent when performance is better than planned and below 100 percent when efficiency drops. This percentage becomes the foundation for calculating Earned Value, turning uniteconomic performance into a measurable indicator of value delivery.

For example, let us say that in March, our cumulative cost per order is $0.54 and our target cost per order is $0.50. The Percent Complete will be 92.6%.

Performance Measurement Baseline (PMB)

The integrated scope, schedule, and cost plan against which project execution is measured. In FinOps EVM, the PMB combines the cloud budget plan with expected value delivery milestones.

Persona

A role archetype within the FinOps Framework, such as FinOps Practitioner, Engineering Lead, Finance Analyst, or Executive, each with distinct responsibilities and perspectives on cloud value management.

Planned Value (PV)

The authorized budget assigned to scheduled work for a specific period. In FinOps EVM, PV represents the expected cloud cost associated with planned value delivery milestones.

R

RACI Matrix

A responsibility assignment chart that defines who is Responsible, Accountable, Consulted, and Informed for each task or decision within the FinOps EVM implementation.

Rate Optimization

The practice of reducing the per-unit cost of cloud resources through commitment-based discounts, spot or preemptible instances, and negotiated pricing without changing usage patterns.

Reserved Instance (RI)

A commitment-based pricing option offered by cloud providers in which the customer reserves capacity for a one- or three-year term in exchange for significant discounts compared to on-demand rates.

Resource Tagging

The practice of applying metadata labels to cloud resources to enable cost allocation, ownership identification, and policy enforcement across the cloud estate.

Rightsizing

The process of adjusting cloud resource specifications, such as instance type or storage tier, to match actual workload requirements, eliminating overprovisioning and reducing waste.

S

Savings Plan

A flexible commitment-based pricing model, primarily in AWS, that provides discounted rates in exchange for a commitment to a consistent amount of usage measured in dollars per hour over a one- or three-year term.

Schedule Performance Index (SPI)

The ratio of Earned Value to Planned Value (EV divided by PV) indicating schedule efficiency. An SPI below 1.0 means value delivery is behind the planned schedule.

Schedule Variance (SV)

The difference between Earned Value and Planned Value (EV minus PV). A negative SV indicates that value delivery is lagging behind the planned timeline.

Shared Cost

Cloud expenditure that benefits multiple teams, products, or business units and must be allocated using agreed-upon rules such as proportional usage, headcount, or fixed percentages.

Showback

A cost allocation model that reports cloud costs to consuming teams for awareness and transparency without directly charging them, encouraging cost-conscious behavior without creating billing overhead.

Spot Instance

A cloud compute option that uses spare provider capacity at deeply discounted prices but can be interrupted with short notice, suitable for fault-tolerant and flexible workloads.

Stakeholder

Any individual or group with an interest in or influence over the FinOps EVM initiative, including executives, engineering teams, finance, product managers, and procurement.

T

Tagging Policy

A set of organizational rules that define required tags, naming conventions, allowed values, and enforcement mechanisms to ensure consistent metadata across cloud resources.

To-Complete Performance Index (TCPI)

The cost performance efficiency that must be achieved on the remaining work to meet a specified budget target, calculated as remaining work divided by remaining funds. A TCPI above 1.0 requires tighter cost control going forward.

Total Cost of Ownership (TCO)

The comprehensive cost of a cloud workload, including not only direct cloud charges, but also operational labor, tooling, migration, training, and opportunity costs.

Trend Analysis

The examination of cost and performance data over time to identify patterns, growth rates, seasonal variations, and trajectories that inform forecasting and decision-making.

U

Unblended Cost

The actual charge for each resource at the specific rate incurred, without averaging across the organization, showing the true cost variation between on-demand and discounted usage.

Unit Cost

The cost per meaningful business unit of output, such as cost per transaction, cost per customer, or cost per API call, enabling efficiency comparisons independent of scale.

Unit Economics

The practice of measuring cloud cost efficiency in terms of cost per meaningful unit of business output providing a value-oriented perspective that connects technical spend to business outcomes.

Usage Optimization

The practice of reducing cloud consumption by eliminating waste, improving application efficiency, scheduling workloads appropriately, and ensuring resources are used only when needed.

V

Value Delivery

The realization of business benefits from cloud investments, measured through outcomes such as features shipped, customers served, revenue generated, or operational improvements achieved.

Value Stream

The end-to-end sequence of activities that delivers value to a customer or stakeholder, used in FinOps EVM to align cloud costs with the business processes they support.

Variance

The measurable difference between planned and actual performance. In FinOps EVM, cost variance and schedule variance are primary indicators of project health.

Variance at Completion (VAC)

See At-Completion Variance.

W

Waste

Cloud spending that delivers no business value, including idle resources, orphaned storage, overprovisioned instances, and unused commitments.

Work Breakdown Structure (WBS)

A hierarchical decomposition of the total scope of work into manageable components, used to organize planning, assign budgets, and track earned value at each level.

Workload

A distinct application, service, or collection of resources that performs a specific business function in the cloud and can be independently measured for cost and value delivery.

Z

Zero-Based Budgeting

A budgeting approach that requires justifying every planned expenditure from scratch for each new period rather than basing budgets on prior-period spending, promoting cost discipline and intentional allocation.

Index

E

F

www.ingramcontent.com/pod-product-compliance
Lightning Source LLC
LaVergne TN
LVHW060447061126
851857LV00016B/1750
* 9 7 8 8 1 6 9 6 4 6 4 9 9 *